Isaac Bashevis Singer

Children's Stories and Childhood Memoirs

Twayne's United States Authors Series

Ruth K. MacDonald, General Editor

Bay Path College

TUSAS 661

ALMA AND ISAAC BASHEVIS SINGER.
Photograph by Ray Fisher; courtesy of Alma Singer.

Isaac Bashevis Singer

Children's Stories and Childhood Memoirs

Alida Allison

San Diego State University

Twayne Publishers
An Imprint of Simon & Schuster Macmillan
New York

Prentice Hall International
London Mexico City New Delhi Singapore Sydney Toronto

Twayne's United States Authors Series No. 661

Isaac Bashevis Singer: Children's Stories and Childhood Memoirs
Alida Allison

Twayne Publishers
An Imprint of Simon & Schuster Macmillan
1633 Broadway
New York, NY 10019

Library of Congress Cataloging-in-Publication Data
Allison, Alida.
    Isaac Bashevis Singer : children's stories and memoirs / Alida
Allison.
        p. cm.—(Twayne's United States authors series ; 661.
Children's literature.)
    Includes bibliographical references (p.) and index.
    ISBN 0-8057-9226-0 (cloth)
        1. Singer, Isaac Bashevis, 1904–1991—Criticism and interpretation.
2. Children's stories, Yiddish—History and criticism.   I. Title.
II. Series: Twayne's United States authors series ; TUSAS 661.
III. Series: Twayne's United States authors series. Children's
literature.
PJ5129.S49Z5825   1996   95-45875
839'.0933—dc20   CIP

The paper used in this publication meets the minimum requirements of American National Standard for Information Sciences—Permanence of Paper for Printed Library Materials. ANSI Z39.48–1984. ∞

10 9 8 7 6 5 4 3 2   (hc)

Printed in the United States of America

Dedicated to Elizabeth (Libby) Shub,
author, editor, and translator,
who persuaded her friend Isaac to write for children

And to my own favorite storytellers,
my grandparents Abe and Eva Slutzky

Contents

Acknowledgments

My special thanks go to Alma Singer for permission to reprint Singer's children's manuscripts and for her hospitality in Miami; to Libby Shub and New York University's Fales Library for permission to use their Singer holdings and to Libby for the many hours she spent with me; to my friend and research assistant extraordinaire, Kate Kordich, whose initiative, hard work, and good company were invaluable; to my editors at Twayne, Ruth MacDonald and Mark Zadrozny; to San Diego State University and to the Children's Literature Association for their support of my research; to Yitz Gefter of San Diego State University for his help with Jewish customs, Yiddish, and Hebrew, and to Ann Proyect of Woodridge, New York, for the same; to Martha E. Casselman and Barbara Schloss of San Diego State University's English and Comparative Literature Department and to Jim Edwards and Rachel Litonjua-Witt of the university's Faculty Computer Room for their help; to Dina Abramowitz of YIVO (Institute for Jewish Research) for her numerous suggestions; to Farrar, Straus and Giroux for use of its library; to the staff of the Olcott Hotel in New York City for their hospitality and to Vic Gordon of Monticello, New York, for the same; to my associates at Mesa State College for their support; to my colleagues in children's literature at San Diego State University, Lois Kuznets, Jerry Griswold, and especially Peter Neumeyer, whose role in this effort was pivotal; and to my family, Byron, Brendan, and Steve, for everything.

Preface

Lucky for all readers, young and old, that Isaac Bashevis Singer wrote for children. Lucky that a writer of such consistent cultural clarity succeeded all the more because he was so ethnic. Lucky that this writer elevated children's literature by depicting child characters who are questioning and deep. They are often involved in cosmic battles right in their own backyard: the Jewish village, or *shtetl*, a colorful, complex microcosm. Singer's children take on the big questions: metaphysical, religious, literary, historic, communal, personal.

Many of the stories are also, as will soon be obvious to the reader, very funny. It has been said that America derived its love of freedom from its first settlers, its love of land from its early settlers, and its sense of humor from its immigrants. Singer's stories are delightful comedy, the humor in them alternately broad, ironic, or clever. His sure touch brings the zany, wise, and earthy world of his own youth in pre–World War I Yiddish Poland to life for a global audience.

To my mind, Singer's largest collection, *Stories for Children*, is one of the best buys in any bookstore. Whatever small help my book may be in spreading the word about Singer's superb stories is a great reward for an enlightening and enjoyable writing assignment.

Preceding this volume in the Twayne series are two useful studies of Singer by Edward Alexander. Alexander places Singer's short stories into types, such as "apocalyptic," "survival," "love and perversion," and "autobiographic." Examples provided by Alexander for each type, respectively, are "The Gentleman from Cracow," the remarkable "The Little Shoemakers," "Blood," and "The Son," in which Singer writes of his awkward first meeting with the son he had not seen for years.

Alexander's framework works well applied to Singer's children's stories, too. Examples would be, respectively, "The Wicked City," "Menashe and Rachel," "Rabbi Leib and the Witch Cunegunde," and "A Hanukkah Eve in Warsaw."

The children's stories allow for other thematic groupings, as is demonstrated below. Following the titles of stories and books are the chapter numbers in which the stories are discussed in this book.

Ghosts, Goblins, Demons, and Imps

"The Lantuch," *Naftali the Storyteller and His Horse, Sus* (N), 5; "Rabbi Leib and the Witch Cunegunde," *When Shlemiel Went to Warsaw* (W), 4; "The Extinguished Lights," *The Power of Light* (P), 6; "Grandmother's Tale," *Zlateh the Goat* (Z), 3; "The Devil's Trick," (Z), 3; "Tsirtsur and Peziza," (W), 5, *The Fearsome Inn*, 7; *Alone in the Wild Forest*, 7.

Stories of Love, Stories of Loss

Joseph and Koza, 7; "The Power of Light" (P), 6; "Menashe and Rachel," (P), 6; "Hanukkah in the Poorhouse," (P), 6; "Topiel and Tekla," *Nimrod* magazine, 8; "Tashlik" (*London Jewish Chronicle*), 8.

Miracle Tales, Visions, and Dreams

"Menaseh's Dream," (W), 4; *A Tale of Three Wishes*, 8; "Utzel and His Daughter, Poverty," (W), 4; "Ole and Trufa," *The Atlantic*, 8; *The Fearsome Inn*, 7; "Why the Geese Shrieked," *A Day of Pleasure* (D), 1.

Fools

The Fools of Chelm and Their History, 7; "The Fools of Chelm and the Stupid Carp," (N), 5; "The Elders of Chelm and Genedel's Key," (W), 4; "Shrewd Todie and Lyzer the Miser," (W), 4; "Dalfunka, Where the Rich Live Forever," (N), 5; "The Mixed Up Feet and the Silly Bridegroom," (Z), 3; "Fool's Paradise," (Z), 3; "Lemel and Tzipa," (N), 5; "The Snow in Chelm," (Z), 3.

Shlemiels

"The First Shlemiel," (Z), 3; "Mr. and Mrs. Shlemiel," (Z), 3; "The Day I Got Lost" (spoof autobiography), *Puffin* magazine, 8; "Shlemiel the Businessman," (W), 4; "When Shlemiel Went to Warsaw," (W), 4.

Bible and Holiday Stories

Why Noah Chose the Dove, 7; *The Wicked City*, 7; *Elijah the Slave*, 7; *A Tale of Three Wishes*, 7; all eight stories in *The Power of Light*, 7.

Originals

"Zlateh the Goat," (Z), 3; "Rabbi Leib and the Witch Cunegunde," (W); "Naftali the Storyteller and His Horse, Sus," (N), 5; "Menaseh's Dream," (W), 4.

Family, Friends, and Neighbors

"Reb Asher the Dairy Man," (D), 1; "A Hanukkah Eve in Warsaw," (N), 5; "A Hanukkah Eve in My Parents' House," (P), 6; "Tashlik," *London Jewish Chronicle*, 8; "The Washwoman," (D), 1; "Hunger," (D), 1.

Writers and Storytellers

"Growing Up," (N), 1 and 5; "Naftali the Storyteller and His Horse, Sus," (N), 1 and 5; "The Lantuch," (N), 5; "A Hanukkah Eve in My Parents' House," (P), 6; "The Extinguished Lights," (P), 6.

Animal Stories

"Zlateh the Goat," (Z), 3; "Naftali the Storyteller and His Horse, Sus," (N), 1 and 5; "A Parakeet Named Dreidel," (P), 6; "The Cat Who Thought She Was a Dog and the Dog Who Thought He Was a Cat," (N), 5; "Hershele and Hanukkah," (P), 6.

Chapters 1 and 2 of this book describe Singer's world and how he came finally to write for children when he was 62, with a nudge from his friend Elizabeth Shub. In the following chapters, Singer's major works for children are organized by format. His four story collections are discussed first, *Zlateh the Goat*, *When Shlemiel Went to Warsaw*, *Naftali the Storyteller and His Horse, Sus*, and *The Power of Light*. Single-story books are analyzed in chapter 7, including long works such as *The Fearsome Inn* and picture books such as *Elijah the Slave*. The concluding chapter uses Singer's anthology *Stories for Children* as its basis for summary and overview.

Chronology

1904–1908   Isaac Singer born in November in Leoncin, a *shtetl*, or Jewish village, in the Polish countryside, to Pinchos-Menachem Singer, a Hasidic rabbi, and Bathsheba Zylberman. The family lives briefly in Radzymin, then moves to Warsaw.

1908–17   The family lives in the Warsaw Ghetto where his father serves as the rabbi of Krochmalna Street, their impoverished neighborhood.

1917–23   World War I exacerbates the family's marginal existence. Singer, his mother, and brother Moshe leave for Bilgoray, the *shtetl* where Singer's maternal grandfather is the rabbi. Singer surreptitiously reads secular literature and philosophy.

1923   Lives the life of a struggling artist in Warsaw translating and writing reviews, rooming with the Yiddish poet Aaron Zeitlin.

1924–29   Publishes his first short stories in the Yiddish press. His Communist lover Runia gives birth to a son, Israel, whom she later raises in Israel after Singer emigrates to the United States. Father dies.

1933   First novel, *Satan in Goray*, published in Yiddish in serial, then book, form.

1935–43   With brother's help, joins Joshua and his family in New York City. Begins long association with the *Jewish Daily Forward*, the Yiddish newspaper published in New York. To distinguish himself from Joshua, Isaac adds *Bashevis* to his name, in honor of his mother. Mother and brother Moshe killed by Nazis. Marries Alma Haimann and becomes U.S. citizen. Begins writing fiction again.

1944–53   Brother Joshua dies suddenly. Publishes many short stories later translated into English, such as "The Spinoza of Market Street" and "Gimpel the Fool." *The*

Family Moskat serialized in the *Forward* and later published in English. Saul Bellow translates "Gimpel tam" for the *Partisan Review*.

1954–66   Stories and novels begin to appear with regularity in Yiddish and English. Among works published in English are *Satan in Goray*, *Gimpel the Fool and Other Stories*, *The Magician of Lublin*, *The Slave*, and his memoir *In My Father's Court*.

1966   Friend and colleague Elizabeth (Libby) Shub finally persuades him to write for children. Begins a long association with her as translator of many children's stories from Yiddish to English, including his first, "Zlateh the Goat," which, as part of the book of the same name, receives Newbery Honor Award.

1967   *The Fearsome Inn* and *Mazel and Shlimazel: or, The Milk of a Lioness*, translated with Shub and illustrated by Nonny Hogrogian and Margot Zemach, respectively. *The Fearsome Inn* garners second Newbery Honor Award. *The Manor* nominated for National Book Award. Works appear in the *New Yorker* and other major magazines.

1968   *When Shlemiel Went to Warsaw* wins third Newbery Honor Award and is designated an American Library Association (ALA) Notable book. *The Seance and Other Stories* published.

1969   *A Day of Pleasure* awarded National Book Award for Children's Literature.

1970   *Elijah the Slave, Joseph and Koza: or, The Sacrifice to the Vistula*, and *A Friend of Kafka and Other Stories* published.

1971   *The Topsy-Turvy Emperor of China*, *Alone in the Wild Forest*, and *An Isaac Bashevis Reader* published.

1972   *The Wicked City* is designated an ALA Notable book. *Enemies, a Love Story* published.

1973   *The Fools of Chelm and Their History* published. *A Crown of Feathers and Other Stories* receives National Book Award.

Chapter One
Roots of a Storyteller

"There Is No Literature without Roots"

A "born storyteller" is how Isaac Bashevis Singer is typically described. An admirer of the nineteenth-century masters whom he read as a child against his rabbi father's wishes, Singer is often compared to writers such as Tolstoy[1] and Hawthorne,[2] but the comparison most apt in acknowledging the variety of genres in which Singer wrote is to another great storyteller, Mark Twain. Like Twain, Isaac Singer lived long, wrote prolifically for children as well as for adults, and drew richly from his own childhood for material and inspiration. Both cultural chroniclers exemplify Singer's often-stated conviction that ". . . there is no literature without roots. . . . The more a writer is rooted in his environment, the more he is understood by all people; the more national he is, the more international he becomes . . ." (*Stories*, 335).[3] Singer's early environment and education defined the narrative techniques and traditionalist standards of his stories. To dig into the roots of Singer the storyteller is to discover an unusually well-nourished soil.

Skinny, blue-eyed, red-haired Isaac Singer was born in 1904 in eastern Poland in a small *shtetl*, a village comprised mostly, sometimes exclusively, of Jews. Segregated from the larger community by religious practice as well as by prejudice and persecution, the culture of Isaac Singer's birth preserved traditions hundreds and thousands of years old. The locus of most of his writing, the *shtetl* world was one that had a story for any and everything, an oral and written heritage of extraordinary depth and variety, of soul-searching and fierce devotion, of trenchant humor and debate—albeit sometimes critical of God's evident lapses.

During his childhood and teens, Singer lived both in the insular, inward *shtetl* and in the overcrowded tenement of the big city, the capital Warsaw. Like most of the Jews in Eastern Europe, his family was poor, sometimes penniless. When his father found a rabbinical position in the Warsaw Ghetto, Singer was three. The family moved to a rat-ridden slum without running water or indoor plumbing. Its dark alleys and

1

stairways were the source of many terrors for the young Singer, as he
describes in "The Collector" and "The Shot at Sarajevo" from his autobiography for children, *A Day of Pleasure: Stories of a Boy Growing Up in
Warsaw* (1963).[4] The city itself, though, was a source of wonder. He
describes its first impact on him in "The Trip from Radzymin," also from
A Day of Pleasure. Singer captures more than the color of a time long
gone; by displaying the open emotion of the child he reminds his readers
that the world itself is a marvelous place—whether the world of the
book or the world of the reader's own roots.

Singer lyricizes:

> . . . before I could open my mouth new marvels turned up. Streets lined
> with huge buildings. . . . Ladies on the sidewalk wearing hats trimmed
> with cherries, peaches, plums, grapes. . . . I saw men with top hats who
> carried silver-handled canes. There were many red trolley cars. . . .
>
> I was both delighted and humbled. What value has a small boy,
> compared to such a great, tumultuous world? . . . Whenever the droshky
> [carriage] made a turn, the sky turned with it and my brain rattled in my
> head like a kernel in a nut. . . . My curiosity had no limits.[5]

The title story, "A Day of Pleasure," is about Singer at age seven,
when, without his parents' knowledge, he sneaks all by himself beyond
the ghetto into the delightful and humbling capital. The impecunious
child finds money in the street and splurges it on carriage rides, candy,
and other unholy frivolities. Completely lost, he lies to a stranger, is
found out, and returned home. Wonder, fear, humiliation, honor: the
intensity of the child's experience, the tensions and triumphs of this particular boy's day, are remembered in generous detail. Because the writer
is Singer and the subject is childhood, a memory becomes a work of art
universal in its expression of this one child's initiation into the exercise of
free will and the consequences of pushing one's limits.

Although Singer's education was narrow, it was deep. Stories were
ingrained early in the *cheders,* or religious schools, to which Jewish boys
were sent quite early; Singer was four when he began, as he describes
in "Who I Am," the first memoir in *A Day of Pleasure.* Six days a week
he studied Judaism and Hebrew and quickly became literate in the
cultural store of religious tales and folklore. His narrative model was,
foremost, the Bible, which in his seventies he still described as exemplary—". . . a most beautiful storybook . . . all writers can learn from
it"[6] and "so good as to be translatable into any language."[7] At synagogue and at home, he heard his elders discuss "The Fathers." These

great sages, such as Rabbis Akiba, Hillel, and Jochanan, stood out as distinct characters in the religious literature. As writers themselves centuries ago, they demonstrated the use of many diverse literary techniques in the Talmud, the scriptural compendium of quotation, analysis, parable, and legend, which Singer learned well. Singer also was raised on the religious maxims and parables of more recent storytellers, the mysterious and moody Hasidic masters, each with a distinct style. Of his favorite, nineteenth-century Rabbi Nahman of Bratslav, Singer wrote: "This man was a great mystic . . . a great seer. . . . He was a beautiful storyteller, a man with an unlimited fantasy, with a great heart, a mystic, and crazy also. Everything which is needed to be a great person" (Wolkstein, 141).

Singer *heard* much of this material as a child, told aloud in the studyhouse where the men congregated and talked informally or at his family's kitchen table. The picture he draws of the child who became a writer emphasizes this omnipresent oral tradition that dates back thousands of years and that was fully represented by the important adults in his early life. Repeatedly he portrays himself as a child listening with total absorption. Roderick McGillis discusses the loss of orality in the modern world when children learn to read in school, either using books or computer screens: "Traces of the speaking voice grow faint as literature commits itself more and more to the visual temptations of print."[8] The long oral and literary tradition and cohesive society of Eastern European Jewry meant that a child like Singer could retain the best of both types of literature.

Singer was 16 when he listened to his Aunt Yentl tell stories such as "The Lantuch." He had learned that stories brought people together, stories entertained and enlightened, and he never tired of hearing them. When he was still quite young, as he writes in "Growing Up," Singer also began telling stories himself extemporaneously to schoolmates. Even then, he recognized that creative ability gave him power that his physique and old-fashioned clothes did not.

Another potent influence on Singer's gift for storytelling were the penny storybooks the child saved his money to buy. The turn-of-the-century equivalent of swashbuckler comic fiction, these fueled his imagination; they provided a sense of pacing and plot in creating a satisfying story (Wolkstein, 141). When he was older, Singer read the Yiddish literature of the day, writers such as I. L. Peretz and Sholem Aleichem. He felt a great affinity for nineteenth-century authors such as Poe, E. T. A. Hoffmann, Dostoyevsky, and Maupassant; he read the Yiddish translation of *Crime and Punishment* when he was 12.[9] He especially liked the Norwegian writer Knut Hamsun.[10]

Having a rabbi father meant that the Singer children—one daughter, three sons—were witness daily to the extremes of life. In his autobiographies, Singers recounts a panoply of tales from the lives of visitors: quarreling lovers to washwomen, famous rabbis to impoverished dairymen; strangers, supplicants, sinners, and saints; the devout to the devious—every one who entered 10 Krochmalna Street had a story . . . or was a story, such as the fanatical Reb Moishe Ba-ba-ba who shooed the girls away when he approached so as not to be contaminated by their presence, or the frail rabbi two doors down from Singer, whom he sketches concisely as having "such a pronounced stoop that all one could make out was a white beard, a sable hat, and a small bundle of silk."[11] In "The Collector," Singer transforms a day spent collecting overdue fees for his father from the often wretched inhabitants of the ghetto into sketches of extraordinary impact. It is as Alfred Kazin observes about the content of Singer's writing, that "looking at the sheer density . . . he can never run out of material."[12]

Singer often depicts himself and his siblings as greatly moved by a story, as when their father responds to the challenge raised by his older brother Israel Joshua in "A Hanukkah Evening in My Parents' House," from the 1980 collection *The Power of Light*:[13]

> As if he read my mind, I heard Joshua ask, "Why did God work miracles in ancient times and why doesn't he work miracles in our times?"
> Father pulled at his red beard. His eyes expressed indignation.
> "What are you saying, my son? God works miracles in all generations even though we are not aware of them. Hanukkah especially is a feast of miracles. My grandmother, Hindel—you, my daughter, are named for her—told me the following story. In the village of Tishewitz there was a child named Zaddock. . . ." (5)

By way of answering the question, in traditional fashion the father first asks a counterquestion, then tells a story. One Hanukkah not long ago, the good-hearted Zaddock, upon hearing of a poor sick tailor's inability to buy wood, rushes into the darkening, wintry forest without telling his parents. One thought only occupies the boy: "to gather as much wood as he could and bring it to the sick man" (*Stories*, 173). The unprepared child, losing his way, is likely to freeze to death. Because of his goodness, however, he is saved by the lights of Hanukkah candles that suddenly appear before him and lead him to the poor man's door.

The candle flames become gold coins and all ends well: the sick man recovers and returns to his tailor shop, and Zaddock grows up to become the saintly Rabbi Zaddock. As does another Yiddish author, I. L. Peretz in his short story "If Not Higher," Singer implies that the most powerful acts of charity are those done privately, without regard to recognition.[14]

When the father's story ends, there is quiet enough in the family's front room for the Singer children to hear their own Hanukkah candles sputtering, along with the chirping of the household cricket that keeps warm behind the family hearth. In the serene silence, the mother comes in from the kitchen, holding a plate of steaming holiday potato pancakes, and little Moshe announces he wants to give his money to the poor. The story has had its effect: the warmth of the scene and the closeness of the moment stayed more than half a century in Singer's memory to be conveyed to who knows how many centuries of future readers. In fact, the images of sputtering candles and chirping crickets reappear in several Singer stories.

The author Singer describes the child Isaac as "listening to everything: to the stories of the Chassidim, to my brother's debates with my parents; to the arguments of the litigants who came for a "Din Torah" (a rabbinical court where rabbis such as his father passed judgment on questions of ritual, law, and diet).[15] The author-to-be realized that "each person had his or her own manner of speaking" (*Stories*, 173). The child's attentiveness to distinctive personalities and modes of self-expression paid off: one of Singer's strongest gifts as a writer is his instinct for realistic, distinct dialogue. Many of his stories include monologues, as in "Aunt Yentl" from *In My Father's Court*, or "A Hanukkah in the Poorhouse" from *The Power of Light* (1980). Singer won critical acclaim for his novella *The Penitent*, in which the main character tells the story of his return to traditional Judaism in an almost uninterrupted monologue.[16]

Both poverty and piety are notable among the people whose lives become stories Singer tells. In "The Washwoman" from *A Day of Pleasure*, Singer portrays one of the few Gentiles the family had steady contact with, the wrinkled old woman who washes their clothes. Her two-month disappearance is a hardship for the Singers because she has taken their laundry with her and the Singers have no clothes to spare. The old woman does finally return. She has been deathly ill but has revived sufficiently to fulfill her obligations to her customers by returning their laundry—cleaned, of course; the Singer family never sees her again. Yet her heroism makes a lasting impression on the boy.

Reb Asher the dairyman, in the story named after him, expands the young Singer's world, to the child's great and lasting delight, by taking him for daylong rides in the countryside as he makes his rounds. The impoverished and pious milk vendor, a follower of Singer's father, rises to greatness when he rouses the rabbi's family late one night to save them all from a fire; only Reb Asher's enormous strength enables him to accomplish the rescue.

A Family of Storytellers

Singer was able to fulfill his own requirement that he "must have the illusion that I am the only one who can write such a story" (Colwin, 23), stories about *shtetl* people such as Aunt Yentl and other village characters, because of the second-most significant move in his life, which, like the first, from the countryside to the capital, was a function of economics. Singer was 10 when World War I began, and he was a teenager during the Russian Revolution. The deprivations resulting from the international tensions were severe in Poland, as Singer writes in "Hunger" and "The Journey" from *A Day of Pleasure*. For Jews special dangers existed. His older brother Israel Joshua was forced to hide out to escape the draft, and Singer's father's congregation dwindled, leaving the family with no means of support. Therefore, in his early teens, Singer moved with his mother and younger brother back to the countryside, to the *shtetl* where her father, an Orthodox rabbi of substantial reputation, ruled the little town of Bilgoray. There Singer spent most of his adolescent years. Although Singer always considered himself a "city boy," he wrote repeatedly about the impact upon him of this move back in time, back to a world not all that much removed in its outlook from a "medieval" village: "In this world of old Jewishness," he wrote, "I found a spiritual treasure trove. I had a chance to see our past as it really was. . . . I lived Jewish history" (*Court*, 290).

For centuries Jews had existed precariously in Eastern Europe, drawn together in response to the severe restrictions imposed by the various governments to which they had alternately owed political allegiance: Russian, Polish, German, Austrian. The Jewish community itself, however, was not uniform. The most basic split was between the increasingly assimilated Jews of Western Europe and the typically old-fashioned Eastern European Jews. The former often discarded traditional Jewish dress and religious observance, scandalizing their Eastern kin, whereas the backwardness and inflexibility of the Eastern Jews threatened what

the more Western Jews saw as their opportunity to prosper as full
Europeans.

But deep religious divides were found even among the Eastern
European Jews. The most central was between the Talmudists, or traditional Orthodox Jews such as Singer's maternal grandfather, and the
Hasidim such as his father, followers of an ecstatic fundamentalism that
arose in Poland during the 1700s, largely in response to the terrors of
European Jewish history in the 1600s—massacres and false messiahs
predominant among them. Furthermore, the scientific discoveries and
speculations of the late nineteenth and early twentieth centuries had
not left the Jews unaffected, although less so in Poland and Russia than
in Germany. Secular ideas such as evolution, psychoanalysis, and emancipated art had the effect of detaching members of the younger generation, such as Singer's brother Joshua, from the hold of any religious
observance. Tremendous conflicts developed within families and communities.

In Singer's own front room these three majors worldviews collided:
Hasidic, Orthodox, and secular. Singer remembers that ". . . our house
was always filled with problems, doubts, and unrest" (*Court*, 162). In
fact, if conflict is fruitful for authors, it is no wonder the Singer family
produced so many writers. His older sister, Hinde Esther, wrote several
books but received little recognition. *Deborah*, her autobiography, is well-
written and revealing. Singer's older brother, Joshua, was a major
Yiddish writer long before his brother Isaac became famous. Joshua's
autobiography, *Of a World That Is No More*, is superb reading, but in a
style very different than either of his siblings' memoirs. And Isaac Singer
has written that he believes his mother, Bathsheba, wrote an autobiography that she destroyed.[17] His father also wrote.

Thus, in addition to being born into a storytelling culture, Singer
happened to be born into a family of extremely intelligent, expressive
storytellers, all different, all dissatisfied, and all very verbal.

Singer writes:

> My parents, my older brother, and my sister all liked to tell stories.
> My father would often tell of the miracles performed by various rabbis,
> also of ghosts, devils, and imps. He wanted in this way to strengthen our
> belief in God and in the good and evil powers that reign in the world. My
> mother told us stories about Bilgoray, where her father was the rabbi and
> ran the community with a strong hand. My brother Joshua became
> worldly and started to read books that were not religious. He told me
> stories about Germany, France, America, about unfamiliar nations and

races, about peculiar beliefs and customs. My sister told romantic stories about counts who fell in love with servant girls. I had my own fantasies. (*Day*, 9)

In *Of a World That Is No More*, Joshua Singer writes about the "mismatch" between his parents: ". . . my mother and my father . . . would have been a well-mated couple if she had been the husband and he had been the wife. . . . They were as different in spirit as in physique" (30). Singer's father believed in spirits and miracles, believed everything in the Holy Books, believed in the unquestionable spiritual authority of the Hasidic patriarchs called *Tzaddikim*. Rabbi Singer was a mystic, simple, emotional, and certain in his faith; his attitude toward the world was one of disinterest and distaste. A telling sketch is drawn by Singer of his father habitually turning his back on the apartment's tiny balcony because it overlooked the *tref*, or unclean, world below. Pinchos-Menachem Singer is portrayed in the three autobiographies written by his children as a mixture of merriness, gentleness, incompetence, intransigence, and fulmination. The elder Singer's refusal even to attempt to learn the Russian required to take the civil exam that would have qualified him as an "official" rabbi in the eyes of the Russian government— allowing him to openly perform some of the more remunerative rabbinical functions—was a source of enduring disappointment to his wife, Bathsheba, and economic hardship for his family. Singer's sister Hinde devotes several detailed pages in her neglected autobiography *Deborah* to describing this "old score" between her father and her mother (10). Joshua Singer also wrote about it:

> Mother finished the course in record time. If it had been she who had to pass the examination instead of Father, our troubles would have been over. But she was only a female and her quick intelligence was more of a detriment than a virtue. Both my sister and I leafed through the textbooks and soon we were chattering away in Russian like magpies. (*World*, 140)

But if the father clashed often with his wife and skeptical oldest son and ignored his daughter, if he were both impractical and obstinate, he nonetheless passed down to his younger sons a temperamental tendency toward the supernatural. Isaac Singer's little brother Moshe was the only brother to become a rabbi—though not for long; along with Bathsheba Singer, he was killed by the Nazis in the 1930s. (Singer's father had already died.) Throughout his long life, Isaac Singer maintained, if not

his father's conviction, at least his receptivity to the inexplicable workings of the world.

Dorothea Straus, a friend and translator of Singer and wife of one of
his publishers, Roger Straus, tells of a day he visited their country home.
The first thing Singer asked was, "Where is the ghost room?" He had
heard Straus recount the tale of a haunted room in the house. Singer
spent the day there, didn't find anything, but told his hosts, "You know
that it is usually those who scoff at the existence of spirits who will most
probably meet one. All my life I have searched for them, but so far, I
have had no success."[18] The key phrase in Singer's sentence is "so far." He
believed, simply, that all the facts were not yet in. "After all, let's not fool
ourselves," Singer often said, "a few hundred years ago we didn't know
about the existence of microbes. . . ."[19]

Singer's mother was as religious as his father, but more fretful and
cerebral, a well-read, frustrated intellectual whose children wrote sym-
pathetically of her. She was open at least to hearing new ideas—which
Singer's father was not. In *A Little Boy in Search of God*, Singer remembers that she would surreptitiously read the short stories Joshua was
beginning to publish. And occasionally, although his father considered
secular books to be "abominations,"[20] she would leaf through one of the
worldly books Joshua Singer brought home. She was a misfit, in this like
her only daughter, Singer's unhappy sister Hinde who married when
Singer was a child and essentially disappeared from his life. Although for
different reasons, both women were severely handicapped by their gender. They may have been in Singer's mind when he wrote stories such as
"Yentl the Yeshiva Boy" and "A Crown of Feathers," about the terrible
frustrations suffered in Yiddish culture by intelligent women. In his stories for children too, stories about the seven fools who rule Chelm or
about the Shlemiel family, wives are always smarter and more capable
than their husbands, but they lack the power to do anything about their
spouses' idiotic decisions. Examples are *The Fools of Chelm and Their
History* and "The Elders of Chelm and Genedel's Key," from *When
Shlemiel Went to Warsaw*.[21]

In "Why the Geese Shrieked" from *A Day of Pleasure*, Singer crystal-
lizes his parents' characters by dramatizing the clash between them.
Many readers can remember from childhood a moment when fact and
faith collided, when the vectoring of a personal belief system was set,
and the side the child rooted for perhaps did not win. Singer captures
that moment, with its tension and its intensity, in a scene from a distant

slum in a vanished part of Poland. Singer makes it a story any reader can understand.

One day, when Singer is eight, a woman suddenly enters the tiny apartment, her eyes full of fear. She lays two dead geese on the kitchen table and says, "Rabbi, I have a very unusual problem."

Her problem is that the geese, though ritually slaughtered, shriek in unholy voices. The woman fears they are possessed. Singer's father pales and the child feels himself fill with dread. This could be proof that the world of spirits really does exist: a sign from heaven that Singer's father is a gifted rabbi elected to perform an exorcism—or it could be a sign from hell. Singer's mother, however, "came from a family of rationalists. . . ." "'Slaughtered geese don't shriek,' she said."

But these geese, although "headless, disemboweled—in short, ordinary dead geese," when the woman strikes one against the other, emit such a mournful and otherworldly sound that Singer himself shrieks and gathers himself into the maternal skirt. Two times the woman demonstrates the unearthly phenomenon.

"My father's voice became hoarse," the author remembers, and "broken by sobs" as he says, "Well, can anyone still doubt that there *is* a creator?" Angrily, he looks at his wife and demands, "And what do you say now, eh?" (*Day*, 41–42).

> "I cannot understand what is going on here," she said, with a certain resentment. . . .
> Suddenly my mother laughed. . . . "Did you remove the windpipes?" . . .
> Mother took hold of one of the geese . . . and with all her might pulled out the thin tube . . . I stood trembling. . . . Her hands had become bloodied. On her face could be seen the wrath of the rationalist whom someone has tried to frighten in broad daylight. (*Day*, 43–44)

And Singer's father's face? "He knew what had happened here: logic, cold logic, was again tearing down faith, mocking it. . . ."

One more time, and this time with faith or fact hanging in the balance, the goose woman prepares to slap the birds against each other. The child's hope? "Although I was afraid I prayed inwardly the geese *would* shriek, shriek so loud that people in the street would hear. . . ." (*Day*, 44).

But the windpipeless fowl no longer shriek. Again there are tears in the boy's eyes.

Victoriously announcing "That's all it was!" and ". . . there is always an explanation," the mother returns to the kitchen. Father and son sit together and suddenly the father speaks, Singer writes, "as if I were an adult. 'Your mother takes after your grandfather, the Rabbi of Bilgoray. He is a great scholar, but a cold-blooded rationalist. People warned me before our betrothal . . .'" (*Day*, 44–45).

When Singer refers to himself as both a mystic and a skeptic, it is as if the two parental points of view merged, creating a highly individualistic perspective:

> I'm a sceptic. I'm a sceptic about making a better world. When it comes to this business where you tell me that this-or-that regime, one sociological order or another, will bring happiness to people, I know it will never work. . . . People will remain people, and they have remained people under . . . all kinds of isms. But I am not a sceptic when it comes to belief in God. I do believe. I always did.[22]

Brother and Mentor

Clearly the most influential person both in terms of ideas and way of life during the first decades of Singer's life was Israel Joshua Singer, whose commitment to literature and *Haskalah*, the Jewish movement toward emancipated ideas translated usually as "Enlightenment," took him far from the *shtetl* world of his roots.

"A Boy Philosopher," from *A Day of Pleasure*, opens with Singer's mother and older brother discussing Isaac's prospects as a Jewish boy in Poland. These are not promising, and the animated discussion turns to the Jewish condition in general, which is also not promising. In fact, Joshua Singer found little to be promising about Jewish life in Poland. The tall, blond, robust, and outgoing older Singer disdained a life spent studying the Torah. Whatever their other differences, both Singer parents agreed that to have two sons who forsook traditional ways was "a tragedy" (Howe, 62). Watching his older brother discard his ritual dress of a gabardine coat, skullcap, and earlocks, Singer recalls: "Every word which he said to me was a bomb, a real spiritual kind of explosion. And my parents were not really able to answer him. Because sooner or later my father began to scream, 'You Unbeliever, you wicked man.' The fact that he screamed proved he couldn't answer" (Sinclair, 22).

In a scene from Singer's story "Growing Up" Joshua's secularist hackles are raised by a visitor displaying a fine storytelling technique, asking a rhetorical question:

> "How did Warsaw become Warsaw? First they built one house, then another, and gradually a city emerged. Everything grows. Even stones grow."
> "Stones don't grow, Reb Wolf Bear," my brother, Joshua, interjected.
> "No? Well, so be it."

The guest goes on to describe the gateway to *Gehenna* (hell) at the hollow center of the earth. Joshua objects that the earth is not hollow. The amiable storyteller answers with a question, "why not?" and the entrenched opinion that "anything is possible," an opinion echoed often throughout his life by Singer himself.

Undaunted by factual objections, the guest continues, recounting the abbreviated life history of a "Yenuka," a wonder child. The child grows a beard at age three, sermonizes in the synagogue at age five, marries at age seven, and, his beard white as snow, dies at age nine.

> "Did you see this Yenuka with your own eyes?" Joshua asked.
> "See him? No. But the whole world knows about it. . . ."
> "It isn't true," Joshua said. He turned pale and his blue eyes reflected scorn.
> "Have you been everywhere and do you know the truth?" Father asked. "The world is full of wonders. Only God the Almighty knows what goes on down here." (*Stories*, 229)

Singer says, "My brother was a rationalist and I was a mystic, but I loved him very much" (Burgin, 23); "he is the only hero I ever worshipped" (Sinclair, 22). The younger brother benefitted from his sibling's benevolence, from the days he spent as a preteen visiting his brother's garret in Warsaw to the job Joshua found for him as a proofreader in Warsaw. It paid a pittance but allowed the younger Singer to survive, to study literature, and occasionally to write for the new Yiddish journals. When the older Singer's growing literary reputation earned him an invitation to live and work in New York, he soon invited his younger brother to join him and his family.

Transported Roots

Singer was 31 years old when he left Europe, "convinced that 'it was inevitable after Hitler came to power that the Germans would invade Poland'" (Howe, 62). He had already separated from his politically committed left-wing lover; she had borne him a son, Singer's only child, whom she raised in Israel. Singer saw his son seldom but the two were reunited in later years. Israel Zamir's 1995 memoir is *Journey to My Father*.

Singer's *A Young Man in Search of Love* and many of his short stories for adults, such as "The Cafeteria," describe the difficulties he had establishing a home in his new world. Before beginning his own writing career in America, he accepted Joshua's suggestion that he add *Bashevis* to his name so that readers could clearly distinguish between the brothers. *Bashevis* was selected as a tribute to Bathsheba Singer, whose name in Yiddish was *Basheva*. Although literarily the distinction between them remained—Joshua more realistic, Isaac more richly wild—Singer repeatedly quoted his brother's advice about writing; he followed it scrupulously, too:

> He (I. J. Singer) had two words which he used: images and sayings. Sayings were for him essays, interpretations. He called sayings *zugerts*. It means you just talk. . . . You don't paint a picture, or bring out an image. He said, leave the *zugerts* to others. You tell them a story. Because you may know stories that they (the readers) don't know—but you don't know more about life than they do. (Sinclair, 22)

Overwhelmed by a feeling of dislocation, Singer wrote relatively little during his early years in America. By the mid-1940s, however, Singer's dry period of adjustment was over. He had married Alma Haimann, and he published copiously in the *Jewish Daily Forward*, much of which material was later translated and published in English. In 1957 Saul Bellow translated his story "Gimpel the Fool." Singer's reputation began to grow among non-Jewish readers through the efforts of supporters such as Cecil Hemley of the Noonday Press, which later became Farrar, Straus and Giroux, Singer's long-time publishers. In the following decades, the second half of Singer's life, his productivity was remarkable. His friend Elizabeth Shub recalls his capacity to concentrate:

> . . . he used to visit us and he had such facility in writing that it was amazing. One day he came, we were sitting around the living room

talking. He was a wonderful conversationalist, always amusing, never a dull moment with him. And he said "Excuse me, I have to go into Boris' study." I said, "Why do you have to go into the study?" He said "Oh, I have to do a column for tomorrow, for the *Jewish Daily Forward*." So we said, "All right, he'll be gone for half an hour to an hour, whatever," and we proceeded to do whatever we had to do. But in ten minutes he was back in the living room. We said, "What's the matter, do you need something?" He said, "No, I'm finished." And that was kind of facility he had. This man, he was almost a writing machine. He wrote, literally, all of the time, in his head or in a little notebook he carried everywhere.[23]

By the time he died in 1991, Singer had published more than a dozen novels and eight collections of short stories, in addition to memoirs, essays, newspaper columns, and at least 100 interviews. He lectured frequently and enjoyed it. His audiences enjoyed themselves, too; Singer was an accomplished performer who was able to evoke laughter on topics such as free will, the nature of evil, and his own eclectic but firm belief in God. His having been raised in the midst of storytellers contributed more than a mine of material; he had also learned how to captivate an audience.

One of Singer's best fictions is "Naftali the Storyteller and His Horse, Sus," his portrait of the idealized storyteller, gentle, single-minded Naftali. The storyteller is the culture's mentor and memory, the collective's essential member, the bard who preserves reality, even if in edited form. Like Singer himself, Naftali is a "born storyteller." Like Singer, Naftali enriches the world with his stories. And much like Singer whose comments on the necessity of roots to the creation of literature were quoted earlier, Naftali never travels far from home in the stories he collects and tells. But, unlike Singer, Naftali, the son of a coachman, has a placid, uncomplicated life. He realizes young that he is destined for a life devoted to—and fulfilled by—stories; he never wavers, never marries, never longs for material things. By the time he comes to be called "Grandpa" by the children who adore him, he finally settles down and adds the printing of books to his lifelong labor of collecting them. When he eases into a quiet death, he is buried beside his lifelong companion, Sus, his horse. The narrator of the story provides a consoling eulogy in which he likens the world to "one endless and wondrous story that only God knows in its entirety" (*Stories*, 183). The very metaphor Singer selects to conclude his story of Naftali, a natural storyteller like Singer himself, therefore, is that of a story.

In "Growing Up," also found in the collection *Naftali the Storyteller and His Horse, Sus,* Singer depicts himself as a born storyteller. The comparison between Singer's fictional and autobiographical versions of the "born" literary artist make this book especially interesting.

"Growing Up" begins with two paragraphs about young Singer's unusually intense dreams and fantasies. In his imagination, the rabbi's son, the brilliant boy, flies to Jerusalem, envisions the Messiah, Adam and Eve, and revelation. But by the third paragraph he has bitten into reality, acknowledging the writer's dual world: reverie is one thing, reality another; fiction and fact.

But neither reverie nor reality has a more potent claim on the child than that of the writing life. Comically he relates a detailed if ultimately impracticable scheme that he and his stolid, loyal friend Feivel cooked up to publish Isaac's stories. Although the plan falls through, the child's sense of mission, of destiny, of difference, survives.

Although other writers have depicted themselves as children, it is not only the singularity of Singer's setting that sets him apart. It is the depth and detail with which he draws upon his own history: personal, religious, and communal. His portrait of himself as child, and of children in general, is respectful. Perhaps this is because even as an old man in New York City writing memoirs of days long gone, he shared with children the conviction that the world is full of wonder and that human life is full of surprises.

In the final story in *A Day of Pleasure,* "Shosha," the grown-up Singer, the actualized and active writer, returns for one last time to his old Warsaw neighborhood to say good-bye to his memories of his youth before emigrating to America. On Krochmalna Street, he finds not Shosha, his beloved childhood playmate, but her daughter, whom he has never met. He is touched to learn that his story has been told—the daughter has heard of him from her mother.

And what does the young man, the 30-year-old soon to leave his roots behind, do to reach out to the child? He tells the girl a story. In this closing image of himself, the author impresses in our minds himself as the very storyteller the child in "Growing Up" so fiercely envisioned. He chooses to close his memoirs by depicting continuity in the face of change, a continuity based on storytellers. He closes by reaffirming childhood and storytelling, leaving a lasting picture of the power of story to connect teller and audience, to connect the teller to the roots he or she draws upon, to effect a bond both through and centered upon the Work—the story. Metaphorically, it is not too far an artistic or religious leap for Singer to imbue this human bond with profound microcosmic meaning; for, ultimately, the universe is God's story.

Singer ends his autobiography for children with a scene that drama- tizes the idea of linkage. The author lingers in Shosha's kitchen, listening to the chirping of a cricket who lives behind Shosha's family stove, just as young Singer himself listened to the hearth cricket in the memoir "A Hanukkah Evening in My Parents' House." And, in addition to its men- tion in the memoir, the hearth cricket has a story written about it in "Tsirtsur and Peziza," from *When Shlemiel Went to Warsaw*. Tsirtsur is the cricket and Peziza is a friendly imp identified as the daughter of the *lan- tuch* in the story of the same name in *Naftali the Storyteller and His Horse, Sus*. The cricket in Shosha's house reminds him of his own youth: "Could it be the cricket of my childhood? Certainly not. Perhaps her great- great-great-granddaughter. But she was telling the same story, as ancient as time, as puzzling as the world, and as long as the dark winter nights of Warsaw" (*Day*, 226).

In his autobiographies, Singer rewards his adult readers by providing a renewed vision of childhood. He affirms that roots laid down in earli- est memories can provide the nourishment for a lifetime of stories. For his young readers, he expresses in their behalf the belief that, though readers age, the stories they read—or live through—are timeless.

Chapter Two
Singer the Children's Author

Better Late Than Never

Isaac Bashevis Singer did not write his first story for children until he was 62 years old, and then only due to the insistence of an old friend, Elizabeth (Libby) Shub, who was at that time a juvenile editor at Harper and Row. Once Singer began writing for children, however, he was prolific: 18 books. He was also successful—three Newbery Honor Award books: *Zlateh the Goat* (1966), *The Fearsome Inn* (1967), and *When Shlemiel Went to Warsaw* (1968). *The Golem* (1982) and *Stories for Children* (1984) were American Library Association (ALA) Notable books, and *A Day of Pleasure* (1974), the memoirs he selected and augmented for children from his highly praised autobiography *In My Father's Court* (1962), garnered his first National Book Award. According to Farrar, Straus and Giroux, Singer's most popular children's books in hardcover are *When Shlemiel Went to Warsaw* and *The Power of Light*. In paperback, his biggest sellers are *The Power of Light* and *Stories for Children*.[1]

Singer was also serious about his audience, as two famous Singer essays reveal. "Are Children the Ultimate Literary Critics?" opens with "Children are the best readers of genuine literature" (*Stories*, 332). And in "I See the Child as the Last Refuge," a front-page essay for the *New York Times Book Review*, Singer decries "literary fads and barren experiments . . . which often reveal nothing but a writer's boring and selfish personality . . . literature . . . ready for suicide."[2] Any renaissance of an adult literature "gone berserk," he writes, will only come through children's literature.[3]

During the Nobel Prize ceremonies in 1978, he had the essay published a year earlier in *Children's Literature*, "Why I Write for Children," read aloud to the distinguished assemblage. In it, Singer provides 10 reasons why he regards children so highly as an audience, at the same time reaffirming his own opinions about literature with characteristically strong conviction:

There are five hundred reasons why I began to write for children, but to save time I will mention only ten of them.

Number 1. Children read books, not reviews. They don't give a hoot about the critics.

Number 2. Children don't read to find their identity.

Number 3. They don't read to free themselves of guilt, to quench their thirst for rebellion, or to get rid of alienation.

Number 4. They have no use for psychology.

Number 5. They detest sociology.

Number 6. They don't try to understand Kafka or *Finnegans Wake*.

Number 7. They still believe in God, the family, angels, devils, witches, goblins, logic, clarity, punctuation, and other such obsolete stuff.

Number 8. They love interesting stories, not commentary, guides, or footnotes.

Number 9. When a book is boring, they yawn openly, without any shame or fear of authority.

Number 10. They don't expect their beloved writer to redeem humanity. Young as they are, they know that it is not in his power. Only the adults have such childish illusions.[4]

Singer's children's books, together with the books and stories he wrote about his own childhood and his numerous essays and interviews about writing for children, comprise a substantial part of his work. In fact, Singer wrote more about childhood and/or for children than any of the other Nobel Prize–winning authors.

In 1962, Singer published 49 memoirs under the title *In My Father's Court*. The "court," or *Beth Din*, of the title refers the religious/judicial/counseling role played by Singer's father, Rabbi Pinchos-Menachem Singer. The court was held in the Singers' ghetto apartment. A center of religious life, of prayers and study and debate, the household was also the home of unexpurgated exposure to human experiences, experiences Singer would grow up to write about. As Singer wrote in *In My Father's Court*, "This book tells the story of a family and of a rabbinical court that were so close together it was hard to tell where one ended and the other began" (*Court*, 13–14).

Written originally in Yiddish—as was almost all of Singer's work—many of the individual stories printed in *In My Father's Court* had been published earlier in the *Jewish Daily Forward*, the New York City newspaper that bonded the Yiddish-speaking immigrants and that was the premier outlet for the literary talents of many Yiddish writers. One of Singer's translators for these stories was his nephew, Joseph Singer, son of Singer's older brother Israel Joshua whose own ascending career had ended abruptly when a heart attack struck him down in his early fifties. Both of Isaac Singer's older siblings, Israel Joshua, senior by 10 years, and Hinde Esther, senior by 12 years, published autobiographies of their childhoods in the *shtetl* world of Eastern Europe. Joshua Singer's powerful *Of a World That Is No More* was translated by Joseph Singer and published in 1970; Hinde Esther (Singer) Kreitman's *Deborah* was translated by her son, the writer Maurice Carr, and published in 1983. The autobiographies of these three siblings comprise an extraordinary literary record.

The exercise of writing so copiously about his own childhood no doubt enhanced Isaac Singer's subsequent writing of fiction for children. It lubricated his memory, which he often described as "extraordinary." Actually, the reverse is probably true as well: that writing so copiously for children as he did once he began reciprocally lubricated his memories of childhood. For he wrote the bulk of his memoirs in the years he was also publishing for children. *A Little Boy in Search of God: or, Mysticism in a Personal Light* (1976), *A Young Man in Search of Love* (1978), *Lost in America* (1981), and *In the Beginning* (1984)—which covered his earliest years and family life—were combined in one volume, *Love and Exile* (1984), the same year his extraordinary collected children's stories were published as *Stories for Children*. "I have," wrote Singer in *A Day of Pleasure*, "a good deal more to say about myself, my family and the Poland of days gone by. I hope to . . . reveal a world that is little known to you but which is rich in comedy and tragedy; rich in its individuality, wisdom, foolishness, wildness, and goodness" (*Day*, Foreword).

Writing for children opened a rich new mine of material for Singer. He remembered stories he had enjoyed hearing from family, friends, and visitors; he drew upon folklore and biblical characters such as the *golem* and the prophet Elijah; and he "invented" stories (Wolkstein, 139), gems of originality, such as his very first effort, "Zlateh the Goat"; his serene ode to storytellers, "Naftali the Storyteller and His Horse, Sus"; and his meditation upon the compensatory value of dreams, "Menaseh's Dream."

Writing for children also allowed Singer to portray a side of human reality other than the tragic character of many of his adult stories: life as it is experienced by children and—sometimes—by adults. By the time *Zlateh the Goat* was published in 1966, Singer was world famous as an author of novels and short stories that depicted his vibrant but doomed Eastern European culture. Many of these stories necessarily dealt with fates too intense for children—everything from persecutions and demon possession to infidelity and incontinence. But, as Singer told an interviewer, "It is not in the nature of a child to tell a story with an unhappy ending. A child expects justice to be done" (Wolkstein, 140). Once tapped, Singer's affinity for the kinds of stories characteristic of children's literature resulted in some of his very best work: stories of joy, amiable silliness, loyalty, supernatural struggles, suspense . . . and happy endings.

Cruelty—demonic or human—is never denied in Singer's children's books, but it is always defeated; examples are stories such as "The Devil's Trick," *The Fearsome Inn, Joseph and Koza,* and "Rabbi Leib and the Witch Cunegunde." Singer's heroes are simple people, the pure-at-heart, the religious, the resourceful, the loving, whether child or adult character. This innocent, optimistic mode of perception is not, however, solely the realm of children, neither inferior nor juvenile. Several of Singer's stories for adults, notably "Gimpel the Fool," seem to state that a belief in essential goodness is an expression of the closest kinship with God.

The recollection of himself as a probing and philosophical child reinforced the esteem with which Singer treated his child characters and, inferentially through them, his child readers. He saw in his young readers not only a discerning and intelligent audience, but also the only hope that literature may indeed have an impact on the future. In "Are Children the Ultimate Literary Critics," he wrote:

> Children think about and ponder such matters as justice, the purpose of life, the why of suffering. They are bewildered and frightened by death. They cannot accept the fact that the strong should rule the weak.
> Many grownups have made up their minds that there is no purpose in asking questions and that one should accept the facts as they are. But the child is often a philosopher and a seeker of God. (*Stories*, 337)

Singer's worldwide recognition is fortunate because his writing has uniquely contributed to keeping the memory of Eastern European Yiddish culture alive. The very buildings on Warsaw's Krochmalna Street in the ghetto where Singer grew up were demolished by the Germans, along with their inhabitants. The Warsaw Ghetto was rebuilt after World War II by the Poles, who replaced it with "row on row of Soviet-style apartment houses . . . all drab, all gray. . . . There is no trace left of the taverns, the shops, the bakeries, the prayer-houses. These remain alive only in Isaac's books and stories."[5] Critic Irving Howe observes that "Here is a man living in New York City, a sophisticated and clever writer, who composes stories about places like Frampol, Bilgoray, Kreshev, *as if they were still there*" (60). Singer demonstrates in many of his stories and essays that people and cultures can survive when they are remembered in literature.

In *Great Jewish Short Stories*, Saul Bellow cautions that when "opening a book in order to pay our respects to a vanished culture, a world destroyed to the eternal reproach of mankind, we may be tempted to put literary standards aside."[6] But the warning does not apply to Singer's writing. Singer transformed history unsentimentally into enduring literature. Without glossing over the privation and persecution that the Jews of Eastern Europe endured, when he wrote for children Singer depicted his deracinated world and at the same time expressed a faith that its roots would find receptive soil in the humanity natural to children everywhere. The forewords to Singer's many children's book are eloquent reading. His foreword to *Zlateh the Goat*, for example, reveals his awareness of the past and of readers lost, and his hopes that good children will become good adults: "I dedicate this book to the many children who had no chance to grow up because of stupid wars and cruel persecutions which devastated cities and destroyed innocent families. I hope that when the readers of these stories become men and women they will love not only their own children but good children everywhere."[7]

Translating Itseleh

Another remarkable fact about Singer's writing is its broad appeal, that it did attain an audience "everywhere." Singer's stories take place in a locale, culture, and time very foreign to most of his readers. Singer's specialized European setting—Russian and Polish in particular, and poor—his Yiddish culture, the fervent religion he was schooled in, even the climactic environment, the extreme Polish winter, would have been too formidable as barriers to communication in a lesser writer, especially one writing in Yiddish. In its broadest sense as a bridge between cultures and centuries as well as across languages, translation was crucial to Singer's work.

Translation had always been important to Singer. Yiddish was a minority language if ever there were one, and his worldwide fame rested on his works in translation. Once he acquired an English-reading audience, he became, as he says, "one of those rare writers who works with his translators . . . I check my translators constantly—I mean those who translate me into English or Hebrew. What happens to me in Italian, Portuguese or Finnish I will never know" ("Translating," 110–11).

Without translator/editor Elizabeth Shub, "Zlateh the Goat," Singer's first venture for children, would never have been written. Singer had many translators in his long career, from Saul Bellow to his own nephew Joseph Singer, but of them all, only Elizabeth Shub thought of him in regard to children's books. Singer recalls:

> I had been writing for forty years and it never occurred to me that I would ever write for children. . . . But my friend, Elizabeth Shub, who was then an editor of juvenile books at Harper, had different ideas. For a long time she tried to persuade me . . . that I was, at least potentially, a writer for children.[8]
>
> The net result was that she translated many stories into English from Yiddish and now, whenever I get a check, she gets a check. Which proves that sometimes altruism pays off.[9]

Elizabeth Shub had known Singer since she was a teenager and he a young new immigrant to New York. Her father, "S." Niger, was an influential Yiddish literary critic, and Isaac Singer soon joined his brother Israel Joshua as a guest in the Niger home. Singer spoke no English when he arrived in 1935; by the time he began writing for children 30 years later, his English was fluent. But it was not native English; Shub's was. "It just seemed natural," Shub said, "when he asked me to translate for him" (Interview, 1992). In addition, Shub worked in and knew children's literature; Singer did not; as he observed, "It did not exist among the Jewish people in my time."[10] Shub's skills, her having already translated many of his adult stories, her tact with Singer and, significantly, her familiarity, though second generation, with the world Isaac Singer had come from, contributed to a solid working friendship.

Oddly enough, however, there was one thing Elizabeth Shub could not do; she could not read Isaac Singer's handwriting. "Other translators of Singer, such as Mirra Ginsburg, worked alone," Shub says, "her Yiddish was better and she could read everything" (Interview, 1992). Shub spoke Yiddish and read it in typeset, but Singer's longhand was beyond her. As a consequence, Shub says:

> The way we mostly worked, at least on the first draft, is that he would come to my house and read it to me in Yiddish. He would sit in a nice easy chair and I would sit at the typewriter and do a rough immediate translation. If there was a word I didn't understand, he was there to

help me. Then I would read it to him and he would correct whatever he didn't think was right. Then I would type the whole thing out clean and I would edit it to correct anything that I thought was wrong. And then he would go over it and correct anything he didn't like. Then I would read it to him and he would make corrections again or if I felt something wasn't working, he would immediately, if he agreed, fix it.

Bringing the manuscript over didn't mean that as he read to me he didn't change things. He never felt that the manuscripts he brought over were just as they had to be. Once it was done, however, it was done. He wasn't a writer, like some of my others, who went back and said, "Oh, I hate this."

Until I got used to working with him I would sometimes not understand what he was doing. I would have a questioning look or frown a little bit. He'd get very angry and he would say "Why do you look like that? How can I work when you look like that? . . ." I would smile and say "I'm sorry." And then, by the end of the story, usually he had pulled it together and what didn't have any meaning to me in the middle certainly meant exactly what he wanted it to at the end. And that was a lesson I learned . . . not to take anything for granted till the story was finished. His instinct for the right word in another language was very, very keen (Interview, 1992).

The spontaneous oral exchange between author and translator drew out the best of Singer's storytelling ability. Alternately, he and Shub served as on-site audience. "My translators," says Singer, "are my best critics. I can tell by their expressions when they don't like a story of mine or any part of it" ("Translating," 111). Telling the stories aloud also drew out from him what Roderick McGillis calls "the speaking voice of literature,"[11] the narrative cadences of his young days in Eastern Europe as the son of a rabbi in whose drawing room all kinds of people came to tell their stories. Singer has often depicted himself in his memoirs as a child who listened carefully and consciously to the ways in which people spoke.

Elizabeth Shub remembers when Singer finally agreed to try his hand at telling stories for children. He brought his first attempts, Hanukkah poems, to her apartment. It took her until the next day to find the courage to reject the saccharine, heavily rhymed poems, a response Singer wasn't at all pleased about.

Shub continues:

It was maybe a day and a half later when I got this phone call. He said, "I wrote another story."

"Oh great, that's wonderful, do you want to come to my house?'"

"No, meet me at Famous" [his favorite deli on Seventy-second Street].

So I met him in the cafeteria and he handed me "Zlateh the Goat" and that's how we got started. (Interview, 1992)

Singer's debut as a children's writer won the first of his three Newbery Honor Awards; all three were won for books Shub translated with him.

Singer donated more than 20 manuscripts for children's and adults' stories to New York University's Fales Library, including the drafts of the seven stories in *Zlateh the Goat* and the stories Singer wrote specifically for *A Day of Pleasure*. These manuscripts are concrete documentation of a creative process that word processing has made obsolete.

Figures 1 through 3 are pages from the manuscripts Singer and Shub translated collaboratively. Page 1 of "Zlateh the Goat" (Figure 1) has very little editing. The large signature on top is Singer's, appended when he donated the manuscripts; interestingly, it looks as though he spelled his last name wrong. The rest of the handwriting is Elizabeth Shub's. The editorial improvement is clear: midpage, "For that money one could buy Hanukkah candles" becomes the more resonant "Such a sum would buy Hanukkah candles," and below "began to cry out" becomes "cried out loud," and finally "cried loudly."

On page 3 of the manuscript (Figure 2), the collaborative translating is more evident; we find many more revisions in Shub's hand. Midpage, the dramatic "She could walk no longer" replaces the bulky and flat "She no longer wanted to or was able to walk"; the strongly cadenced "did not want to admit the danger" replaces the polysyllabic "was reluctant to admit the danger." And at the bottom of the page, the bland "a large stack of hay covered with snow" becomes "a large hay stack which the snow had blanketed." The manuscript's final page (Figure 3) shows how spontaneous working on the story had become. In Shub's hand is written the final flawless paragraph of Zlateh: "utter" and "bleat" are crossed out, replaced with "come out with a single sound which expressed." The perfect last sentence is refined through crossings-out from "all her feelings, all her thoughts, and all her love" to "all her thoughts, and all her love." Love *is* a feeling, after all, so why be repetitive?

There is a particularly lively page from one of the several manuscript versions now owned by the University of Texas, Austin, of Singer's 1983 *The Fools of Chelm and Their History*. The novella is an Orwellian Yiddish

Zlateh, the Goat
by Isaac *Bashevis Singer*

At Hanukah time the road from the village to the town is
usually covered with snow, but this year the winter ~~was a~~ had been mild
one. Hanukah had almost come, yet little snow had fallen.
The sun shone most of the time. The peasants complained
that because ~~it was a a dry weather~~ of the dry weather there would be
a poor harvest of winter grain. New grass sprouted and the
peasants sent their cattle out to pasture.

For Reuven, the furrier, it was a bad year and after
long hesitation he decided to sell Zlateh, the goat. She
was old and gave little milk. Feyvel, the town butcher,
had offered eight gulden for her. ~~For that money one could~~ Such a sum would
buy Hanukah candles, potatoes and oil for pancakes, ~~give~~ gifts for the
children ~~gifts and buy~~ and other holiday necessaries for the house. Rueven
told his oldest boy Aaron to take the goat to town.

Aaron understood what taking the goat ~~to town~~ to Feyvel meant,
but he ~~couldxxxx~~ had to obey his father. Leah, his mother,
wiped the tears from her eyes when she heard ~~plainxxix~~ the news.
Aaron's ~~xix~~ younger sisters, Anna and Miriam ~~began to cry out loud~~ cried loudly.
Aaron put on his quilted jacket, a cap with ear muffs, bound
a rope around Zlateh's neck, and took along two slices of bread
with cheese to eat on the road. Aaron was supposed to deliver
the goat by evening, spend the night at the butchers, and return
the next day with the money.

While the family said goodbye to the goat and Aaron placed
the rope around her neck, Zlateh stood as patiently and goodnaturedly
as ever. She licked Reuven's hand. She shook her small white
beard. Zlateh trusted human beings. She knew that they fed her

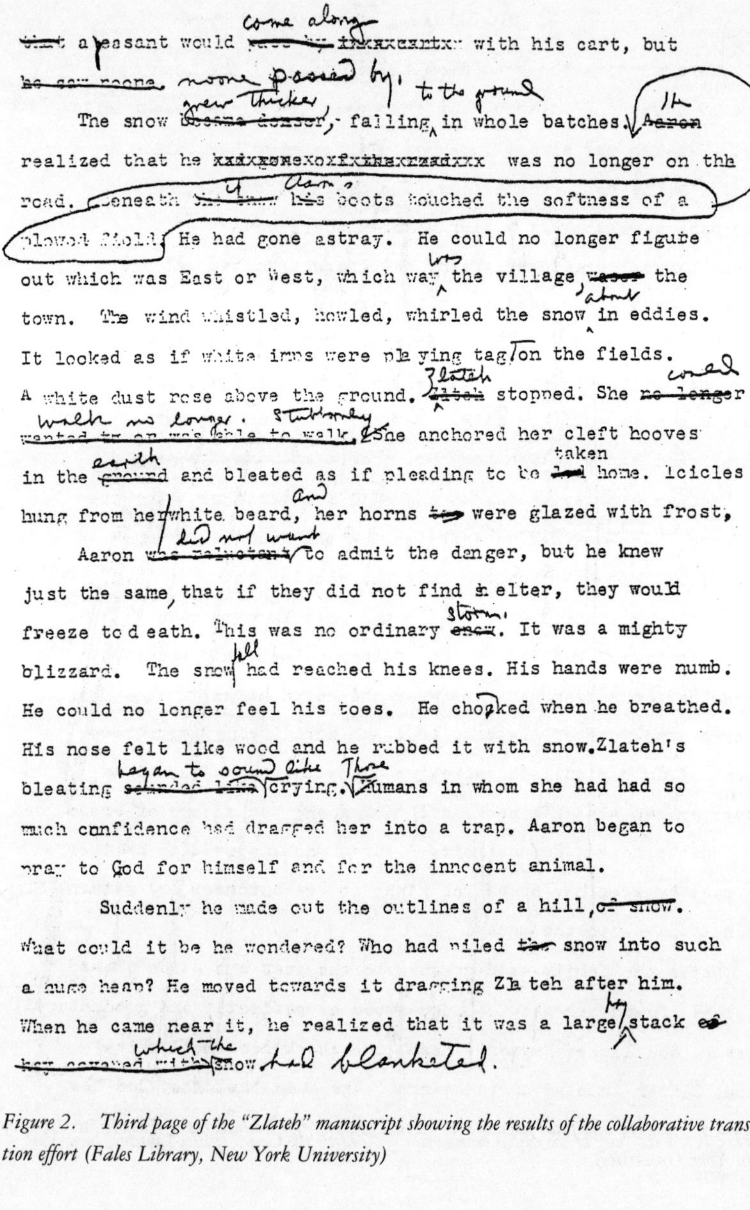

~~that~~ a peasant would ^come along^ ~~~~ ~~fxxxxxxxx~~ with his cart, but ~~he saw none.~~ noone passed by. ^grew thicker,^

The snow ~~became denser,~~ falling in whole batches. ^to the ground^ ~~Aaron~~ realized that he ~~xxxxxxxxxxxxxxxxxx~~ was no longer on the road. Beneath ~~the snow~~ ^Clean^ his boots touched the softness of a plowed field. He had gone astray. He could no longer figure out which was East or West, which way ^lay^ the village, ~~where~~ the ^about^ town. The wind whistled, howled, whirled the snow in eddies. It looked as if white imps were playing tag/on the fields. A white dust rose above the ground. ~~Zlateh~~ ^Zlateh^ stopped. She ~~no longer~~ ~~walk no longer. Suddenly~~ ~~wanted to or was able to walk,~~ She anchored her cleft hooves ^earth^ ^taken^ in the ~~ground~~ and bleated as if pleading to be ~~led~~ home. Icicles hung from her white beard, her horns ~~to~~ ^and^ were glazed with frost,

Aaron ~~who reluctant~~ ^did not want^ to admit the danger, but he knew just the same, that if they did not find shelter, they would freeze to death. This was no ordinary ~~snow.~~ ^storm.^ It was a mighty ^fell^ blizzard. The snow had reached his knees. His hands were numb. He could no longer feel his toes. He choked when he breathed. His nose felt like wood and he rubbed it with snow. Zlateh's ^began to sound like^ ^Those^ bleating ~~sounded like~~ crying. Humans in whom she had had so much confidence had dragged her into a trap. Aaron began to pray to God for himself and for the innocent animal.

Suddenly he made out the outlines of a hill, ~~of snow.~~ What could it be he wondered? Who had piled ~~the~~ snow into such a huge heap? He moved towards it dragging Zlateh after him. When he came near it, he realized that it was a large stack ~~of~~ ^by^ ~~hay covered with~~ ^which the^ snow ~~had~~ ^had blanketed.^

Figure 2. *Third page of the "Zlateh" manuscript showing the results of the collaborative translation effort (Fales Library, New York University)*

Figure 3. Eighth and final page of the "Zlateh" manuscript with working notes (Fales Library, New York University)

political comedy about the famous folklore fools, the so-called sages of Chelm and the consequences of their harebrained imperialism. Humor is notoriously difficult to translate, and, as Singer says, "Yiddish is a language with a built-in humor . . . [it] can take a lot of overstatement . . . English or French must be much more precise, logical, lean" ("Translating," 111–12). The deadpan parody that begins with the inflated opening of the "history"—that "God said, 'Let there be Chelm.' And there was Chelm"—does translate, in no small part because of the precision of the editing. At the bottom of the page, sentence structure and delivery are refined through translation: "It is said that the first Chelmites were primitive people, or maybe just fools" becomes "It is said that the earliest Chelmites were primitive people. Some said they were just plain fools." Wording is definitely punchier the second time around.

Elizabeth Shub and Isaac Singer together translated nearly all of Singer's children's books. He credits six other translators as having worked on stories appearing in *A Day of Pleasure*, including his nephew Joseph who had already translated many of the stories originally printed in *In My Father's Court*; Elizabeth Shub translated such new material as "Who I Am," the first story in the book. Almost 20 years after their first endeavor, Singer reaffirmed his debt to his old friend Elizabeth in the "Author's Note" for *Stories for Children*: "But editors often know more about writers than the writers themselves." Singer's stories are good enough to be good in any language, but Elizabeth Shub made them good in *English*.

Zlateh the Goat was published in 1966 by Harper and Row, where Elizabeth Shub was employed. Singer followed Shub when she changed publishers and his second book, *The Fearsome Inn*, was published by Charles Scribner's Sons. Singer did not, however, follow Shub once more when she moved to Greenwillow Books, where she has been ever since. By this time, Farrar, Straus and Giroux, the publishers of Singer's adult fiction who had been initially skeptical about Singer writing for children, wanted his children's books too. He published the rest of his children's fiction with its children's book division, and worked with editors Michael di Capua and Stephen Roxburgh. His autobiographies, however, he published with Doubleday: *Love and Exile*, *A Little Boy in Search of God*, *A Young Man in Search of Love* (1978), and *Lost in America* (1981).

Singer's native tongue necessitated translation and his career depended upon it. For him, however, the ultimate justification for struggling with translation was "that my work will be good enough to be translated or to be read, and I work accordingly" (Colwin, 23–24).

In his last published interview before his death in 1991 he said: "I would like people to remember me as a good writer, not as a bad writer. I would like people to remember me as a good person, not a bad person. But whether this will come out is a big question."[12]

Illustrating Isaac

Another kind of translation occurs when an author's words are illustrated. The words will be transformed into a visual medium that both enlightens and limits the reader.

Singer was ambivalent about illustration. He reminisces about his "Jewish puritanical" basic training in aesthetics in a story from *In My Father's Court* (1962), "The Purim Gift": "In our neighbors' homes I had seen carpets, pictures on the wall, copper bowls, lamps, and figurines. But in our house, a rabbi's house, such luxuries were frowned upon. Pictures and statuary were out of the question; my parents regarded them as idolatrous. . . . My Father . . . cited the Commandment: 'Thou shalt not make unto thee any graven image, or any likeness . . .'" (67–68).

He expresses his own adult views on art and artists in the Introduction to his major collection, *Stories for Children* (1984):

> Although I love illustrations to stories for children and in many cases they are a very propitious addition to the story, I still think that the power of the word is the best medium to inform and entertain the mind of our youngsters. Most of the stories I read as a young boy were not illustrated. Needless to say, the stories in the Bible . . . had no illustrations. In this volume I'm happy to speak to my young readers in just words. I still believe that in the beginning was the Logos, the power of the word. (Foreword)

In 1975 Singer was asked if he were happy with the illustrations in his children's books. He replied, "I never interfere. I am not always completely happy, but I decided to leave this to the publisher" (Wolkstein, 138). The only illustrator whose work he asked Farrar, Straus and Giroux to consider for a book was that of his *landtsman*, Irene Leiblich, a woman from his area of Poland. The publisher agreed. Leiblich used oil paint to illustrate first *A Tale of Three Wishes* and then *The Power of Light* with a lush primitive style reminiscent of Chagall and Grandma Moses. Farrar, Straus and Giroux produced a handsome Sunburst edition printed on bright white paper that highlights Leiblich's deep blues and glowing yellows.

Singer's other children's books were illustrated by a publishers' wish list of artists, including Maurice Sendak, Margot Zemach, Uri Shulevitz, Eric Carle, Leonard Everett Fisher, Nonny Hogrogian, William Pene du Bois, and photographer Roman Vishniac.

Singer's illustrators have employed wide-ranging techniques and media: *The Wicked City* and *Yentl* done in stark woodcuts, *Joseph and Koza* in a cocoa brown conté crayon, *Why Noah Chose the Dove* in a collage mixed with paint, *Elijah the Slave* in mixed media, *The Golem* in a pen-and-ink wash, and *The Fools of Chelm*, *Zlateh the Goat*, and Margot Zemach's numerous books done in pen and ink.[13]

Critiquing Singer

In recent years, assessment of Singer's body of works, acknowledging that he is a literary giant, has tended to favor his short fiction over his novels. Because his children's stories are all short, it is no surprise that among them are found some of Singer's finest work; "Zlateh the Goat," "Naftali the Storyteller and His Horse, Sus," "The Lantuch," "Menaseh's Dream," "Hanukkah in the Poorhouse," and his many Chelm and Shlemiel stories are examples. What is surprising is how little has been written exclusively on his children's stories. The usual pattern of criticism has been to discuss his adult works at length and his children's books in passing. Nonetheless, several fine essays have been penned, among them commentaries by Thomas P. Riggio, Naomi S. Morse, and Eric A. Kimmel. Singer wrote about writing for children and gave several informative interviews, such as those by Francelia Butler, Diane Wolkstein, and Laurie Colwin. Extensive interviews, which covered many facets of his works, were conducted by Irving Howe, Richard Burgin, and Paul Rosenblatt among many others. Grace Farrell's 1991 book *Conversations* presents several decades of interviews with Singer. The title of one essay reaffirms the interwoven nature of Singer's fiction and his fact, his children's stories and his childhood autobiographies—David Miller's essay, "Isaac Bashevis Singer: The Interview as a Fictional Genre."

Many critics believe the best of Singer's children's books is his first, *Zlateh the Goat*. For its translator, editor, and initiator, Elizabeth Shub, it remains first and foremost.

Chapter Three
First and Foremost
Zlateh the Goat

Haystack Haven

Singer's first publication for children, the collection *Zlateh the Goat*, remains his standard. In it, he demarcated and transmitted his lively world in full dimension, establishing from the first page that his craft would undergo no diminution due to audience. The turns of phrase and imagery in these stories equal Singer's best work anywhere. Several critics note, for example, the first appearance of Singer's powerful descriptions of the devil's homeland, where "no people walk, no cattle tread, where the sky is copper and the earth is iron" (*Zlateh* 73). Singer demonstrated the complexity and originality of his use of his native material, his *Stoffe*, the stories he knew so well from childhood that they were, as his translator Elizabeth Shub remarked, "part of the world he breathed" (Interview, 1992). As pointed out by Edward Alexander in his analysis of Singer's adult stories, Singer in his early work in all genres drew first upon historic and folkloric material, as distinct from the autobiographic stories he included in his later collections. The later the work, in children's collections as well as in adult ones, the more likely it was to contain one or more memoirs. While *Zlateh the Goat* has no autobiographic tales, "Growing Up" from *Naftali the Storyteller and His Horse, Sus* and "A Hanukkah Evening in My Parents' House," from *The Power of Light*, are stories about Singer as a child. Even the Foreword is more generic in his first publication for children than in his later forewords, in which he usually mentions his family.

The seven stories in *Zlateh the Goat* also exemplified Singer's range, from gothic in "Grandmother's Tale" to realistic in "Zlateh the Goat" and slapstick in "The Mixed-Up Feet and the Silly Bridegroom." Singer's reappearing characters are introduced: the Shlemiel family, the fools of Chelm, devils and witches, affectionate animals, storytellers, working people, exasperated wives, steadfast children. The author's return as a teenager from Warsaw to the rural Polish countryside rounded out his experience of Jewish life in Eastern Europe, equipping him to describe the wintry landscapes of Poland's cities and villages, the marketplaces and forests, the wind-whipped streets, and hearthsides in which his stories are set. The locations are those of his youth: the towns and villages of Bilgoray, Frampol, Lublin, Cracow, the Vistula River, and the Carpathian Mountains.

Children are respectful to parents, and men are very much in power, if not exactly in control. Objects are everyday—onions, kerchiefs, brooms, and haystacks, and only one story, "Fool's Paradise," is set in explicitly comfortable surroundings. Life is public; the poor have no privacy. People are dramatic; there is much excited gesturing, such as slapping of foreheads and pulling of beards. People are also forgiving of each other's faults—although that attitude ranges from affectionate acceptance to resigned rage. Under difficult conditions, tolerance was essential: "Surrounded by physical hostility and social uncertainty, the *shtetl* imposed law and decorum upon its cohesive, intimate, vulnerable community. Group and family came first. The individual was not ignored, but neither was he exalted."[1]

In truth Singer's stories have an uncommon lot of fools, and by way of accepting them himself, he lets their goodness of heart earn its reward. Lemel and Yenta from "The Mixed-Up Feet and the Silly Bridegroom" truly love each other; that fact bodes better for their continued happiness than business acumen or material abundance—and fortunately so, for they possess neither.

Although its title tale is unique, the core of *Zlateh the Goat* is folkloric. In Singer's stories, devils, ogres, and neutral and benevolent spirits interact with the human world; crickets talk to each other and imps of the hearth contribute to household expenses. Two of the stories, "Grandmother's Tale" and "The Devil's Trick," are based on *Bubbe meises*, literally oral "Grandmother's Tales" which he developed into polished narratives. In "The Mixed-Up Feet and the Silly Bridegroom," Singer incorporates a widespread comedic trope about ridiculously tangled feet into a folktale-like story by filling in dialogue and description.[2] In "The Snow in Chelm" he expands upon one of many established cultural jokes about a recognizable set of characters and circumstances—the so-called sages of Chelm and their unworldly foolishness.[3] In "The First Shlemiel" Singer brilliantly builds a world, a family, and a history for the hapless incompetent of Jewish humor, the *shlemiel*. Yiddish is rich in nouns describing character types; a *shlemiel* is a bungler, a dimwit, inept but not malicious, simply incapable of doing much more than providing fodder for jokes. This stock character is fleshed out in Singer's prose.

The *shlemiel* story turned out to be the first of several. Similarly, the appearance of the fools of Chelm in two stories in this collection presaged their development in many future stories, including an entire book, *The Fools of Chelm and Their History*. Other Shlemiel and Elders stories are "Dalfunka, Where the Rich Live Forever," "The Elders of Chelm and Genedel's Key," "The Fools of Chelm and the Stupid Carp," "Shlemiel the Businessman," "The Snow in Chelm," "When Shlemiel Went to Warsaw," and "The Day I Got Lost."

"A Grandmother's Tale," in *Zlateh the Goat*, like many of Singer's stories, resembles a fairy tale in its unquestioned acceptance of the supernatural. In it, no surprise is expressed when demons appear, and no explanation of their presence is provided. In the *shtetl* world, as Singer often depicted it in his stories for adults, the existence of spirits was consensual reality.

Like fairy tales in this too, Singer's children's stories have happy endings, an explicit decision on his part. Even in scary stories like "A Grandmother's Tale" in which the intrusion of the supernatural into the everyday world remains unexplained, evil is at least only evanescent. In other stories, evil is clearly defeated. In *Zlateh the Goat*, several stories have refrains and rhymes, reminiscent of the Grimms' stories and Afanasiev stories Singer read as a youth[4] and of the delivery common to the oral tradition.

Singer's children's stories are unlike fairy tales in that his characters are everyday people. *Zlateh the Goat* has no castles; instead we find synagogues, studyhouses, inns, and tenements. Royalty is uncommon, as are jewels and material rewards, and "happily ever after" does not automatically equate with power and rulership. Avarice and stinginess are ridiculed. Physical beauty is less valued than knowledge, goodness of heart, and charitable action. Heroic feats are accomplished on a small scale by children such as David in "The Devil's Trick," who is described as a "poor boy with a pale face" (71). All by himself and far from public view, David saves his parents and his baby brother and outsmarts the devil. Singer is saying that in the *shtetl*, as in one's own tiny personal backyard, the stakes are enormous, eternal: souls there hang in the balance no less than in the courtyards of kings. Within the cramped microcosm of the ghetto, greatness of spirit is possible, and it too, rather than material gain, is its own reward. Without sentimentalizing, Singer exalts both childhood in general and the culture of his own childhood.

Family love and the warmth of the holiday, human/animal dependence, and harsh reality—economic and environmental—are all part of Singer's first children's story. "Zlateh the Goat" is about the Russian Jewish family of Reuven, the furrier. An unusually warm winter spells disaster for them, and reluctantly they are forced to sell their beloved old goat Zlateh to raise a few gulden for necessities. Zlateh must be butchered because Reuven has no choice. Even so, he hesitates. Aaron's mother, Leah, and his two sisters weep, but they do not argue. Not only Aaron but everyone in the family knows why Zlateh must go; it is a matter of survival. Singer lays out the situation: "Reuven told his oldest son Aaron to take the goat to town. Aaron understood what taking the goat to Feivel meant, but he had to obey his father" (80).

Matter-of-factly Singer conveys the father's plan: Aaron and Zlateh are to go to town, both will stay overnight, but only Aaron will return home the next day. Singer's dramatic pacing is impeccable, for no sooner does he baldly state the itinerary than he shifts the scene and the sympathy to Zlateh, patiently waiting upon the humans: "Zlateh trusted human beings. She knew that they always fed her and never did her any harm" (80). This situation and the reactions of the family members can be contrasted to the opening scene in *Charlotte's Web*. Fern beseeches her father not to slaughter Wilbur, and dubiously but affectionately, her father can acquiesce; he is in an economic position to indulge his daughter by sparing the runt piglet's life. Reuven is not in a position to do so and his children, although upset, do not ask him to. Indeed, few pets are found in Singer's stories, notably the parakeet Dreidel in *The Power of Light*; pets are a luxury and ones such as dogs and cats are infrequent. Much more prevalent are peasant-pleasing and productive animals such as goats, geese, and horses.

The day Zlateh and Aaron set off is blue and clear but it does not remain that balmy for long. The boy and the goat are caught in a blizzard. Much like the emotional writer he admired, Edgar Allan Poe, Singer uses weather like a character in his stories and as a means to mark crescendos in plot. The Eastern European-born author knew firsthand the wild weather on the open fields and rural roads of Russia—it was his neighborhood. In a vivid paragraph he concocts a storm ferocious in its magnitude yet entirely natural. Describing the snowy turbulence with his trademark mention of imps, Singer writes "[it] looked as if white imps were playing tag on the fields" (81), stipulating "as if" because this is a realistic story.

On the verge of freezing, Aaron and Zlateh are saved by a mound of snow. Aaron realizes it covers a large haystack. This is no deus ex machina salvation; as a country boy, Aaron is credible as a resourceful character. He tunnels a way in for him and Zlateh. The storm rages during the three days they share there. They converse—the boy with words, Zlateh with the always appropriate "maaaa": "Aaron had always loved Zlateh, but in those three days he loved her more and more. She fed him with her milk and helped him keep warm. She comforted him with her patience. He told her many stories, and she always cocked her ear and listened. When he patted her, she licked his hand and his face. Then she said, 'Maaaa,' and he knew it meant, I love you too" (86).

Singer had used the image of a vocalizing goat before as expressive of the rapport between man and beast. Because animals respond so readily to kindness, the goat's polyvalent and guileless sound of affirmation is also a literary means to confirm the purity of the human character involved. In "Gimpel the Fool," Singer's breakthrough story translated in the mid-1950s, he uses the response of the goat to reconfirm the translucent goodness of Gimpel:

> I have forgotten to say that we had a goat. When I heard she was unwell I went into the yard. The nanny goat was a good little creature. I had a nearly human feeling for her. With hesitant steps I went up to the shed and opened the door. The goat stood there on her four feet. I felt her everywhere, drew her by the horns, examined her udders, and found nothing wrong. She had probably eaten too much bark. "Good night, little goat," I said. "Keep well." And the little beast answered with a 'Maa' as though to thank me for the good will. (*Collected Stories*, 11)

The goat communicates, but in the manner of a real life—if extraordinarily sensitive—goat. Zlateh is never personified as are Wilbur and Charlotte, again in contrast to *Charlotte's Web*.

Inside the snow womb Zlateh and Aaron share, the boy forgets time. His dreams are depicted by Singer with characteristic lyricism; the descriptive prose here, as elsewhere, is lovely, but Singer disciplines his use of it, accomplishing in a few sentences and images what many writers must take many more words to present. When the storm subsides, Aaron and Zlateh emerge and look at the world: "It was all white, quiet, dreaming dreams of heavenly splendor. The stars were large and close. The moon swam in the sky as in a sea" (89).

Aaron turns not toward town but toward home, resolved to keep Zlateh. The frantic family rejoices to see them; the snow has alleviated their economic straits, and by mutual consent Zlateh indeed remains at home. Not only has she saved Aaron, Zlateh has herself been reborn twice; once when she and Aaron emerge after the mystical three days in the darkness of their home of hay, and once again when reprieved from the death sentence hanging over her. After her return, Zlateh is treated as one of the family. She scratches on the door with her horn when she wants to visit the house and responds to Aaron's loving words with her contented "maaaa." Singer ends with perfect details: "Aaron's sisters . . . gave her a special treat of chopped carrots and potato peels, which Zlateh gobbled up hungrily" and "When Hanukkah came, Aaron's mother was able to fry pancakes every evening, and Zlateh got her portion too" (90). Singer's story of trust, self-reliance, mutual aid, and poetic justice overcoming poverty and the elements is one that stays in the memory of its readers.

Dealing with Dumbos and Devils

A completely different kind of story opens the collection. "Fool's Paradise" is a deadpan bildungsroman in which the educational journey takes place in the living room of the rich man Kadish. This living room is "somewhere, sometime" (5), that is, in the fairy-tale world where the improbable is unquestioned; although, except for the exceeding foolishness of Atzel, this story is not even that unbelievable.

Atzel's name means "Lazy One" in Hebrew.[5] He has grown up in comfortable surroundings, along with an orphan girl, Aksah; they plan to marry. But, true to his name, Atzel prefers the visions inculcated in him early by the family's servants of an easeful and abundant paradise to his father's explicit expectations that he work. Like many an impressionable teen, Atzel has succumbed to a fictionalized perfection that is located somewhere other than the familiar family surroundings. Although generation conflict and clinging to the nest are elements common to myriad stories, Atzel's solution is extraordinary: he steadfastly imagines himself dead. In paradise he will be able to partake of the high-protein diet described to him by the servants and to blissfully avoid all responsibility. The obvious fact that he lives and breathes, confirmed by all his relatives and a stream of doctors, fails to convince Atzel; after all, if he were logical, there would be no story. As Naomi S. Morse observes, "His wish to die is not regarded as sinful or deranged, but as a condition that requires attention."[6]

Atzel's father Kadish, whose name is identical with the Hebrew name for the prayer said for the dead, finally seeks out the specialist, Dr. Yoetz. His name means "adviser." Dr. Yoetz agrees to cure Atzel, but on condition that the family go along with whatever the doctor says and does. Ingeniously using reverse psychology, the doctor humors his peculiar patient. Everyone agrees to pretend that Atzel really has died and a paradise is concocted for him in the house. The stolid servants of Maurice Sendak's illustrations look suitably absurd masquerading as angels with tiny wings, but Atzel finally rests easy in his perceived Heaven. Except for one problem: perfection is monotonous. He gets bored. Inquiring of an "angel" the whereabouts of Aksah, he even gets a little jealous when told that Aksah misses him now, but will eventually adjust. It will be decades, he learns, before anyone comes to join him in his serene seclusion. Atzel complains to an angel:

> "I would rather chop wood and carry stones than sit here. And how long will this last?"
> "Forever."
> "Stay here forever?" Atzel began to tear his hair in grief. "I'd rather kill myself."
> "A dead man cannot kill himself." (*Zlateh*, 12)

The logic of the punch line captures both Atzel's lesson and his dilemma. Now that he has gotten where he wanted to go, he does not want to be there anymore: it is Dorothy's story in L. Frank Baum's *The Wizard of Oz* all over again. Atzel too has learned that home is where the heart is, but he does not appear to have a way out of paradise. Singer has set up the manner of Atzel's "rebirth" by having earlier established the cleverness of Dr. Yoetz. Following the doctor's prearranged directions, after eight days the winged servant announces to Atzel that his death was, after all, a misdiagnosis. Atzel learns that he is still alive.

Characteristically, Atzel does not question the logic of his good luck. He allows the servant to blindfold his eyes and lead him through the hallways back to the joyful family. At the wedding of Atzel and Aksah, Dr. Yoetz is the guest of honor. The happy couple lives long and often marvels with their children at the doctor's "wonderful cure" (16).

The loving scene of the family at the story's end is followed by a final pithy sentence, like one of the sayings of the Talmudic Fathers. This is the pattern of Singer's extraordinary endings—with an affecting detail of human emotion, then an abstraction, Singer resolves and elevates a story in a few memorable sentences. Fittingly, the once-and-future paradise dweller Atzel speaks the story's last words that lift a slapstick fool's tale to one tinged with the metaphysical: "But, of course, what paradise is like, no one can tell" (16).

In one rare story in which Singer does depict paradise, it is much like earth—only nicer. Families are reunited in "Menaseh's Dream," and that alone is paradise for the orphan Menaseh. This story is not comic; it is dreamy and the dream Menaseh has in it immediately begins turning into reality upon his awakening into the real world. This major story is discussed in chapter 4.

The characters in the humorous "Fool's Paradise" are colorful and quirky; they are indulgent to a fault, loyal, bourgeois. The story has been called "paternalistic" as opposed to the "maternalistic" "Zlateh the Goat"[7] because the father is asserting his will through the all-knowing male doctor.

Much more mysterious and ambivalent a character is Grandmother in "Grandmother's Tale," who tells a horror story to her grandchildren one Hanukkah night. The brief, powerful story represents another characteristic of Singer stories in addition to the suspended disbelief.

If a holiday is depicted in a Singer story, it is almost always Hanukkah; occasionally, it is the carefree springtime holiday, Purim. Hanukkah is a festive break in the dark winter, a celebration of legendary miracles and glowing candles; a children's holiday in a ritual calendar that often commemorates suffering. Presents are exchanged. Insofar as they can afford, women lay out a feast of *latkes*, or potato pancakes, jam, and sour cream.

Singer frames "Grandmother's Tale" concisely. Grandmother Leah is telling her excited grandchildren a bedtime story. The children in it stay up late, absorbed in a game of *dreidel*. A strange young man appears at the door, joins them in the game, and extravagantly loses. The night ages. When the clock strikes 13, the oldest child sees that the stranger casts no shadow: indeed, "Their guest was not a man but a demon" (22). The scene becomes ominous. The devil rises with a loud laugh; the house spins; goblins appear. The devil sprouts wings, crows like a rooster, and, along with his entire company, suddenly disappears. Grandmother Leah's story ends immediately—she provides no explanation of the events.

But Singer's story continues, first with a comical verse,[8] then with a closure of the frame, showing the Grandmother hustling her young charges off to bed. The ghoulishness of the tale told so matter-of-factly by the matriarch is juxtaposed to the visual image Singer provides of her as incongruously knitting socks for her youngest grandchild.

A similarly related, similarly received supernatural tale is told by another credible character in "Naftali the Storyteller and His Horse, Sus." In it, Naftali's coachman father frequently tells of meeting a demon on the road, and provides neither notice nor explanation of anything particularly surprising about the contact.

"The Devil's Trick" could equally be called "David's Trick," for the boy dents the devil's pride. David's situation is desperate. It is the first night of Hanukkah. A storm of Singer's cosmic proportions is raking the "soot-covered walls" of the family hut, and both the boy's parents are missing. There is no food and David is alone with his baby brother. Snow "somersault[s] in the cold air" (71) and falls "dry and heavy as salt" (72). Singer describes the demons abroad in the storm: "The devil's wife rode on her hoop, with a broom in one hand and a rope in the other. Before her ran a white goat with a black beard and twisted horns. Behind her strode the devil with his cobweb face, holes instead of eyes, hair to his shoulders, and legs long as stilts" (71).

Having lighted the one Hanukkah candle, David tucks his brother in and steps out to find his parents. Notably the hero in this Jewish story is going to save his parents, rather than, in familiar fairy-tale form, being cast out by them or sent on a journey. But for David to step into their territory is exactly what the demons want. The storm redoubles in fury and it seems certain David will be overwhelmed and captured by the superior forces, just as his parents were. As so often in Singer's stories, the simple pure gesture made without ulterior motive proves the salvation; in this story the beacon of the candle David lighted earlier for Hanukkah guides him through the darkness back to his hut—just as the single candle lighted the way for the young boy Tzaddock in the story told by Rabbi Singer to his young son. David slips inside the house just ahead of the devil; the devil in fact is so close behind that in the confusion his tail gets caught in the door. Refusing to release him, David manages to leverage his advantage, winning the return of his parents, and singeing the devil's tail with the same miraculously multipurpose Hanukkah candle that had guided him home.

In the tradition of the fighting Maccabee brothers whose heroism is remembered in the holiday, exultantly David yells, "Now devil, you will remember, Hanukkah is no time for making trouble" (73). Without having David win fame or fortune, Singer has portrayed a victory that confirms the story's theme:

No matter how shrewd he is, the devil will always make a mistake, especially on Hanukkah.

The powers of evil had managed to hide the stars, but they could
not extinguish the single Hanukkah candle. (72)

Chelm on Earth

The remaining three stories in *Zlateh the Goat* share a common location;
they all take place in the Polish *shtetl* of Chelm. Here Singer's folklore
roots are broad. *Chelm* is the Yiddish code word for the central locus of
foolishness, a medieval backwater impervious to modernity. The very
recognizable name elicits immediate humorous association. Except for its
high percentage of nitwits, Chelm is a typical village: people work hard
and are poor. Its problems are entrenched—poverty, provincialism, and
prejudice. The town muddles along—the Yiddish word would be
shleps—despite the incompetence of the authorities in charge: the legendary seven elders known as the sages of Chelm.

Some modicum of twisted coherence in the sages' solutions is always
found, around which the well-known humorous incidents revolve.
Collections such as Nathan Ausubel's *A Treasury of Jewish Folklore* present
these jokes in the shorter forms Singer embellished upon in creating his
narratives.

The sages of Chelm are Jewish slapstick counterparts of the seven
dwarves. The dwarves are industrious in Grimm and endearing in
Disney. They operate in the forest isolated from society and power. The
Elders of Chelm are much more complex, however, stars of their own
stories. They are industrious only in producing inane schemes, endearing
but also exasperating. They are unthinkingly sexist and self-satisfied,
and they have a taste for sweets. That they are much respected by the
general populace does not reflect well on the villagers' judgment: "Of all
the fools of Chelm, the most famous were its seven Elders. Because they
were the village's oldest and greatest fools, they ruled in Chelm" (29).

The chief sage, Gronam the Great Fool, or Gronam Ox, as he is called
in subsequent Chelm stories, is regarded as brilliant:

> "Is the child a boy?" the Elder asked.
> "No."
> "Is it a girl?"
> "How did you guess?" Lemel asked in amazement.
> And the Elder of Chelm replied, "For the wise men in Chelm there
> are no secrets." (50)

While no secrets exist in Chelm, problems do. Singer introduces his version of the legendary town in "The Snow in Chelm." The village is broke, and the sages do not know what to do. It is Hanukkah; snow blankets everything "like a silver tablecloth." When Gronam sees this, a light bulb goes off in his head: "The snow is silver," he proclaims, and the other Elders readily see diamonds and pearls: "It became clear to the Elders that a treasure had fallen from the sky."

But no sooner is one problem solved—now that income is to be secured from the fallen snow—than it is replaced by another. The sages realize that once the people of Chelm walk on the snow, they will trample it. Singer strings out the joke as the characters debate. Silly Tudras solves the problem: the Elders will send a messenger to tell the townsfolk to stay indoors. "For a while," writes Singer, "the Elders were satisfied" but eventually, Dopey Lekisch realizes that the messenger, by delivering the message, will trample the snow (30).

By this time, in a couple of pages, Singer has established the characteristics of the Elders, not only their thought processes, language, and gestures, but their looks. They are old, white bearded, and have "high foreheads from thinking too much" (30). Confronted with a dilemma such as Dopey Lekisch's objection, the Elders react characteristically by wrinkling their foreheads and clutching their beards. The next solution is the brainchild of Shmerel Ox: if the messenger is carried around town on a table, then he will not trample the snow. The Elders, "clapping their hands, admired their own wisdom" (33).

The difficult thinking successfully concluded, the Elders employ the working people around them to carry out their plan, for Jewish scholars do not do physical tasks. Sendak's illustration shows a wide-eyed Gimpel the errand boy borne aloft by the burly figures of "Treitle the cook, Berel the potato peeler, Yukel the salad maker, and Yontel, who was in charge of the community goat." They dutifully convey the boy around town and he warns one and all to stay inside: "A treasure has fallen from the sky and it is forbidden to step on it" (33). The acquiescent town obeys the Elders, for, after all, they are fools too.

Henry D. Spalding's *Encyclopedia of Jewish Humor* (1969) provides a basic form of this joke. It is much shorter and peopled by the stock characters of Chelm. The reason for preserving the snow is aesthetic, rather than economic, and it is the rabbi who strikes a "sad note": "The *shammes* [sexton] will soon be passing through town to call on people to prepare for the *Shabbes* [Sabbath]. He will leave ugly tracks in the beautiful snow when he walks on it." The punch line is the same: the *shammes* is conveyed over the snow on a table—in this version carried by none other than the "seven Council members!"[9]

During the night the sages devise schemes for spending the money to come. One of these is the first of several sly jabs Singer makes at the ability of rulers to dupe people by playing around with words. Dopey Lekisch proposes that the money be used to give the townspeople magnifying glasses because if everything *looks* bigger, they will think things are bigger and, therefore, better. Civic pride is a factor in Dopey's plan, too; if Chelm looks bigger, it will look like a city instead of a village. In a later story, "The Elders of Chelm and Genedel's Key" from *When Shlemiel Went to Warsaw*, also set in a time of community privation, the Elders actually consider resolving the shortage of sour cream for the holidays by decreeing that sour cream thenceforth be called "water" and water "sour cream." Because "sour cream" will therefore be plentiful, who can complain?

Several years after *Zlateh the Goat*, Singer wrote a self-contained political burlesque, *The Fools of Chelm and Their History*, in which Chelm goes disastrously to war; this story is discussed in chapter 7. Singer's political writing is less ominous than, for example, George Orwell's in *Animal Farm* and *1984* because the characters in Singer's stories are ridiculous rather than murderous. They are sincere rather than calculating. Equally as dimwitted as their constituents, they believe their own moronic judgments. This is not to say that Singer was a political writer; he was in fact conservative in most matters. For example, his friend Dorothy Straus relates that even after years in New York City, Singer still wore heavy dark European suits, "neckties, and heavy, polished oxford shoes," making no concession to the fashions of the New World in this and other matters.[10] It is to say, however, that he was a astute observer of human psychology, and that, as concerned leaders, followers, causes, and "isms," he usually found little to admire.

In "The Snow in Chelm," the Elders' "clever ideas" evaporate with the morning sun. The snow treasure has been trampled during the night, but the Elders, notwithstanding, manage to preserve their optimism. They admit their mistake, but vow to correct it the following year when the four carriers of the messenger boy will themselves be carried, thereby preventing the carriers' footprints from marring the treasure. While the Elders prepare impractically for the future, the town is still impoverished in the present; nevertheless, the villagers "were full of hope for the next year and praised their Elders, who they know could always be counted on to find a way, no matter how difficult the problem" (34). The

zany stasis depicted in the countryside exists perhaps because there really was no way to solve the problems of the Eastern European Jews. To
react with humor to a mad world was a rational response.

In the role of consultants, the Elders of Chelm appear in "The Mixed-
Up Feet and the Silly Bridegroom" and in "The First Shlemiel." Gronam
saves the day several times in the former story by providing reasonable
solutions to the absurd dilemmas that arise in Chelm. Chelm itself is a
joke, but Singer compounds it by locating this story in East Chelm, as if
Chelm proper were important enough to spawn suburbs. There the four
daughters of Shmelka and Shmelkicha, the diminutive name signifying
affection, work hard on the farm and share a broad bed: typical peasant
girls of Chelm.

"The Mixed-Up Feet and the Silly Bridegroom" has two parts. In the
first, one morning the girls' feet get hopelessly tangled in the bed. With
utterly serious concern, the mother runs to the Elder for advice: "When
Shmelkicha arrived in Chelm and told the Elder about what had happened to her daughters, he clutched his white beard with one hand,
placed the other on his forehead, and was immediately lost in thought.
As he pondered he hummed a Chelm melody" (40).

Although the sage grumbles that no certain way to resolve the problem of mixed-up feet exists, he counsels Shmelkicha not only to carry a
big stick, but to sneak into her daughters' room and quickly smack their
feet with it. The cure works, and townsfolk marvel at the Elder's acumen. The girls' parents then implement the second part of the Elder's
advice—that the girls be married off. Living in their own houses, he reasons, they will not be able to get their feet tangled.

The eldest daughter Yenta is matched to Lemel, a coachman's son.
As his generic name "Fool" denotes, Lemel is not too bright. Singer
shows this lack of perspicuity in a humorous series of folklore-like repe-
titions: Lemel receives gift after gift from Yenta's family, but so inept is
he that Yenta's mother finally observes to her daughter that "whatever
you gave him either died or got lost" (49). The Elder is once more con-
sulted: "After much pondering and humming, he proclaimed, 'The road
between Chelm and East Chelm is fraught with all kinds of dangers,
and that is why such misfortunes occur. The best thing is to have a
quick marriage. Then Lemel and Yenta will be together, and Lemel will
not have to drag his gifts from one place to another, and no misfortunes
will befall them'" (50).

The sage's advice is logical, tactful, practical, constructive, and non-
judgmental. He is rewarded for it with blintzes and borscht, which he is

served first. Singer remarks the sage's appetite was "particularly good that day" (42).

Sometimes, however, Gronam's advice is not very helpful. In no story is this clearer than in one of Singer's funniest, "The First Shlemiel." In its conciseness, the story's first sentence proceeds from a universal truth that establishes a tongue-in-cheek tone, "There are many shlemiels in the world," to a precise identification of the particular *shlemiel* of the story and his one claim to fame: that of all the world's *shlemiels*, he is the first. The original *shlemiel* is, naturally, from Chelm. Singer devises for the first *shlemiel* a wife, Mrs. Shlemiel, and a child, Small Shlemiel. Next Singer reveals exactly why Mr. Shlemiel is a *shlemiel*, a fact that also sets the plot in motion: "he could not provide for his family" (55). In books to come, Singer would develop a history of the Shlemiel couple in their earlier years. In all the stories Shlemiel is a loser; the family's income comes through his hard-working, long-suffering wife. This is not to say Mrs. Shlemiel possesses a stellar intellect herself, but in "The First Shlemiel" it is she who must rise early to sell vegetables in the market. Mr. Shlemiel is incapable of this, and worse, is even unable to mind the baby and the family rooster while Mrs. Shlemiel is at work.

Mrs. Shlemiel knows her husband well, that he is "unhandy and lazy. He also loved to sleep and had a sweet tooth," (55) so she is careful to instruct him in the day's responsibilities. He is to keep the baby in his cradle and the rooster in the house. Knowing, however, that he will not be able to refrain from devouring the pot of jam she has just made for Hanukkah, she decides to trick him. She tells him the pot high in the cupboard is filled not with jam, but with poison. It is this simple plot device that Singer develops; the trope of the mislabeled jam is not exclusive to Yiddish folklore.[11]

The simple dialogue between husband and wife emphasizes Mr. Shlemiel's very narrow capacities. Mrs. Shlemiel treats her foolish husband like a child, and with good reason. Once she leaves, he sings a silly song to the baby, then dozes. In his dream he is a king, but not a great and glorious king; Shlemiel is a simple peasant king whose fondest desires are congruent with his real life experience. Mrs. Shlemiel, now a queen, no longer hawks vegetables but sits next to him: ". . . they share a huge pancake spread with jam between them. He ate from one side and she from the other until their mouths met" (57).

Shlemiel's return to real life is abrupt. The rooster crows; he mistakes the sound for that of the town's fire alarm bell. Jumping up, Shlemiel overturns the baby's cradle, and the baby bumps his head; Shlemiel opens the window to ascertain the location of the fire, and the rooster escapes. Shlemiel rights the baby's cradle and replaces the bumped-up baby in it, but only, as Singer masterfully details, "with great effort" (58). Knowing his wife will berate him for the damage, he sings:

> In my dream I was a rich Shlemiel
> But awake I am poor Shlemiel.
> In my dreams I ate pancakes with jam
> Awake I chew bread and onion.
> In my dream I was Shlemiel the King
> But awake I am just Shlemiel. (58)

There is only one way to escape Mrs. Shlemiel's recriminations: Shlemiel decides to kill himself by eating the poison in the jam pot: "A dead Shlemiel does not hear when he is screamed at" (58). Because Shlemiel is short—again Singer's telling details—he has to climb on a stool to reach the jam pot. Because the "poison" is sweet, he eats it all and then lies down to die. After an hour of waiting, he becomes thirsty. Being lazy, Shlemiel decides that instead of going to fetch water, as all the residents of Chlem must do, he will drink the expensive apple cider his wife has also been saving for Hanukkah: ". . . when a man is about to die, what is the point in saving money?" (61). His belly full, he dozes again and dreams he wears not one but three golden crowns. He eats from three pots: "One filled with pancakes, one with jam, and one with apple cider. Whenever he soiled his beard with eating, a servant wiped it off for him with a napkin" (61).

In his dream his wife the queen praises her good luck in being married to "such a king," but when the real Mrs. Shlemiel returns home from market to find her house in darkness and disarray, what she shrieks is far from praise. When Shlemiel tells her not to yell at a dying man and confesses he has eaten all the poison, Mrs. Shlemiels' no-win situation becomes abundantly clear to her. The baby is hurt, the rooster is gone, the jam and cider have been devoured: Mrs. Shlemiel begins to cry.

Shlemiel cries too, but from joy at discovering that he is not going to die. Awakened by his parents, Small Shlemiel joins in the sobbing familial chorus and the ruckus rouses the neighbors. All ends well when the charitable, understanding villagers replace the holiday fare, and the rooster returns to the roost.

The story is not concluded, however, until the philosophers of Chelm meet to decide its import. Demonstrating again their perspicacity, their topsy-turvy, unintentionally funny conclusion goes a long way to explaining why nothing ever changes in Chelm. After seven days and seven nights of forehead wrinkling and beard tugging, they opine: "A wife who has a child in the cradle and a rooster to take care of should never lie to her husband and tell him that a pot of jam is a pot of poison, or that a pot of poison is a pot of jam, even if he is lazy, and is a shlemiel besides" (65).

The manuscript for "The First Shlemiel" shows Singer and Shub refining the ending, adding the details about the child in the cradle, the rooster to take care of, and the pots of jam and poison. Shub has said Singer enjoyed writing for children and that the two of them, up on the nineteenth floor of her building overlooking the Hudson River, often laughed aloud as they worked.

The majority of the book's reviewers were also delighted. Naomi S. Morse, writing in *Children's Literature*, praises both author and artist, for example in commenting on the values in "Zlateh the Goat" as representative of the book as a whole: "It is an initiation rite in a world that looks dangerous on the surface, yet ultimately proves safe. God, animals, and the earth itself provide refuge from cold and hunger. The world is found to be warm, maternal, nuturant."[12]

Alison Lurie, commenting in her *New York Review of Books* article that writing for children is actually harder than writing for adults, calls *Zlateh the Goat* "a triumph . . . even for someone as famous as I. B. Singer."[13] She assesses Sendak's drawings as "marvelous" combinations of "mystery and a subtly comic realism," and recommends if "you have no older children on your list," that "you buy it for yourself" (29).

Other reviewers were ambivalent. *Book Week*'s Irving Feldman compliments *Zlateh the Goat* by writing, "I doubt that any child . . . will be displeased to see this handsome book on a cold December morning among his other gifts lying at the foot of the 'Hanukkah bush.'" (A *Hanukkah bush* is the satirical name for the Christmas tree many assimilated American Jews buy for their homes during the holiday season. The joke that goes along with the practice is that some Jews are so reformed, that is, liberal in their beliefs, that the most apt name for them is "Catholics.") However, Feldman suggests that adults who are knowledgeable about Singer's adult stories will be disappointed by these "thin and perfunctory" renditions of "Eastern European *shtetl* tales." The implication seems to be that because the core of the stories was not original, the writer's accomplishment is diminished. The exception is "Zlateh the Goat," which Feldman calls "moving."[14]

Thomas P. Riggio makes the opposite point: "Of course, Singer's success depends on his storytelling genius. . . . Few writers could translate this material into anything like Singer's superbly graphic prose. . . . What distinguishes Singer as a writer . . . is his ability to dramatize the points at which the rhythms of Jewish/Yiddish lore coincide with the broader curve of Western fables, fairy tales, and myths."[15]

Feldman is appreciative, however, of the book's illustrations, "Maurice Sendak's . . . somber stumpy figures solidly posed in their timeless gestures . . . underscore the commemorative intention of which Singer speaks in his brief foreword" (4).

Morse also observes that Sendak's illustrations deserve more than "passing mention" in contributing to the book's success: "Sendak takes these characters seriously and renders them by means of hundreds and hundreds of carefully cross hatched lines that show contour, features, depth and detail. . . . These delicate and loving illustrations invest the stories with dignity, detail and gravity (18–19).

Others, however, find that Sendak's renditions of Singer's characters, while technically superb, lack charm overall—for example, the sisters in "The Mixed-Up Feet and the Silly Bridegroom." As depicted by Sendak, the Shlemiel parents look too old, as if they were the baby's grandparents.

After the success of *Zlateh the Goat*, Singer needed no more persuasion from Elizabeth Shub to continue writing for children. His first publication won not only a Newbery Honor Award, but a firm place for him in children's literature, a niche of the sort he was delighted to fill. The particular location of his children's stories in the same Polish neighborhood as the stories he wrote for adults reconfirmed his belief that these were indeed stories only he could tell.

And his audience? Not only Jewish children, not only children, but adults. Mark A. Bernheim repeats Singer's anecdote: "Isaac, in fact, tells of meeting a woman at a party shortly after the publication of *Zlateh the Goat* who asked him to autograph a copy for her. 'Who is the child?' Isaac inquired. 'It's for me,' the woman confessed, 'I am the child.'"[16]

Chapter Four

Silver Spoons, Simpletons, and Dreamers

When Shlemiel Went to Warsaw

Shrewd versus Miserly

Following *Zlateh the Goat*, Singer published four more collections of stories: in 1968, 1973, 1980, and 1984. *When Shlemiel Went to Warsaw*, *Naftali the Storyteller and His Horse, Sus*, and *The Power of Light* contain eight stories each. In 1984, Singer, along with the editor, Stephen Roxburgh, selected the stories for his crowning collection, *Stories for Children*. By then, he had published more than 30 stories in collections and children's magazines, and more than a dozen single-story books. The latter are richly illustrated, in full color for the most part. There are shorter picture books such as *Why Noah Chose the Dove* and *Elijah the Slave*, as well as stories of some length and complexity. As usual with Singer, the range of the longer stories is extraordinary. In *The Golem* and *The Fools of Chelm and Their History*, he uses traditional characters in a novel narrative. In *The Fearsome Inn* and *Mazel and Shlimazel*, he employs the form of the fairy tale to write a Yiddish-flavored story. In *Joseph and Koza* and *Alone in the Wild Forest*, he creates unique stories of fierce imagination.

Zlateh the Goat won a Newbery Honor Award. So did Singer's next collection, *When Shlemiel Went to Warsaw*. It too displayed the breadth of Singer's personal repository. He credits his sources for the book's Chelm and Shlemiel stories by acknowledging his mother as a storyteller, and her mother and her grandmother. These stories and original ones, such as the cricket and imp idyll "Tsirtsur and Peziza" and the haunting "Menaseh's Dream," all come from "a way of life rich in fantasy and make-believe."[1] The book itself he dedicates to both his parents: ". . . persons of deep faith and love of man, especially of all Shlemiels, old and young." As with all of Singer's books, the publisher Farrar, Straus and

Giroux produced a substantial volume that feels good in a reader's hands; the paper is heavy and each of Margot Zemach's drawings occupies a page to itself.

When Shlemiel Went to Warsaw was one of several pairings of Singer's stories with Margot Zemach's pen-and-ink art. Zemach's light, whimsical touch and affectionate sense of humor were fine matches for Singer's quirky characters and Jewish expressions and settings. Zemach also illustrated *Mazel and Shlimazel, Alone in the Wild Forest, Naftali the Storyteller and His Horse, Sus,* and several others. In 1977 Naomi S. Morse wrote: "Her pictures emphasize the fabulous, folk character of the tales in their decorative quality. They have the rhythm and movement of a folk dance in contrast to the weight and stasis of Sendak's illustrations (19).

After discussing several of Singer's earlier works and the artwork accompanying them, Morse contrasts the works of Singer to those of Hans Christian Andersen, pointing out, for example, Andersen's unhappy endings as contrasted to Singer's hopeful ones.

In "Shrewd Todie and Lyzer the Miser," from *When Shlemiel Went to Warsaw,* Singer expands upon an old Chelm joke as he had done in *Zlateh the Goat,* by developing "plot, detail, and point of view." So successful was the story that it became the title of a collection issued by Little Barefoot Books, an imprint of Random House, which publishes classic children's literature in high-quality, child-sized books. *Shrewd Todie and Lyzer the Miser*—the book—also contains five other Singer stories selected by series editor Jonathan Cott. In the series, Singer joins authors such as Lewis Carroll and Rudyard Kipling.

To develop the fundamental Chelm joke into a story, first Singer builds up the two character types: shrewd and miser(ly), personifying them in the unscrupulous Todie and the gulden-retentive Lyzer. Then he sets the scene: Todie lives in the Ukraine in a village and is poor. He has a wife, Shaindel, and seven hungry children. Todie fails at all trades: "It is was said of Todie that if he decided to deal in candles the sun would never set"(S, 3), and that if he ever made money, it was only through dubious means. As a well-known one-liner, the joke about the candles and the sun appears in Hanan J. Ayalti's *Yiddish Proverbs.*[2]

In his *Treasury of Jewish Folklore,* Nathan Ausubel provides a source for the ubiquitous story:

> In the Twelfth Century a *schlimazel* of genius, the poet Abraham ibn Ezra (of whom the poet Robert Browning has written) laughed at his own mistakes with mirthful irony:

If I sold shrouds
No one would die
If I sold lamps,
Then, in the sky
The sun, for spite,
Would shine by
night. (343)

A narrative version of the joke is provided by Ausubel on pages 354–55. So well-known were these jokes that there can be little doubt that Singer heard them as a child.

The winter is unusually cold and Todie has no wood to build a fire for his family: "When the frost burns outside, hunger is stronger than ever" (S, 4). Writing from personal experience, Singer combines weather and economics to build atmosphere and suspense. Todie's children must stay in bed all day to keep warm, as Singer wrote in *A Day of Pleasure* he had had to do while growing up. Shaindel despairs and speaks of divorce.

Wives in Singer's stories typically do not fare well. Whether this expressed a personal bias or a satirical representation of women's real status in Yiddish society is unknown—probably a little of both. Examples are Genedel and Yenta, the wives of Gronam Ox, chief sage of Chelm, and the suicidal servant girl Miriam from *The Golem*. An example from Singer's own family was his capable, mismatched mother, Bathsheba. In most of Singer's stories, the only women who are happy are the ones who are too blissfully dumb to realize how stupid their husbands are, such as Mrs. Shlemiel early in her marriage and Yenta and Tzipa, both married to fools named Lemel.

In *When Shlemiel Went to Warsaw*, Gronam's wife is named Genedel. In the subsequent *Naftali the Storyteller and His Horse, Sus* and *The Fools of Chelm and Their History*, she is named Yente Pesha. No history of a divorce or a death is provided by way of explaining the inconsistency. *Yenta* or *yente* is a Yiddish noun that has developed a negative connotation, meaning a busybody or a shrew. Used as a proper name in Singer's stories for characters other than Gronam Ox's wife, the name seems innocent of such connotations. Yenta, for example, is the name of the foolish bride in "The Mixed-Up Feet and the Silly Bridegroom"; she is not clever enough to be shrewish.

Shaindel, however, is simply trapped in her marriage and unable to do more than mouth despairing threats. Todie's response when Shaindel wails "If you can't feed your children, I will go to the rabbi and get a divorce," is as realistic as it is uncomforting: "And what will you do with it, eat it?"

In Todie's town lives a rich man, Lyzer. Unfortunately for Todie, Lyzer stays rich by practicing the most absurd frugalities—detailed humorously by Singer—and by denying all of Todie's appeals for loans. One day, motivated by both necessity and revenge, Todie finally finagles a silver spoon out of Lyzer. Todie tells him the silver is needed to impress a suitor for his oldest daughter's hand, and he gives Lyzer his holy word that the spoon will be returned. His oath establishes the requirements of the joke: that, however it is that Todie will eventually outsmart Lyzer, it must be within the bounds of his holy word. Somehow Todie will swindle Lyzer and turn a profit, but Lyzer must get his silver spoon back. Within this limitation, Todie is free to maneuver.

He has, in fact, already lied. He can find no suitor for his daughter. What he does have at home are three silver teaspoons, the last of the family's resources. Returning Lyzer's spoon the next day as promised, Todie hands over one of his own spoons as well. He tells Lyzer that Lyzer's spoon gave birth to a new spoon. Lyzer swallows the bait: ". . . his greed overcame his doubt and he happily accepted both spoons" (*S*, 6).

In Singer's narrative, Todie soon returns to request another loan, once again to impress a fictitious suitor. Before Todie can even finish his fib, Lyzer interrupts eagerly to offer him the loan of another spoon. The pattern is repeated when Todie returns two spoons the next day to Lyzer, who joyfully accepts the baby spoon and therefore the premise behind the story of its birth. A third time Todie borrows and a third time returns two spoons to Lyzer.

A week passes before Todie returns, this time to ask Lyzer for a "special favor" (*S*, 9). This time, the fictitious suitor for his daughter is said to come from the big city, Lublin, and to be a good catch. Todie needs to borrow not only a spoon but expensive silver candlesticks. Lyzer willingly loans him eight. Noticeably, Todie has said nothing about his holy word this time, so he can take the candlesticks right to the pawn shop without violating the rules of his swindle.

When Shaindel asks him where he got so much money, Todie replies, ". . . a cow flew over our roof and dropped a dozen silver eggs. . . . I sold them and here is the money" (*S*, 10). When she persists, he plays realpolitik, "If you don't want the money, give it back to me." Enough said—Shaindel buys the children clothes and food. "Even some nuts and raisins for a pudding," Singer adds with characteristic vividness.

The next day Todie returns to Lyzer only the spoon:

"Your candlesticks died," he explains.
"You fool!" [Lyzer is apoplectic.] "How can candlesticks die?"
"If spoons can give birth, candlesticks can die."

Todie's rejoinder is irrefutable. Like Atzel in "Fool's Paradise" who
cannot commit suicide because he is convinced he is already dead, Lyzer
is hoist on his own logic.

In *A Treasury of Jewish Folklore*, Ausubel relates a variation of this story
under the heading "Cunning and Greed." In this shorter version, the
trickster borrows from the miser first a silver spoon, then a silver goblet,
then a gold watch. No rabbi figures in at the end to make a ruling, as
happens in Singer's version; the cunning character simply states to the
angry cheapskate, "If a spoon can bear little spoons . . . and if a goblet
can bear little goblets, why should it surprise you that a watch can die?"
(368). The folklore joke ends with this punch line, but Singer the storyteller has more story to tell.

The miser takes Todie to a *Din Torah*, a rabbinical court of the sort
Singer's own father would have held. But the rabbi laughs out loud and
dismisses Lyzer's suit. He rules, "If you accept nonsense when it brings
you profit, you must also accept nonsense when it brings you loss" (*S*, 12).

Singer lauds the power of story by stating that the "story of the silver
spoons that gave birth" spread through the village, in the same way that
the joke was shared among his family and friends. He reaffirms the thematic popularity of the poor chiseling the rich by adding that the villagers were happy at Todie's success. This is because they are common
laborers like Todie—like most people—the poor, the oppressed, the
young. The appeal of the small outwitting the big, the poor the rich, the
weak the powerful is good-naturedly spoofed through the shady protagonist's own tongue-in-cheek character. Notwithstanding this, the shoe-
maker's and the tailor's apprentices make up a song to commemorate
the event and to tease Lyzer: ". . . You're the richest man on earth / With
silver spoons that can give birth. . . ." So mundane and of-the-people is
the story that these figures are not merely tradespeople, but apprentices
to tradespeople. As both poetic justice and the real world dictate, Lyzer's
spoons never again reproduce themselves (*S*, 12–13).

Todie and Lyzer are stock types whom Singer's genius renders real
and specific. Both have, to use a frequent Singer metaphor, a "specific
address"[3]; Todie and Lyzer are vivid Eastern European incarnations of

omnicultural kinds of people. Yiddish literature is extremely acute at exhibiting personality types in action. Singer, the admirer of nineteenth-century novelists, himself wrote several multigenerational, family saga historic novels, sweeping in scope and complex in psychological characterization. These same skills are presented more concisely in his children's stories. Todie and Lyzer work well in opposition; one is clearly capable of guile and the other of greed.

"When You Send a Fool to Market . . ."

Returning in two of this collection's stories is Shlemiel, who is capable of neither guile nor greed. He can only manage goofiness. Two other *shlemiel* types in Singer stories are both named Lemel, one the silly bridegroom of *Zlateh the Goat*'s "The Mixed-Up Feet and the Silly Bridegroom" and the other the loving loser of *Naftali the Storyteller and His Horse, Sus*'s "Lemel and Tzipa." The Yiddish word *lemel* denotes an amiable dimwit. Ausubel traces several stereotypes back to the time of the prophets in the writings of Amos and Isaiah: "the hypocrite, the miser, the skinflint, the profligate, the coquette, the self-satisfied and the self-righteous" (266). Singer opposes Shlemiel and the Lemels as stock *shlemiels* to stock characters who are out-and-out cynical thieves. So bold, in fact, does one thief become that he sends a note back to Chelm with the illiterate Lemel that says, "WHEN YOU SEND A FOOL TO MARKET, THE MERCHANTS REJOICE." If there were a Yiddish Barnum, he would have said that there's a *shlemiel* born every minute.

The *shlemiel* has, as Ausubel points out, ". . . no skill in coping with any situation in life. . . . He . . . spoils everything he attempts" (15). But there is a sociohistoric bite to the characterization. In *The Schlemiel as Modern Hero*, Ruth Wisse quotes historian Salo Baron in providing this statistic: "In many communities up to 40 percent of the entire Jewish population consisted of families of so-called *Luftmenschen*, that is persons without any particular skill, capital, or specific occupations.[4]

One of the problems with prejudice, of course, is that those discriminated against are purposely limited in opportunity. Most occupations had been barred to Jews for centuries. Many had to live on *Luft*, air—that is, on their wits. Ausubel writes:

> As identifiable types, *schlemiels* and *schlimazels* must have sprung into being with the first economic discriminations against Jews by the Byzantine emperors, beginning with Justinian (530–60) who froze the

social and economic restrictions against the Jews into ruthless Roman law. The Imperial Code . . . "the Jews shall not" and "the Jews must not . . . ," entered into almost all legal codes in European countries down to the Nuremberg laws of Hitler. As one writer has remarked, "It reduced men, who through the generations had loved to live by the work of their hands, to the necessity of living by the exercise of their wits." (344)

One problem with that situation was that not everybody had sufficient wit. "The First Shlemiel" from *Zlateh the Goat* introduced the ill-witted Shlemiel family, the pinhead husband and his exasperated wife. "Shlemiel, the Businessman" from *When Shlemiel Went to Warsaw* fills in the history of the Shlemiel family before it became destitute. "When Shlemiel Went to Warsaw," the title story, shows the Shlemiel family later on, older but in no way wiser.

Newly wed and funded by the dowry provided by his wife's well-to-do father, in "Shlemiel, the Businessman" Shlemiel attempts to capitalize by going into the goat business. From Chelm—a departure point foreshadowing comical disaster rather than profitability—the earnest simpleton travels to Lublin where he buys a milk goat with full udders. Ignorance is seldom bliss for a patsy; no sooner does Shlemiel stop at an inn in Piask to celebrate on his way home "as befits a successful businessman" than he is duped. Everyone else, it seems, is aware that the village of Piask is "known for its thieves and swindlers" (*S*, 56). Obliviously, Shlemiel feasts, orders brandy, and brags about his goat to the innkeeper. The celebration is premature, for the innkeeper is a thief who switches his emaciated, blind billy goat for Shlemiel's nanny goat. Still sated, Shlemiel doesn't even look at the goat in his hurry to return to Chelm, where friends and in-laws have congregated to welcome the merchant home. Instead of congratulation, however, Shlemiel is greeted with consternation and laughter. "When he saw the old billy goat, he beat his head with his fists" (*S*, 58).

Convinced he was cheated in Lublin, Shlemiel sets out for the city, stopping first at the swindler's inn. He tells the innkeeper his intention to set things right in Lublin or resort to the police. The host, less than eager to be involved with the authorities, switches the goats back. Thus, when the unobservant Shlemiel returns to the goat dealer to complain, he once again is bewildered. At the end of the tether is the same buxom goat he originally bought. First speechless, then apologetic, Shlemiel sets out again for Chelm, once more stopping in Piask. After offering him brandy on the house, the innkeeper again swaps his skinny billy for Shlemiel's goat. Tipsy, Shlemiel departs, not noticing the substitution. Back in Chelm, however, "Word spread quickly and the whole town went wild." How to explain the mystery of Shlemiel's gender-erratic animal?

Fortunately for Chelm, it has its seven sages. After a week of debate, they conclude that "when a nanny goat is taken from Lublin to Chelm it turns into a billy goat on the way." Based on the facts at hand and the perspicacity of the wise ones, the explanation makes sense. To protect Chelm, the sages pass a law prohibiting the import of goats from Lublin. The screwball logic of the sages and the guilelessness of Shlemiel combine to produce a sympathetic response from readers, for the episode adversely affects the Shlemiel family's fortunes: "The old goat soon died and Shlemiel had lost one third of his wife's dowry" (*S*, 61).

This well-known joke appears in Ausubel as "The Chelm Goat Mystery." Its punch line is, "Such is the luck of us Chelm *schlimazels* that, by the time a nanny goat reaches our town, it's sure to turn into a billy!" (327–31). Because Singer depicts several characters in his stories who are themselves telling stories, readers can infer the cadence of a Yiddish storyteller, such as Aunt Yentl and Singer's mother Bathsheba, who most likely told this old story to her young family.

Uneducated but undaunted, in the next episode of Singer's story Shlemiel avoids the reprehensible town of Lublin. No sooner does he arrive in Lemberg than a house across the street from where he is staying erupts in flames. People scream. In lieu of fire alarms, trumpets blare. Assured by a servant at the inn that there is no danger, the tired traveler sleeps through the rest of the commotion.

Later, Shlemiel asks a stranger whether the fire was put out "merely by blowing a trumpet?" The stranger, sensing an easy mark, in short order sells Shlemiel a miraculous trumpet that comes guaranteed, when blown, to put out fires. This device, reasons Shlemiel, would be invaluable in Chelm, where most houses burn down before the "ancient nag" that pulls the dilapidated fire cart can be roused to deliver its one bucket of water. Here again, the social reality behind the joke reminds readers of the poverty out of which the tradition of humor paradoxically grew.

Back in Chelm, villagers' opinions about the trumpet's efficacy are divided. Shlemiel's father-in-law perceptively calls the trumpet "another billy goat." But so confident is Shlemiel that, to demonstrate the trumpet's worth, he sets his father-in-law's house on fire. After all, to put out the fire, Shlemiel only has to blow the trumpet. He does, but it does not work. No one is hurt, but the family loses everything.

In a weeklong emergency session, the Elders ponder and declare that "for some unknown reason,"(*S*, 64) fire-quenching trumpets from Lemberg lose their power in Chelm. Reasonably, they pass a new law prohibiting the import of trumpets to Chelm.

For his final business venture, Shlemiel decides there is no place like home. Shlemiel is fond of the local sweet brandy. He buys a keg and figures, at three groschen a glass, he can "make three-gulden profit a day." He even has the help of Mrs. Shlemiel. Together, "they set up a small stand in the marketplace, placed the keg and a few glasses on it, and began hawking their drink to passers-by. . . ."

But their price is too high. By midday they have had only one customer, who pays with a three-groschen piece. Disheartened, Shlemiel decides he needs a drink. Taking out the three-groschen coin, he says to his wife, "In what way is my money inferior to another man's? Here is three groschen and sell me a drink" (*S*, 65).

That makes sense to Mrs. Shlemiel; she takes the coin and gives Shlemiel a glass of brandy from the keg. Soon she is thirsty, and, following the same logic, she pays Shlemiel for her drink with the three-groschen piece. At day's end, the keg is nearly empty and the Shlemiels have only three groschen to show for their day. They cannot figure out how they had "sold almost an entire keg of sweet brandy for cash, but the cash was not to be seen" (*S*, 66). Shlemiel believes not even the sages could explain what happened to the money.

This is a watershed in the Shlemiels' history. After this, Shlemiel gives up on business. He stays home and Mrs. Shlemiel sells vegetables in the market, as they are depicted in "The First Shlemiel." Disgusted, Mrs. Shlemiel's father becomes the first person to emigrate from Chelm. But loyal to the end, Mrs. Shlemiel states with a straight-face to her husband, "You may be poor, Shlemiel, but you are certainly wise. Wisdom such as yours is rare even in Chelm" (*S*, 67).

That Mrs. Shlemiel is being sincere rather than sarcastic allows readers an ironic delight. Irony, as Israel Knox observes, has been and will be the salient feature of Jewish humor as long as ". . . the actual and the ideal are disparate, so long as the hopes of the heart are not embodied in the contexture of things."[5] Part of the appeal of fools, naturally, is that everyone else feels superior, even Singer's youngest readers. Mrs. Shlemiel's heartfelt admiration also adds to the humor by lightening the tone of what, treated differently, would be tragic. *Shlemiel*-ness is a tragic flaw, after all; its affinity for comedy rests on the benevolent stupidity of the character. In contrast to this is the glorious intransigence of, say,

Oedipus or Achilles. Shlemiels, basically, are modest. They operate on a very small stage. They do not commit the sin of *hubris*. They are not violent, and fortunately so, for they would only shoot themselves in the foot. The worst that can be said about them is that they are unbelievably dense.

By the time Shlemiel decides to indulge his wanderlust by going to Warsaw in the book's last story, Mrs. Shlemiel's patience has frayed. So he doesn't tell her he is leaving. He ties up bread, onion, and garlic in a bag, instructs the older children to watch the younger ones, and sets out. After walking for miles, he tires and lies down on the ground to sleep.

Fearful he will waken and not remember which way is Warsaw and which way is Chelm, Shlemiel puts his boots out with the toes pointing toward Warsaw. While he dreams a sweet *shlemiel* dream of being the king of Chelm and of lovingly sharing strawberry jam and hot onion rolls with his wife and children, he is once again tricked. This time, it is a prankster who sees Shlemiel "carefully placing his boots" (*S*, 101), and he turns Shlemiel's boots around as a joke.

Shlemiel wakens, puts on his boots, and sets off, unknowingly retracing exactly the same route he had traveled the day before. Soon he remarks to himself upon the peculiar familiarity of houses, people, family. But he manages to figure it out all: "There were two Chelms and he had reached the second one" (*S*, 102). When he opens the door of a house exactly like his own in Chelm One and is greeted by a look-alike family asking where he has been, Shlemiel answers:

> "Mrs. Shlemiel, I am not your husband. Children, I am not your father."
> "Have you lost your mind?" Mrs. Shlemiel screamed.
> "I am Shlemiel of Chelm One and this is Chelm Two."
> Mrs. Shlemiel clapped her hands so hard that the chickens sleeping under the stove awoke in fright and flew out all over the room.
> "Children, your father has gone crazy," she wailed. (*S*, 105)

Shlemiel explains himself in the same way when his neighbors crowd in the room: ". . . between Chelm One and Warsaw there is a Chelm Two. And that is where I am."

"Don't you recognize your chickens?" his neighbors ask.

Some of the neighbors cannot help laughing; others pity the family. Gimpel, the healer, announces that he knows no remedy for such an illness. After some time, everybody goes home (*S*, 109).

Left alone with him, Mrs. Shlemiel says to Shlemiel, "You may be a madman, but even madmen have to eat" (S, 107).
When she gives him his favorite dish, noodles and beans, he tells her, "Mrs. Shlemiel, you're a good woman. My wife wouldn't feed a stranger. . . ."
"As if being a Shlemiel wasn't enough, he has to go crazy in addition," she wails. "God in heaven, what I have done to deserve this?"
Still, she makes a bed for Shlemiel, and in his dreams he redeems himself. He is again the king of Chelm; "Shlemiel ate twenty blintzes all at once and hid the remainder in his crown for later" (S, 107).
In the morning, Shlemiel wakes to find himself surrounded by townspeople who are passionately debating his future while Mrs. Shlemiel weeps and screams. They agree to take him to the house of Gronam Ox, chief sage of Chelm.

> As the crowd came in, one of the Elders, Dopey Lekisch, was saying, "Maybe there are two Chelms."
> "If there are two, why can't there be three, four, or even a hundred Chelms?" Sender Donkey interrupted.
> "And even if there are a hundred Chelms, must there be a Shlemiel in each one of them?" argued Shmendrick Numskull. . . .
> "Isn't it possible that you turned around and came back to Chelm?" Gronam inquired.
> "Why should I turn around? I'm not a windmill," Shlemiel replied.
> (S, 109)

This kind of exchange parodies the *pilpul*, that is, extreme cases of the Talmudic debates of the learned. Leo Rosten defines *pilpul* as "unproductive hair-splitting . . . or logic-chopping."[6] Nero may have played the violin while Rome burned, but to withdraw from the outside world to debate questions of meaning in the ancient Torah was often, Singer implies, a misguided response to reality, not unlike his father's habitual retreat from the messy life below his balcony on Krochmalna Street.
Ultimately, the Elder rules that Shlemiel must stay until the other Shlemiel returns: "Dear Elders, my Shlemiel has come back," Mrs. Shlemiel screams. "I don't need two Shlemiels. . . ."
Because he insists he is not married to Mrs. Shlemiel, the Elders rule that Shlemiel will have to go to the poorhouse to live. But then who will take care of the little Shlemiels while Mrs. Shlemiel sells vegetables in

the market? Gronam Ox has an excellent idea: ". . . the town will have to hire someone to take care of Mrs. Shlemiel's children. . . . Why not hire Shlemiel for that?" (*S*, 113).

Gronam asks Shlemiel how much he wants to be paid to take care of the children.

> For a moment Shlemiel stood there completely bewildered. Then he said, "Three groschen a day."
> "Idiot, moron, ass!" screamed Mrs. Shlemiel. . . . You shouldn't do it for less than six a day. She ran over to Shlemiel and pinched him on the arm. . . . Shlemiel winced and cried out, "She pinches just like my wife."
> (*S*, 113)

The townsfolk decide to pay Shlemiel five groschen a day. When he turns it over daily to Mrs. Shlemiel for room and board, she is delighted. After all, this is the first time he has ever brought home money from any source.

The other Shlemiel never returns. Ingenuously, both Shlemiel and Mrs. Shlemiel admit to each other they are "quite happy with matters as they stood" (*S*, 114).

The Elders come to their own conclusions in another satire of learned discussion: the original Shlemiel has fallen off the edge of the earth, for example, or has been eaten by cannibals over the mountains. Gronam Ox, however, believes that Shlemiel has indeed gone to Chelm Two, where he is living a parallel life, hired by that community for five groschen a day to watch over the other Mrs. Shlemiel's children.

In Ausubel, this story is called "The Columbus of Chelm." The Chelmite in this story is Reb Selig, and his boots are turned around in a different manner. A Polish peasant passes, picks up the boots to steal them, sees how full of holes they are, and drops them carelessly. Selig also returns to Chelm, thinking he has gone to Warsaw, and links up in the similar way to a "second" Selig family (334–36).

As for Singer's Shlemiel, the experience gives him something to think about, not that he can figure it out. He wonders about his wife and about the other Shlemiel. Sometimes he thinks of traveling again, but doesn't, wondering what the point would be of travel that went nowhere.

With help from Elizabeth Shub and her poetic skills, Singer ends his story with Shlemiel humming to himself:

Those who leave Chelm
End up in Chelm.
Those who remain in Chelm
Are certainly in Chelm.
All roads lead to Chelm
All the world is one big Chelm. (*S*, 116)

The rhyming finale is equally funny and philosophical, as suits a Chelm poem. Natalie S. Morse comments: "For Shlemiel, as for everyman, the external world is unimportant. Since he takes himself along, wherever he goes, all roads do lead to Chelm, 'all the world is one big Chelm.' The journey takes place, not in space, but within the self" (27).

In his children's stories, Singer makes accessible to younger readers his belief in struggle, mystery, and the ultimate triumph of goodness. Life is a journey from Chelm One to Chelm Two, with a bit of Piask and Lemberg thrown in for good measure.

Cosmic Confrontation

Very different in tone is a thoroughly original Singer creation, "Rabbi Leib and the Witch Cunegunde." This elemental demon tale seems drawn from the passionate reveries of Singer's youth, such as he describes in "Growing Up" and "Tashlik," among other stories. As an adult, Singer wrote: "We call supernatural the things which we don't know, for which we have no evidence. . . . But in my view, ghosts, spirits, premonitions, telepathy, clairvoyance, are actually a part of nature. . . . Actually, our knowledge is a little island in a great ocean of non-knowledge. The supernatural is like the ocean, while the so-called natural is only a little island in it. And even this island is a great riddle."[7]

Critic Mark A. Bernheim observed of Singer: "The world of his children's books is inhabited by as many demons and agents of Satan as are his most fantastic adult tales and novels, and the lovers in his children's books are almost as passionate in their own ways as their counterparts in adult books such as *The Slave*" (31).

Both Rabbi Leib and Cunegunde are "miracle workers," but he is a holy man and she uses "the power of the devil." More than 60 years old and mother of a rapacious highway bandit, Cunegunde[8] has a potion that keeps her young-looking. Although the witch and the rabbi are enemies and he bests her constantly, Cunegunde admires the rabbi's power and lusts after him (*S*, 89).

Singer's stories often have to do with different kinds of love between men and women, boys and girls, even monsters and girls, as in *The Golem.* "Menashe and Rachel," from *The Power of Light*, is a pristine tale whereas "Rabbi Leib and the Witch Cunegunde" is an almost erotic story. Singer is renowned for his passionate, often erotic and perverse adult stories, such as "A Crown of Feathers," "The Magician of Lublin," *The Slave*, and *Satan in Goray*. Singer was unusually uncensored for a Jewish writer of his background. In fact, critic Eugene Goodheart has declared Singer's use of eroticism unprecedented in Yiddish letters.[9] In his autobiographic stories, Singer reveals himself to have been a passionate child, an unflinching dreamer possessed of a fervid imagination. In "Tashlik," his adolescent reveries are fevered. In later years, Singer's willingness to portray irrationality and extremity became a trademark that shocked some Yiddish-language readers from the Old Country (Goodheart, 88). On the other hand, his passionate ambiguities had a real appeal to what Alfred Kazin described as Singer's "fascinated American readers."[10] Singer did not mince words on the subject of censorship. In "Indecent Language and Sex in Literature" he wrote:

> Some people still maintain that literature must drink only from "pure springs." But where are they to be found, these "pure springs"? Not in our consciousness, and certainly not in dreams. Whether we pour over Bible or the Talmud . . . physiology or psychology, history, anatomy, or sociology—in none of these can we escape the phenomenon of evil. . . .
> Man cannot learn to know God without confronting Satan.[11]

The plot of "Rabbi Leib and the Witch Cunegunde" is exemplary of the cosmic duels to the death found in so many of Singer's stories. In this child-accessible version, the duel manifests in alternating attraction and deception between the sexes. The relationship between Leib and Cunegunde smolders; the story is the exception to Bernheim's otherwise sound observation: "Throughout [Singer's] entire work the reader is in fact invited to . . . view the world with what has sometimes been termed a child's innocent eyes. If any line at all is to be found between the two directions of his writings, it may be the absence of overt sexuality in the one and of pictorial illustration in the other. But spiritually, the distance is slight" . . . (32).

It is the rabbi's ability to defeat her that turns Cunegunde's emotions toward him from hate to "admiration." Singer next presents an episto-

lary exchange between the combative lovers. Cunegunde writes to Rabbi
Leib: "If we got married, we could rule the world," but he replies, "I'd
rather live with a snake than with you." Then Cunegunde feels hate as
well as love and writes back ". . . you will have the same bitter end as my
five husbands before you" (S, 31).

The precise and rhythmic prose of the previous sentence results from
Singer's genius and from editing during translation. Rabbi and witch
occupy the same mushroomy forest. He lives by the river, is a vegetarian, and always buys seed to feed the birds. Hundreds of them come "to
feed in the clearing in front of his hut." In this image, Singer once again
uses animals to confirm the goodness of a character. In the latter two
characteristics—being vegetarian and religiously feeding the birds—
Rabbi Leib is like Singer himself, a vegetarian whom Shub and Straus,
among many others, remember as avidly feeding pigeons in Central
Park.

Cunegunde lives underground, luxuriously. Soon she sends evil things
to invade the rabbi's space. Even the river is muddied. One evening a
demon appears on the roof of Leib's hut. The rabbi chants him away, but
in a delightful twist on the expected, Singer has the demon rather cheek-
ily demanding, "I will not move until you listen to what I have to say"
(S, 92).

What he has to say is that Cunegunde is "pining away for love of
you" (S, 92). The wild-eyed demon threatens and bribes, but is banished
by the rabbi. Fearing for his friends, however, the heroic rabbi realizes he
must devise a means of defeating the witch. When Hurzimah, the
cheeky bat-winged demon, returns the next night, Rabbi Leib tells him
he will marry Cunegunde.

Hurzimah is alternated with Kurzimah and Burzimah in the doodle
sketched by Singer (Figure 4). He was doodling while translating with
Elizabeth Shub, for the sketch was found among her collection of Singer
papers.

Cunegunde wastes no time. Dressing in diamonds, she mounts "a
broom with silver whisks," followed by her retinue of screaming, laughing, hooting, and blaspheming creatures (S, 94). Hurzimah gives the
bride away, and she gloats over the success of her treachery. Cunegunde
intends to learn the rabbi's holy incantations so she can destroy him and
the forces of good. Had Rabbi Leib actually put onto Cunegunde's finger
the black wedding ring given to him by one of the devils, he would have
been lost forever. But first he asks Cunegunde to accept a present, a

Figure 4.   Sketches made by Singer while translating "Rabbi Leib and the Witch Cunegunde" with Elizabeth Shub (from Elizabeth Shub's collection of Singer papers)

golden locket that he wants to place around her neck. Smugly, Cunegunde assents.

The locket is blessed, so the touch of it on her skin is excruciating to the witch. She becomes "powerless"; the rabbi has outsmarted her. She begs, unsuccessfully. Singer in his moralistic mode shows his hard edge:

> Rabbi Leib had learned there could be no compassion for the creatures of the netherworld.
>
> He knew what had happened in olden times to Joseph della Reina, the famous saint, who had captured Satan and bound him in chains. Satan had begged for some snuff and when Rabbi Joseph took pity and gave it to him, Satan turned the snuff into a fire that melted his chains. . . . (S, 95)[12]

Rabbi Leib banishes his former fiancée to the wastelands near the pillar of salt that was at one time Lot's wife. Cunegunde dies, divested of evil. Without her protection, her robber son is soon arrested and dies in prison. Rabbi Leib lives out his days "in peace"; the river water clears; birds gather. The holy man "supported the poor, cured the sick, and helped those who were possessed by evil spirits." As long as he lives, the evil ones are kept away. But even when he dies, the cosmic duel is not lost. Singer ends this story again by stressing the continuity of experience; he writes, ". . . and the ancient war between good and evil started all over again" when Reb Berish, a new "miracle worker," appears (S, 97).

Dreamscape

In addition to respect for children, love of animals, love of humble humans and of a good joke, and affinity for the supernatural, Singer had yet another major preoccupation: dreams. And not a preoccupation only as an adult—Singer wrote of himself as a child: "My dreams were filled with demons, ghosts, devils, corpses. Sometimes before falling asleep I saw shapes. They danced around my bed, hovered in the air."[13]

Singer believed dreams fulfilled many purposes; in our sleep, all humans are geniuses, he told Richard Burgin, "but the artist dreams while he is awake. The making of art is a way of dreaming."[14]

Milton F. Hindus quotes Gimpel the Fool's famous line about dreams, then interprets its significance in Singer's writing: "'Whatever doesn't really happen is dreamed at night.' This conception of the imaginative realm bathes [Singer's] pages with mysterious poetic light and an air of symbolic suggestiveness. In the most humble characters and most commonplace situations, Singer deciphers the message that the world is a much more mysterious place than appears to our unaided sight. The people in his pages seem to be emissaries of unseen powers. . . . Like Herman Melville, Singer aims to penetrate the mask of deceptively-simply looking phenomena to discover the unfathomable depths below depths."[15]

"Menaseh's Dream" from *When Shlemiel Went to Warsaw* is most satisfying in its subtle reassurance of meaning in life—and in death. It is one of Singer's most popular stories, one he was often asked about during interviews.

Menaseh is an orphan, a very poor orphan. He is 12, and he is alienated from his hard-working aunt and uncle who struggle to care for their own children. He is also a child full of questions, as Singer had portrayed himself in *A Day of Pleasure.*

After an argument with his Aunt Dvosha, Menaseh leaves lunch uneaten to grab a book and head for the forest. The book he picks up mirrors his action: *Alone in the Wild Forest*, later the title of a real book by Singer.

"Menaseh's Dream" is one of the few stories Singer sets in the northern European summer, on a hot, humid day. It contains prose as lovely and lyrical as any Andersen ever wrote: "Once Menaseh entered the forest, it was cooler. The pine trees stood straight as pillars and on their brownish bark hung golden necklaces, the light of the sun shining through the pine needles" (*S*, 85).

Wandering deeper into the trees, the usually careful Menaseh fails to mark his path with stones. Hungry and lonely, he begins to think of his own death and of being with his parents. He lies down among intoxicating flowers and soon begins to dream.

In his dream he spies a beautiful crystal castle with many tall windows. He goes up to one and sees his own portrait hanging on the walls. In it, he is richly dressed and seems to be alive. Doors suddenly open and into the room come his family members, dressed in white satin and holding finely decorated prayer books. On the outside of the glass, the child dreamer begins to cry. The people inside hear him and his grandfather comes to him.

The child and the grandfather share a poignant moment. Menaseh is told by the white-bearded patriarch that the castle belongs to them all, but that the time has not yet come for him to join his family. Menaseh says he is tired of being an orphan, and he pleads to enter for just a few moments.

The family confers and agrees to let the child in, but no sooner is Menaseh over the threshold of the castle than his earthly concerns fall away. He is no longer tired or hungry. His parents kiss and hug him silently, and he feels "strangely light" (*S*, 88). The family floats along together, and, as the grandfather opens the doors, Menaseh is amazed to see rooms full of his possessions, his clothes, his toys, his soap bubbles, the sounds of his laughter with playmates, and all the characters from stories he had heard growing up, including *Alone in the Wild Forest*.

The sixth and seventh doors are special. Behind the sixth flash scenes of Menaseh as King Solomon or among giants. This room is full of Menaseh's dreams. The seventh door, the mystic and perfect one, opens onto sights Menaseh does not recognize, including the vision of a girl with golden braids.

"These are the people and events of your future," his grandfather tells him, adding that Menaseh is in a castle "with many names. We like to call it the place where nothing is lost." Menaseh wants to stay, and although he sees his parents would like him to, he understands he will have to leave. The castle is "forbidden" for him. His family kisses him good-bye, and everything disappears.

A barefoot girl wearing a patched skirt is shaking him, her golden hair shining in the moonlight. She introduces herself as Channeleh, a new arrival to the village. Suddenly Menaseh recognizes her as the girl in the seventh room. He tells her he has been dreaming, but circumspectly, she does not press him to reveal what. They like each other immediately and start toward the village together, surrounded by the sounds of the summer night: crickets, frogs.

Menaseh knows he will be in trouble coming home so late. But these things hardly matter. In his dream he has visited a mysterious world. He has found a friend. Channeleh and he have already decided to go berry picking the next day.

Menaseh is mature enough to accept the consequences of his angry flight into the forest; he is also mature enough to understand the magnitude of what he has undergone. He has made a friend, been reassured that his family loves him, and been admitted to his future home. For any reader, there can hardly been a more comforting outcome, yet the story is saved from what in Yiddish would be called *shmaltz*, or excess sentiment (literally "chicken fat"), by the hard truth of the orphaned Menaseh's return to the world.

Singer ratchets the story up yet another notch in his final paragraph. Its matter-of-fact sense of wonder and its profound address to children as "those who know" are among the finest conclusions of any story. As Menaseh and Channeleh walk away into their future, their happiness is confirmed by the antics of yet another type of beings "who know": "Among the undergrowth and wild mushrooms, little people in red jackets, gold caps, and green boots emerged. They danced in a circle and sang a song which is heard only by those who know that everything lives and nothing in time is ever lost" (*S*, 96).

Rivers of Sour Cream

In other stories, Singer is grimly funny or playful. In the manner of Roald Dahl describing his protagonists' home lives, as in *James and the Giant Peach*, he describes the living conditions of Utzel and his daughter Poverty, after whom the story is named: "There had been a time when mice had lived there, but now there weren't any because there was nothing for them to eat. Utzel's wife had starved to death, but before she died she had given birth to a baby girl. . . . Utzel . . . called her Poverty" (*S*, 74).

This is an allegory about laziness; the name Utzel, like Atzel in "Fool's Paradise," means lazy. The more laziness exists, the more poverty grows. Singer takes an adage and transforms it into a humorous story. Singer's work is so good that a mediocre story from him is the same as most authors' finest efforts.

"The Elders of Chelm and Genedel's Key" is a series of Chelm jokes. It contains one of the most famous, a solution to the town's problem of an insufficient supply of sour cream: "Let us make a law that water is to be called sour cream and sour cream is to be called water. Since there is plenty of water in the wells of Chelm, each housewife will have a full barrel of sour cream" (*S*, 49).

It is precisely this harebrained thinking that drives Genedel, the chief sage's wife, to threaten to expose him as a fool. But she is also practical. She knows if Gronam's bluff is called, she too will fall from power in the town. So she tells him she will bring in the key to their strongbox at such time as he makes a foolish ruling. Thus he will be clued in and can alter his pronouncement.

Naturally, not much time passes before her plan is put to the test. The seven sages congregate regularly at Gronam's house to ponder philosophy and eat blintzes. Gronam shares his realization with them that the reason it is hot in summer is that the stoves have been going all winter and "this heat stays in Chelm and makes the summer hot." Winter is cold, the sage continues, because the "stoves are not heated in summer, so there is no heat left over for the winter" (S, 50).

When Genedel brings in the key to the strongbox, Gronam is so surprised that he turns to his council of sages for support. To a man, they defend their chief. They assert: "We are the Elders of Chelm, and we understand everything. No woman can tell us what is wise and what is silly" (S, 51).

They pass a new law: Genedel can bring in the key to the strongbox to signify the foolishness of her husband whenever she likes, but the final arbiters will be the council of sages. And if they agree that Gronam, not Genedel, is correct, then Genedel will have to prepare blintzes and tea for all of them. Perhaps they are not such fools after all, for immediately after hearing the sages' pronouncement, Genedel ceases bringing in the key to the strongbox.

The Chelmites find that their wells are full of sour cream, but there is a shortage of water in the town. Nevertheless, they praise their chief for finding ample "sour cream," and decide they will wait for next year for him to solve the water shortage: "Gronam Ox became famous all over the world as the sage who—by passing a law—gave Chelm a whole river and many wells full of sour cream" (S, 51).

In the foreword to *When Shlemiel Went to Warsaw*, Singer affirms that his writing is basically the same for children as for adults, the same spirit, the same settings. "In our time, when literature is losing its address and the telling of stories is becoming a forgotten art, children are the best readers."

One of Margot Zemach's colored drawings decorates the cover of the 1968 and subsequent Farrar, Straus and Giroux editions. It is one of her best, showing Shlemiel and Mrs. Shlemiel for all eternity toasting each other with the brandy they had planned to sell. For them, the barrel is half full, not half empty. Whether young or old, we are like the parents to whom Singer dedicated this book, we love people, "especially all shlemiels, old and young." And we like Singer's stories about them.

Chapter Five

A Confused Cat and a Stupid Carp

Naftali the Storyteller and His Horse, Sus

Naftali and Isaac: Storytellers

In the remarkably productive decade from 1968 to 1978 when he won the Nobel Prize, Singer published more than 20 books. Four of these were major story collections: *The Seance and Other Stories*, *A Friend of Kafka and Other Stories*, *A Crown of Feathers*, and *Passions and Other Stories*. Three were major novels: *The Estate*, *Enemies, a Love Story*, and *Shosha*. Two were substantial autobiographies: *A Little Boy in Search of God* and *A Young Man in Search of Love*. A full 11 were children's books. *Naftali the Storyteller and His Horse, Sus* followed *When Shlemiel Went to Warsaw* in 1973. By that time, Singer was in his late sixties.

Naftali, his third collection of children's stories, was his longest, 143 pages, handsomely produced, as usual, by Farrar, Straus and Giroux. On Margot Zemach's cover, Naftali and Sus cart books in a straw-filled wagon down a small village street. A pen-and-ink of the oak beneath which Naftali and Sus are later buried decorates the frontispiece. Zemach's animated small-town Jews inhabit the pages of Singer's world with a simple sweetness, as in her illustration of Lemel and Tzipa. Norma Rosen is one critic, however, who faults the drawings, finding in them expressions so "vacant" as to exceed even the blankness of Chelm (56); Naomi S. Morse calls them "earthy" (22).[1] The draughtsmanship, compared to Sendak, is skimpy.

Bracketing the collection are two stories sharing the born storyteller theme. The first is the fictional version, "Naftali the Storyteller and His Horse, Sus"; the closing story is the autobiographic "Growing Up." Storytellers appear and reappear in Singer's stories: Reb Zebulun, Reb Falik, Reb Berish, Wolf Bear, Menashe, Singer himself, his brother and parents, aunt and sister, the old man in "Hanukkah in the Poorhouse." Singer's most famous character, Gimpel, comes late in life to footloose storytelling. He lives so long that the children call him "Grandfather," running after him to hear his tales. Thomas P. Riggio points out a profound similarity: "Naftali is a child's version of Gimpel" (136); Naftali grows in his story from a child to the old tale spinner. This "grandfather," the generic storyteller who speaks to the children and grandchildren, plays a role in Singer's fiction comparable to what he himself played in real life as storyteller/author to current and upcoming generations. Singer is himself a one-man Grimm Brothers. Singer biographer Paul Kresh says, "Isaac has often said that he himself is Gimpel" (quoted in Riggio, 136). As Naftali's mentor Reb Zebulun says, "Whoever has eyes that see and ears that hear absorbs enough stories to last a lifetime and to tell to his children and grandchildren."[2]

Grace Farrell describes the importance of these kindly tale makers in Singer's writing: "Singer creates Gimpel in such a way that the character is finally made in the author's own image and likeness, spinning improbable yarns . . . defying . . . the narrow conventions of the 'real' . . . such is the stuff of fiction as it gropes its way towards truth."[3]

Naftali loves stories and saves up to buy them, as did young Isaac Singer, but Naftali's path toward storytelling is easier than Isaac's. No expectations are laid upon Naftali as are laid upon the rabbi's son. It is true Naftali is encouraged to become a coachman like his father, but he holds out for being a bookseller. He wants his own horse and wagon like Reb Zebulun, the avuncular peddler who sells books along with pots, pans, needles, and other supplies. Naftali's parents try to dissuade him, but their son is blessed with singleness of purpose and his vocation is clear. In contrast, pressured himself by his parents and by the dislocations at the end of World War I, Isaac Singer went to rabbinical school for nearly a year in Warsaw when he was 19. He called it the worst year of his life and left to work as a proofreader, a job his older brother secured for him.

The value of Naftali's drive is confirmed explicitly in Singer's story, "When a person does his work not only for money but out of love, he brings out the best in others" (N, 14). Young Naftali decides not only to tell stories but to be a "writer of storybooks." He knows the craft requires of him that he study books—and people, too. He asks his mentor, Reb Zebulun, where stories come from and is told: "First of all, many unusual things happen in the world. A day doesn't go by without some rare event happening. Besides, there are writers who make up such stories" (*N*, 9).

Naftali says such writers must be liars. Gently his teacher tells him that the human brain with its dreams, fantasies, and fictions is the work of God. Anything is possible—if not now, then soon; if not here, then there, even on other worlds. Naftali understands, unlike Joshua Singer who is outraged by the fabrications of their guest, Reb Wolf Bear, in "A Hanukkah Evening in My Parents' House."

Ten years pass during which Naftali raises his father's mare's colt and names it Sus, or "horse." He builds his own wagon and soon is traveling from town to town. His first cargo of wares is the storybooks he himself bought as a child. These he either sells or reads to illiterate youngsters as he and Sus cover the countryside.

Naftali is a *shtetl* cowboy, itinerant, sleeping under the stars, close to his horse and his wagon. Unlike the archetypal American cowboy, Naftali never travels far; he doesn't need to. For it is not restlessness that drives him ever onward, but rather its opposite, a sense of belonging, a desire to play out his role within the larger community of telling stories to children. He is a rebel, but with an amiable cause. Enriched by his roots, he is everywhere loved. He tells stories, writes stories, and remembers stories. He takes his own experiences and turns them into stories, for example, when he goes to the circus in the big city of Lublin and has his store of wonders recharged and transformed into new stories for children in the *shtetl*.

Life goes on. Naftali meets girls but never marries. His parents pass away. Naftali is gray and Sus at the remarkable age of 40 is beginning to show signs of age. Then one spring day Naftali comes to the estate of Reb Falik, a landowner fond of books and storytellers. The two men share many a tale, and Sus is welcomed by Reb Falik's horses.

Sus's name means "horse" in Hebrew. Naftali learns from his horse that there are many kinds of conversation; when the children bring Sus pieces of turnips, Sus waves his tail and shakes his head to say "Thank you." It is as if Naftali were the ideal of storytellers and his relationship to Sus the ideal of relationships to the ideal horse. This tale of quiet and complete contentment is in sharp contrast to the more jagged cultural experiences of Singer's own life.

The meeting of Naftali and Falik is providential. In Reb Falik's forest a huge, deep-rooted oak changes Naftali and Sus's lives: "When Naftali saw the giant oak, . . . it occurred to him: 'What a shame an oak hasn't a mouth to tell a story with!'" The traveler now seeks to lay his own roots: ". . . Naftali suddenly realized that he was tired of wandering. He now envied the oak for standing so long in one place, deeply rooted in God's earth. . . . He also thought of his horse. Sus was undoubtably tired . . ." (N, 17).

Reb Falik offers to build a place for Naftali and Sus, and Naftali accepts with joy. The storyteller has found a supporter, and the wise Reb expresses both Naftali's and Singer's creed: "Those who don't tell stories and those who don't hear stories live only for that moment, and that isn't enough" (N, 19).

In fact, Reb Falik's plans are much larger than Naftali's; the landowner wants a library and a printing shop, all to be run by Naftali. When the storyteller hears this, he says: "Of all the stories I have ever heard or told, for me this will be by far the nicest" (N, 20).

Naftali's simple diction and his foreign syntax express the depth of his feelings. He is poor in wealth but rich in life. He settles in. Reb Falik contributes his own world of tales and Sus, in his own way, participates, seeming to share stories with his new horse friends. Naftali writes all winter; he sets the stories in type and prints them by hand. When the weather lifts, he travels again to nearby towns and sells his books, or gives them away. Sometimes Reb Falik comes along and the two men collect more stories from the people they meet. For those with ears and eyes, such as Naftali, Zebulun, and Falik, the world is an ongoing coincidence of stories.

Sus begins to weaken, or, as Singer puts it, became "ready to end his story on earth" (N, 22). The horse dies and Naftali places above the horse's grave as a marker the oak-handled whip he had never used. Weeks later Naftali sees the whip has sprouted into a sapling, nourished by the body of Sus. Birds gather in its branches, and it blossoms. Its twigs intertwine with those of the marvelous old oak. In some of his biblical-based stories, Singer's moralistic hand is heavy, as in *The Wicked City*. But in his benevolent religious mode, when he wrote of the lighter side of existence, including death, his faith was sure and his words were comforting: "Yes, individual creatures die, but this doesn't end the story of the world. The whole earth, all the stars, all the planets, all the comets represent within them one divine history, one source of life, one endless and wondrous story that only God knows in its entirety" (N, 23).

Reb Falik dies and Naftali dies, too. As the storyteller had wished, he is buried next to Sus beneath the young oak. "Naftali the Storyteller and

His Horse, Sus" has become the story of a man, his horse . . . and his oak tree. Scriptural words are carved on the tombstone:

> LOVELY AND PLEASANT IN THEIR LIVES,
> AND IN THEIR DEATH
> THEY WERE NOT DIVIDED. (N, 24)

Singer restated this in his final interview in 1991, the year he died: "We may die privately, but as far as we are part of the universe, we are very much alive. The universe doesn't look to me like a dead body; it looks full of wisdom and purpose. Life is not a kind of chemical accident. . . ."[4]

Fittingly, these are Singer's last published words.

In the collection's bookend story "Growing Up," Singer writes of himself as Isaac—or "Itseleh," (It' seh leh) as his family and friends called him, using the Yiddish diminutive of Isaac. His friends in the United States used his Yiddish nickname as well. Itseleh struggles with what it means to be a writer. "Growing Up" is a rather long story of several sections, which is also discussed in chapter 1. In one part of the story, Isaac is making up a story about young Haiml that has all the grand elements of a heroic rescue fairy tale, including ogres and an attractive kidnapee named Rebecca. The pubescent author, however, backs himself into a plot corner. He is 11 years old and is already experiencing failure: "I had just launched my literary career and already I had fallen into a literary dilemma" (N, 2). Though Singer was in his sixties and seventies when he wrote these stories about his own childhood and undoubtably has some selective memory, he consistently puts himself onto paper as a child of unusual creative intensity. He does so, for example, in "A Hanukkah Eve in Warsaw," the other memoir in this collection. Singer wrote in *A Day of Pleasure* that he knew he wanted to be a writer by the time he was 16 or 17, but he often depicts himself as much younger telling stories to friends, schoolmates, and to his treasured neighbor, young Shosha.

God Loves Fools

The collection's Chelm stories are swiftly paced. "Dalfunka, Where the Rich Live Forever" was originally published in the *New York Times*. It revolves around Reb Zalman Typpesh, the richest man in Chelm and the stingiest. He approaches the Council of Elders with a request. He wants a way to live forever, and he will pay handsomely for the privilege. Ever desperate for cash, the council members pull their beards and debate. It is the beadle, or custodian, Shlemiel who comes up with an answer. He indicates this to Gronam by sticking out his tongue and touching the tip of his nose with his finger. He has noticed in the records of Dalfunka— the poorest section of town where beggars and paupers live—that no one rich ever dies there. He advises that Zalman should "buy a house in Dalfunka, settle there, and live forever" (N, 32–33).

The advice is well-received.

But Zalman won't pay until the advice is proved true—that is, until he has lived forever. Zalman lives well in Dalfunka for five years and then dies. The sages discuss the possible reasons—all ridiculous ones— until they agree that Zalman died because he spent all his money living well in Dalfunka, and so became a pauper like all the others there.

"The Fools of Chelm and the Stupid Carp" spins out another Chelm joke, that of punishment to be wrought on a fish. Singer establishes the centrality of fish to the Eastern European Jews: "In Chelm, a city of fools, every housewife bought fish for the Sabbath. The rich bought large fish, the poor small ones. They were bought on Thursday, cut up, chopped, and made into gefilte fish on Friday, and eaten on the Sabbath" (N, 75).

One appreciates, therefore, the honor being done to Gronam by the other wise men of Chelm when they present him with the "largest carp ever caught in the Lake of Chelm . . ." (N, 76). But the fish proves unwise. When its new owner bends to inspect it, it slaps him in the face with its tail.

Gronam proclaims, "this carp is a fool, and malicious to boot. . . . This fish should be punished" (N, 76–77).

But how? While Gronam weighs the council's suggestions, one more absurd than the other, the fish is kept at town expense in a large fresh water trough. It is guarded, too, lest a Chelmite wife steal it for gefilte fish.

Finally Gronam announces how the fish will meet its end: it is to be drowned. The town assembles festively to see the sentence carried out, although some fault-finders grumble that a fish will not drown in water. The fact that once returned to water, however, the fish never reappears convinces the majority it is indeed dead. So seriously do the sages consider the issue, nevertheless, that they devise and post a decree that if the fish is ever caught again, it should be imprisoned by the town in a special pool of water for the rest of its life. Gronam and his sages all sign in big block letters.

Two other fools star in "Lemel and Tzipa." Singer opens by stating that he is telling the story as closely as possible to the way he heard it from his mother: Tzipa's father is well-to-do but can't marry off his dolt of a daughter. The groom made in heaven appears in the person of a bona fide fool named Lemel, or "fool." Much like the Lemel and Yenta from "The Mixed-Up Feet and the Silly Bridegroom" in *Zlateh the Goat*, this couple compensates in affection for what it lacks in acumen. Lemel's own mother asks, "What girl would want to marry such a dunderhead?" (*N*, 87). The answer is, Tzipa would, and the couple is betrothed. Once married, Lemel is encouraged by his father-in-law to go into business. The plot line is familiar: this is the ubiquitous joke of the rube who goes to town; it is similar to "Shlemiel the Businessman." Part of the pleasure of the joke comes from its familiarity. We wonder only what the particular circumstances in the story will be.

This time, the fool goes to town and stops along the way to eat the chicken his new bride Tzipa has sent with him. Only she was not told to cook it and she did not know she should; even Lemel knows not to eat a raw chicken. He must stop at an inn to eat. The inn symbolizes the crossroads of commerce, the wide world where the hayseed from the *shtetl* is dazzled by that most basic of pleasures: food. As did Shlemiel on his way to Lublin lose himself on the road, so does Lemel on his way to Lublin. At the inn, he orders, "Give me everything you have and I'll eat until I'm full" (*N*, 89).

Singer begins the next paragraph with the sentence "Said and done" (*N*, 89). This is an oral storyteller's expression, and reminds the reader in the midst of the story that Singer says his own mother told it to him. She no doubt cadenced her telling with exclamations such as "Said and done."

Lemel stuffs himself. As so many fine children's authors—Kenneth Grahame and Russell Hoban come to mind—write about the pleasures of food in details children enjoy, Singer spins a paragraph full of Eastern European Jewish cuisine: noodle soup, meat with potatoes, carrots, and cabbage; apple, pear, and raisin compote; tea and honey cake. But Lemel is still hungry. So the innkeeper gives him a cookie. Lemel eats it and states: "Now I'm full. Had I known you can get full from a cookie, I needn't have ordered all those other dishes" (*N*, 90).

Said and done, indeed. The fool has revealed himself, and the innkeeper immediately swoops in. Come back, he tells Lemel, and next time I'll give you a cookie right away. In Lublin, Lemel looks around but finds nothing as captivating as the idea of the four-course meal cookie. He returns to the inn. The proprietor tells Lemel he is out of cookies, but will gladly sell the recipe, for "a high price" (N, 91).

The innkeeper knows Lemel can't read. It isn't until the groom returns to Chelm that the recipe is deciphered by his father-in-law. Alas, it turns out to be nothing but very funny nonsense, but it is not so funny if you are related to Lemel.

The family decides Lemel must learn to read. Lemel goes to Lublin. He passes an eyeglasses store and hears a doctor ask, as a customer is trying on a new pair of glasses, "Now can you read?" (N, 93).

Ever eager to avoid effort, Lemel concludes he need not study reading if all he has to do is buy a pair of reading glasses. Alas, reality obtrudes again. Lemel can't read even with glasses, and he is faced with long months of study in Lublin.

Lemel seeks out a teacher—but not to learn from, to dictate a letter to. He writes to Tzipa that he misses her unbearably and wants to come home to find work.

Tzipa responds: ". . . Yes my dear Lemel, come back. I don't need a writer but a good husband and, later, a houseful of children. . . . Come straight home, because if you come back dead and I go crazy, it wouldn't be so good for either of us" (N, 95).

Lemel does return to Chelm, but not before he is swindled yet again. This time what the trickster sells Lemel is a written guarantee that turns out to say "God loves fools. That's why he made so many of them" (N, 97).

Finally Lemel is back where he belongs, back in Chelm; he becomes a coachman, a nonintellectual in touch with the earth. Like Naftali, he is loving toward his horse. Lemel is also back with his devoted Tzipa. Singer blesses both of them with many children, grandchildren, great-grandchildren, and great-great-grandchildren. Love is more important than knowledge, the story says. Zemach's charming back view of the dumpy couple, their chubby arms encircled, says the same as Singer's letters, but with lines. The message is that there is always someone who will love you just the way you are.

Calling it "some careless editing," (56) Norma Rosen points out an unfortunate bit of duplication between this story and "The Mixed-Up Feet and the Silly Bridegroom" from *Zlateh the Goat*, the joke in which both brides-to-be weep to their mothers that they don't want to marry a stranger. Their mothers reply with exasperation that in their time they married strangers too, but that with marriage grows familiarity. The daughters miss the point: "'You married Father,' Yenta answered, 'and I have to marry a complete stranger'" (*Zlateh*, 41); "'You, Mama, married Papa,' Tzipa countered, 'but I have to marry a complete stranger'" (*N*, 102). Rosen excuses Singer by saying an author of hundreds of stories would need help keeping them straight. But between the lines from *Zlateh the Goat*, translated by Elizabeth Shub and published under her eye at Harper and Row, and the same lines in *Naftali the Storyteller and His Horse, Sus*, translated by Joseph Singer and published by Farrar, Straus and Giroux, Singer was the only connection. One can only be glad, however, that if Singer did inadvertently tell the same joke twice, at least it was a good one.

The Heart of an Imp

"The Lantuch" is subtitled "from my Aunt Yentl's stories," and it is the only one of Singer's children's stories so labeled. Yentl figures in stories found in *In My Father's Court* and in *A Day of Pleasure*. Singer met this aunt for the first time when he moved back to Bilgoray from Warsaw in his early teens. She was his uncle's wife, part of the old *shtetl* world. When she smiled, Singer wrote, she smiled "with every wrinkle in her face." She addressed Isaac as "my child" (*N*, 41). Her storytelling was a Sabbath highlight for Singer, neighbors, and relatives.

Aunt Yentl starts her story by defining *lantuch* for her audience. Singer artfully recreates her speech, that of a masterful storyteller: "A lantuch? Yes, there is such a spirit as a lantuch. These days people don't believe in such things, but in my time they knew that everything can't be explained away with reason. The world is full of secrets" (*N*, 41).

Here is our primordial storyteller again, revealing in her words the common denominator in all oral artists: the ability to convey their belief in a multiply manifest, marvelous presence in the everyday world. *Lantuchs* are "like a part of the family" (*N*, 41). For the most part invisible, they do what they can to be helpful. Yentl describes the *lantuch* who lived in her childhood home; it favored her older sister and even brought her an almond cake. The matter-of-fact "authenticity" of her recounting establishes terra firma for marvelous doings, just as Naftali's father's recounting of his brush with the supernatural is told as utter truth, needing no explanation. "There is a proverb," writes Singer in the *New York Times Book Review*: "'You don't ask questions about a tale,' and this is true for the folktales of all nations. They were not told as fact or history, but as a means to entertain the listener, whether he was a child or an adult."[5]

Aunt Yentl continues with her story; *lantuchs* live behind the stove with the crickets. "Lantuchs love crickets. They bring them food and they understand their language" (*N*, 41). These concrete details make the reader feel present at the introduction of a new breed of imaginary being, somewhat akin to reading J. R. R. Tolkien's description of hobbits. With its mysterious ghost and its first-person plural narrator—the talk of the town—"The Lantuch" is also reminiscent of a short story by William Faulkner. Except, unlike "A Rose for Emily" and its ghoulish necrophile, the mysterious imp in "The Lantuch" brings his favorite family members firewood and things to eat. The unknown need not be frightening, says the story; we sometimes find help from unknown quarters.

Singer told Diane Wolkstein in an interview that "The whole business of comparing is a literary invention" (142), yet there is hardly a better story to showcase Singer's attitude toward both the characters in his children's stories and his readers than "The Lantuch." Writing for children enabled Singer to give voice to stories that are "affirmative and nourishing." Naomi S. Morse contrasts the "romantic, fascinating, and highly artistic . . ." stories of Hans Christian Andersen: "Beneath their surface, the morbid and masochistic are often found" (29). The poor and downtrodden in Singer's stories have a wealth of experience to share with listeners, whereas the poor in Andersen's stories are mistreated and abandoned. Very few of them receive altruistic help. Singer is writing for and out of a culture that considered acts of charity to be of primary importance. The cultural cohesion in his life was expressed in his stories.

In Yentl's story, the *lantuch* lives in the home of a poor schoolteacher. His wife is ill and his daughter is blind. The teacher suddenly dies. The first-person town assumes mother and daughter will soon have to enter the poorhouse. This is not a pleasant prospect for anyone, but it is a secure one because each *shtetl* supported a poorhouse through charity. Somehow the helpless women hang on in their home, although they have no money and never go out: "The town grew curious" (*N*, 43).

To express the storyteller's art most fully, Singer here switches to a first-person narrative style for several pages, words spoken by his Aunt Yentl. This direct voice is close, one could assert, to a genuine transcription; it is changed no more than, say, a tale by the Grimms. It is entertaining to hear the words in one's mind: "My dear people, there was a *lantuch* in their house, and when he saw that the breadwinner was gone and the women had been left penniless . . . he assumed the burden himself. You're laughing? It's nothing to laugh at. He brought them everything they needed—bread, sugar, herring. He did it at night" (*N*, 44).

Two townsfolk actually see the *lantuch* out on errands late at night. The girl is questioned by the rabbi; "It must be an angel from heaven," she says (N, 45).

"No," says not the rabbi, but the narrating Aunt Yentl, "it wasn't any angel but the *lantuch*." The end of the story Yentl was telling is "'It must be an angel from heaven,' she says": perfect ending to that story, no explanation provided. But the denouement is provided by the narrator: "After the mother died, the daughter sold the house and went to live with relatives in Galicia" (N, 45). Again Singer provides an apparent authenticity for the strange events of his story by mixing them with mundane minutiae.

A confirmation of Aunt Yentl's skill in storytelling is provided by the first comment from the audience after Yentl has finished: "'The *lantuch* didn't go along?' our neighbor Riva asked." The request for information isn't for explanation; it is a question in which "willing suspension of disbelief" is totally integrated. A question of this sort is a tribute to the storyteller.

She replies, "Who knows? . . . ." "Do they live forever?" Sheindel asked. "No one lives forever," Aunt Yentl replied (N, 45).

Reality and fantasy merge. And being a participant in the storytelling, which includes not just telling but listening and making remarks, is rewarded in Isaac's world as it was to be in Singer's. In the story, Isaac's Aunt Yentl gives him a cookie and fruit; in his later literary years, Singer received accolades and awards. The year he died at age 87 he expressed his attitude toward fame:

> I was translated into many languages and I got prizes. I received the Nobel Prize. I did not foresee this, and it was not the most important condition. I would have continued to do my writing even if I would have had no honors and no awards. . . . Many of the great writers like Dostoevski and Strindberg never got any awards or prizes, and they still did their best work to the last.[6]

"The Lantuch" is one of Singer's most entertaining stories; it has real personality. The characteristic that *lantuchs* are compatible with crickets forms the basis of "Tsirtsur and Peziza," the dreamy cricket and imp friendship story in *When Shlemiel Went to Warsaw*. The *Times Educational Supplement* calls "Tsirtsur and Peziza" "enchanting."[7] It has all the warmth of Singer's other cricket stories, "Shosha" and several other autobiographic ones in which a cricket *tsirtsurs*—the cricket's name is actually the Hebrew verb for the sound a cricket makes, the equivalent of calling a cricket "Chirpy" in English. Peziza, the female *lantuch*'s name, is a feminization of the adjective for "quick" or "zippy."[8] "Tsirtsur and Peziza" is a story of friendship that overcomes differences and difficulties; it is also a story of discovery. It starts mundanely: "In a dark space between the stove and the wall. . . ." The characters are an orphan imp and a thin but uncomplaining cricket. In fact, the cricket is another of Singer's storytellers, for Singer tells us what the noise a cricket makes at night means—the little creature is making stories. For Singer, stories pervade all levels of existence.

Peziza never meets her father *Lantuch*. Here the noun *lantuch* is specific rather than generic as in "The Lantuch." Her mother Pashtida, however, tells her of the wide world outside. Peziza and her cricket friend are thrust into it suddenly when carpentry in the kitchen forces them outside.

It is night, it is dewy, and "myriads of crickets . . . just like Tsirtsur" abound (*S*, 19). Both creatures prepare shelter for themselves, but Peziza has wanderlust. No sooner does she flap her wings than someone calls to her; it is "an imp perched on a weathervane. . . . He had two pairs of wings and his horns were transparent" (*S*, 20). His name is Paziz, the masculine form of Peziza: "quick," "zippy." In an enjoyable version of the typical male-female initiation theme, as in Walt Disney's *Aladdin* where the boy shows the girl "a whole new world," this imp takes Peziza out on the town and woos her with—what else—stories: "of ruined castles, broken windmills, and forsaken houses. How large the world was!" (*S*, 21).

She asks Paziz to return with her to the place where Tsirtsur is waiting. Upon arriving, "she saw that Tsirtsur was not alone." Peziza introduces Paziz and Tsirtsur introduces his new cricket friend Grillida.

The narrator opines that "fate always has surprises up its sleeve." Being forced outdoors has turned out well. They all enjoy the summer together, according to their own inclinations. But soon the nights grow chilly. Not only that, Singer adds with delightful detail, but the autumnal blowing of the ram's horn in the synagogue near where the foursome lives is beginning to rattle the sensitive Peziza's nerves. But "sensitive" does not mean "useless" in Singer's world; it is Peziza who sees smoke coming out of the chimney where she and the cricket used to live, fortunately signaling that the kitchen is livable again. Returning is easy for the flying imps, and they help the cricket couple back to the old space behind the stove. They live happily ever after.

Being near the human household owners has taught Tsirtsur and Peziza human language, and along with it the marvelous truth that ". . . like imps and crickets, humans too dream of love and happiness" (*S*, 26). In Singer's all-inclusive world, loyalty and love are everywhere immanent.

A Winter's Tale

In "A Hanukkah Eve in Warsaw," Isaac is aware of the differences between himself and the other boys at the *cheder* he attends every day. He is dreamy, introspective, and dressed like a provincial rabbi in out-of-date clothes. (Nor in later life in the United States did he make any concessions to fashion. According to his widow Alma, he never went to buy clothes.)[9] His red hair and pale skin contrast with his usually dark-complexioned schoolmates, a complexion confirmed in the Singer home in Miami Beach where many paintings and sketches of Isaac Singer are hung. One, on the wall facing the ocean, is a colored crayon drawing of Singer as a young man. His eyes are a deep blue, like the Atlantic Ocean, and his hair is a carrot red. In addition to his medieval clothes and atypical coloring, Isaac's family is poorer than most, but his father is a rabbi while other children's parents are less prestigious laborers or small-time merchants. Isaac is also different in that his overprotective mother insists he be escorted to and from school, an indignity visited upon none of the other students. "I was ashamed," he writes, "that my mother was such a worrier" (*N*, 65).

One Hanukkah evening, Isaac's escort has his own plans and asks the boy to return to Krochmalna Street alone. Not that the seven-year-old Isaac objects; on the contrary, he willingly colludes and proudly sets out. It is many hours and many adventures later before he reaches home.

Running from bullies, he winds up on a street full of fragrant goods: bagels, potato cakes, hot chick peas. He daydreams about rich foods for his friend Shosha and himself and does not notice the snow that begins to fall. Nor does he notice it until the snow has mixed with sleet and, blinded by it and his own imagination, he becomes thoroughly lost. On the unfamiliar main street, strange forces seem at work. In a description echoing earlier works, such as "The Devil's Trick" and *The Fearsome Inn*, Singer writes that, in the chill wind, he fancied himself dragged off to Mount Sair, "where the ground is copper and the sky is iron" (*N*, 71). Suddenly he is dragged off, but by a rescuer saving him from an oncoming trolley. In response to questions asked by the adult who now faces him, the startled child begins to lie, and once begun, continues. He say he is an orphan who lives with his grandfather, a porter. But inside the restaurant he is taken to, he is recognized as the rabbi's son. Instinctively, he eludes the adults, dashing out into the snow. Concerned about the "sins" he has committed, Isaac decides he must run away—but not alone. Rather than home, where he knows he should go, the boy makes directly for his friend Shosha's house. There he persuades the waif-like child to leave with him for Berlin. But no sooner do the children make plans than the door to Shosha's rooms flies open. Isaac's sister gloats to her flabbergasted mother, "Didn't I tell you he'd be here?" The sister even figures out Isaac and Shosha are planning to run away; all this infuriates Isaac's worried mother who hauls Isaac home where he assumes he will be punished.

But in a famous scene, once they return, his father, in a mellow Hanukkah mood, brushes aside the exclamations of his wife and presents Isaac with a beautiful prayer book all the way from Israel. Hindele objects, "Why does he get a gift. . . . The worst dog gets the best bone." She has not been given a beautiful prayer book because she is only a girl and is not included in the rabbi's vision. Pinchos-Menachem defends his son against his wife and daughter, then turns his attention exclusively upon him. Warming immediately to the subject of holiness and the coming of the Messiah, the rabbi ends his apocalyptic sermon to his son with "The saints will sit with crowns upon their heads and study the secret of the Torah" (*Stories*, 67). Undoubtably the saints are male. Singer, not subtly, shows rather than tells the workings of gender discrimination. Right after the lyrical speech by Pinchos-Menachem, the author Singer has his character Hindele call her father—and the reader—back to reality, back, that is, to her reality. The Father talks saints and Torah, but his daughter can only be concerned with tasks:

> "Mama, the potato pancakes are getting cold," Hindele said.
> "Oh, yes!"
> And my mother and my sister went back to the kitchen. (*N*, 82)

Father and son continue talking about religious matters and what Isaac wants to do when he grows up. But for Hindele, no such discussion occurs. She will be a wife and mother.

The question of Singer's attitude toward women rises frequently in many readers' minds. Such discussion strikes some as anachronistic when applied to Eastern European *shtetl* Jews, an imposition of a late-twentieth century feminist perspective. But awareness of the poor treatment of many women in Singer's stories is impossible to ignore. Singer's attitude is not easily explained. His juxtaposition of the father's visionary sentence and the sister's menial concern is no careless accident. Conservative in life and old-worldly—not about to start a revolution—Singer was nonetheless outside his own tradition sufficiently to observe the follies of its gender dogma, and to write about the consequences of its failings, his mother's and sister's unhappiness and isolation among them. As Rosen points out, ". . . of course Singer who wrote 'Yentl the Yeshiva Boy' knew all about such inequities'" (56).

"A Hanukkah Eve in Warsaw" is a complex story and the characters in it are presented in the round. While Isaac and Pinchos-Menachem in the front room discuss religion and the future, Bathsheba and Hindele cook the holiday feast. When the women emerge smiling from the kitchen, their faces glow with the warmth of Hanukkah and of the kitchen. Everyone is happy, even Isaac. His mother's glance tells him, "I know all your antics, but I love you anyhow."

This story is an older child's version of Sendak's classic *Where the Wild Things Are*. So deeply have both authors tapped into the *Stoffe* of story that their plots are precisely similar. Both their characters, Isaac and Max, are rebellious and angry—not at their fathers, but at their mothers. This signals running away from the home. Both children are disobedient and break rules. Both venture into terra incognita where they pretend to be someone other than themselves. Time is compressed for both. Isaac and Max eventually return home; they are forgiven by their mothers—and fed. The denouements are quick and ambiguous; too much explanation would smother the emotional resonance of both authors' endings. To know our mothers will forgive us is to be securely lovable.

Of Dogs, and Cats, and Superfluous Mirrors

Jan Skiba's Polish family is so poor the peddlers don't even come to the door of their one-room straw hut. How poor is the family? So poor that they don't even own a mirror. The peasants, says Singer somewhat condescendingly, "aren't curious about their appearance" (*N*,119). They are not so poor as to be without pets, however; the good-hearted Skibas own a cat, Kot, and a dog, Burek. But they, like their owners, have no mirror and therefore no conception of their appearance. The dog looks at the cat and thinks he looks like her. The cat looks at her friend the dog and sees herself as a dog.

Things change radically for everyone in the Skiba home when a peddler gets lost and winds up there. The concreteness of Singer's writing provides detailed images of the family, the surroundings, the peddler, and the merchandise: goats, eggs, honey, all kinds of "pretty doodads" that "bedazzle" the Skiba women—and a mirror. Only because he fears the mirror will eventually break as he carts it around does the peddler consent to Mrs. Skiba's offer to buy the mirror on time.

The mirror is a disaster. Looking at themselves for the first time clearly, the Skibas become depressed. Father Skiba has buck teeth; his daughters suffer from freckles, potato noses, and sharp chins. The girls stop working and long for cosmetic solutions such as dentists and freckle-removers. Vanity and envy of the rich have replaced the bliss of ignorance.

But if the humans in the house are adversely affected, the animals are apoplectic. In the mirror Kot and Burek see alien creatures and "for the first time in their lives they turned on each other" (N, 121). Bloodied and perplexed, they are separated and soon stop eating.

Jan Skiba is wise. The mirror has to go. Why look in a mirror, he asks, when you can "see and admire the sky, the sun, the moon . . ." (122). The peddler returns for his monthly installment, but instead gets the mirror back in exchange for more useful goods. Soon all is well. Kot again thinks she is a dog and Burek is again contentedly deluded as well. The girls, Singer adds, all make good matches despite what they themselves perceive as their physical shortcomings.

Characteristically, Singer ends by having a religious authority state the story's moral. This time, however, the wise man is the village priest rather than a rabbi. The priest's concluding remarks are that a mirror only shows the outside of a person. "The real image" is the kindness one displays: "This kind of mirror reveals the very soul of the person" (N, 122).

Who can argue with that? It is the way we all know the world should be. This story is one of the six chosen for inclusion in *Shrewd Todie and Lyzer the Miser* as one of Singer's best.

The madcap but fundamentally sane world of Singer's peasants where everyone eventually does get by contrasts sharply to Lewis Carroll's Wonderland, a world equally or even more madcap but very seldom kind. Reviewing *Naftali the Storyteller and His Horse, Sus*, Rosen observed the innate attractiveness of Singer's vision in the *New York Times Book Review*: ". . . a child of our contemporary culture who reads these stories

. . . steps into a world so centered and balanced and yet so rich that it must feel like stepping into some lost Paradise" (56).

In material terms, Singer's world was hardly paradise. But Naftali, Menaseh, Lemel, Tzipa: these characters are vivid, and, as long as their values are transmitted to readers of Singer's stories, they are never truly lost. Morse makes this point, "Naftali, of the title piece, pays homage to storytelling by devoting his life to telling, selling, giving away, writing, printing, and finally, becoming a story himself" (22). The same can be said of Naftali's creator.

Chapter Six

Holidays and Other Miracles

The Power of Light

A Child's Hanukkah in Poland

Many of Singer's stories are set during holidays that provide immediate associations for Jewish readers. For his non-Jewish readers, many of whom encounter their first depictions of these holidays in his pages, Singer soon establishes the respective festival atmospheres. Purim signifies spring and a carnival-like loosening of inhibitions; Passover is a ritualistic holiday and a close family time; Shavuot follows Passover by seven weeks and is associated in folk tradition with prayers and wishes; Succoth brings to mind the harvest and the grape juice the children drink pretending it is wine; and Hanukkah is heralded by the arrival in the household of the bright blue box of multicolored candles. *A Tale of Three Wishes*, a Singer picture book discussed in chapter 7, is set during Shavuot, the Festival of Tabernacles; "Tashlik," the story chosen by Singer to conclude his final collection, *Stories for Children*, is set during Rosh Hashanah, the Jewish New Year in the fall, when repentance and renewal are foremost.

Singer does not generally set his stories for children during the more somber holidays, such as Yom Kippur. "Tashlik" is an exception, an autobiographic tale of Singer as a teenager experiencing his first adult love; it was first published not as a children's book, but in the *London Jewish Chronicle*.

By the 1980s, Singer could write whatever he liked. He had written Hanukkah stories earlier: In *Zlateh the Goat*, for example, "A Grandmother's Tale," "The Snow in Chelm," and "The Devil's Trick" take place during the early winter holiday. A long Isaac saga in several sections is told in "A Hanukkah Eve in Warsaw" from *Naftali the Storyteller and His Horse, Sus*. Like the earlier "A Day of Pleasure," it is a memoir of initiation and rebellion, grand schemes and stark realities. But it was Singer's own idea to produce a book composed entirely of

Hanukkah stories. *The Power of Light: Eight Stories for Hanukkah* contains a miracle tale for each night of the holiday—quietly powerful stories conveyed with deep feeling.

Between Singer as a representative Jewish child and Hanukkah a special connection exists. It is, as he points out in the book, the only holiday in winter. Then the mystery of candles mingles with a stirring story and, better yet, with the giving of gifts. As the son of a Hasidic rabbi, however, for Singer the light-heartedness of Hanukkah was even more special. In *The Power of Light*'s memoir "A Hanukkah Evening in My Parents' House," he explains the holiday's appeal:

> All year round my father, a rabbi in Warsaw, did not allow his children to play games. . . .
> But on Hanukkah, after Father lit the Hanukkah candles, he allowed us to play dreidel for half an hour. I remember one such night especially.[1]

The author remembers the eighth night of the holiday. On this culminating night, in the *minorah*, the traditional candelabrum, nine candles glow. Starting with just one candle the first night, night by night another candle is added and lighted. The *shammes*, the candle used to light the others, is allowed to burn, for it symbolizes that a supporting role is also to be commemorated. A prayer is said over the small flames, some grandfather's face in the evening speaking the Hebrew words, illuminated. Watching the elemental candles burn as everyone feasts on *latkes*, the children play *dreidel* with a spinning top, a game of chance.

Hanukkah is satisfying because it commemorates the triumph of the underdogs and deals with courage, faith, and religious freedom; so do Singer's stories. They concern, the *New York Times Book Review* reports, "not miracles of the vulgar, splashy, spectacular kind but rather modest, seemingly mundane miracles."[2] The sorrow of a girl ghost is assuaged, a lost city boy comes home, a homeless old man tells a moving tale, the prophet Elijah aids a deserving family, a young couple is brought together by a Yiddish-speaking parakeet, a childless couple is visited prophetically by a deer, another young couple fights the Nazis, and yet another overcomes blindness by virtue of inner awareness. Poverty and cold are the conditions of the stories, and the poorhouse is the most common location, yet *The Power of Light* is one of Singer's most durable creations; it is one of his biggest sellers both in hardcover and in paperback. In 1990, Farrar, Straus and Giroux reprinted the book in a fine Sunburst

edition, with top-of-the-line, very fine, glossy paper and full-color repro-
ductions of Irene Leiblich's illustrations. Of these the *Christian Science
Monitor* writes, her "Chagallesque paintings capture with extraordinary
delicacy and evocative subtlety exactly the heartwarming blend of love
and nostalgia" (15).

Even in the poorhouse, as Singer's prose makes clear, the cheerful
Festival of Light was a favorite in the Jewish calendar. Like Purim,
which celebrates the victory of Queen Esther over the evil Haman,
Hanukkah celebrates a centuries' old Jewish triumph. As related in the
Apocrypha, in 170 B.C. the Seleucid Empire wanted forcibly to convert
the Jews to their pantheist Greek religion. The Jews, led by Judah
Maccabee, though greatly outarmed, refused; *maccabee* means "ham-
mer" in Hebrew. A small force of Jews managed to hold out against the
Greeks. In the newly regained Temple (this is the part children love to
hear), there was only enough oil to light the lamp for one night, but for
these heroes the lamp burned miraculously for eight nights. The
Maccabees chased the Greeks away and reconsecrated the Temple in
Jerusalem. With its drama, collective courage, and concrete miracles,
Hanukkah has become a simple secular holiday everyone can understand as a triumph over assimilation. The deeper meaning to the holi-
day has largely been lost, as pointed out by Theodor H. Gaster in his
Festivals of the Jewish Year.[3]

Singer does not credit a cotranslator for *The Power of Light*, and the
stories, beautifully crafted and often profound, tend to be longer and less
dynamic than those in earlier collections. Perhaps the stories display less
"orality" because Singer did not go through the process of translating
them aloud, as he done before with Elizabeth Shub. In contrast to the
repartee in the earlier books, many of these stories are narrations by an
individual. Three stories are narrated by Reb Berish, a new incarnation
of Singer's ubiquitous grandfatherly storyteller. "The Parakeet Named
Dreidel" is an unusual first-person narration based, according to Singer's
widow Alma, on true life, and "Hanukkah in the Poorhouse," one of
Singer's finest stories, is told by an old itinerant Russian Jew. All the stories in *The Power of Light* are serious—about heroics, as suits the holiday,
rather than about the *narishkeit*, or foolishness, of Chelm. They perhaps
appeal less to a young listener than to an older reader, but they are richly rewarding.

The Power of Light is the first collection not to begin with a foreword.
Rather, Singer opens with "A Hanukkah Evening in My Parents'
House," an intimate family portrait that shows the author's father at his

best and Singer's family at its closest. Writing from Isaac's point of view, knowledge, and feelings, Singer shows the interactions of Joshua, Hindele, and Moishe. Their personalities and comments blend with their pious father's in a threnody of contrasting worldviews: the child's ingenuous, the brother's scientific, the sister's wistful, the rabbi's evangelical. Singer describes himself and Moishe earnestly playing *dreidel* while their older siblings play along, letting the younger ones win. Singer's mother Bathsheba enters, coming in from the kitchen flushed from frying *latkes*, the traditional holiday potato pancakes. Singer's mother surveys the action, asks who is winning, and returns to the kitchen to cook.

In response to a question from Joshua, the father tells his children a contemporary miracle tale. When the story is over, all the children are serenely still. Then mother brings in the fragrant *latkes*. The holiday is flawless. The family atmosphere Singer describes is removed from time, almost archetypal. Knowing the power of such scenes, Singer elevates this one Hanukkah night of his childhood to the timeless, universal plane of domestic love and other quiet miracles. Singer has his father bless the present day by saying, ". . . what God could do two thousand years ago He can also do in our time" (*P*, 7). In his fine essay on the themes of faith in Singer's children's stories, Thomas P. Riggio discusses Singer's connection as an author to this natural attitude in children:

> Modern writers tend to speak to the cognitive, ethical, or psycho-social side of the child's experience. . . . Singer subordinates such contemporary ideals to what can be called, for want of a more elegant term, the child's faith development. . . .
>
> The children's volumes can be read profitably in the context of the adult works, which often center on the tortured fates of those who sever themselves from the support of their heritage. ("Symbols," 135)

Singer closes his book of Hanukkah stories with a very different tale, "Hanukkah in the Poorhouse." In contrast to the secure Singer household of "A Hanukkah Night in My Parents' House," the story narrated by the stranger in the poorhouse, a 92-year-old Russian, is a wrenching recounting of kidnapping, slavery, and desolation.

In the nineteenth-century tsarist Russia of Nicolas I, Jewish boys could be forcibly taken from home and sent far away to work for Christian families and be turned into Christians, ultimately to be conscripted for 25 years into the Russian army. Few survived the experience, either before joining the army or after. Because the Russian army did not take married men, to avert the possibility of conscription young Jewish children were often officially married, although consummation would be many years away. Singer's story is about one such boy; it is not unlikely that Singer as a child heard this story told firsthand by a traveler at his family's table, at the studyhouse, or, as he writes, during his years in his grandfather's *shtetl*: "There was a poorhouse in Bilgoray. . . . I liked to go in and hear people tell stories. . . . In these towns of Poland storytelling was really a part of life. . . . their literature, their theater, their movies, and their TV."[4]

Singer establishes his frame; in the poorhouse on the last night of Hanukkah, the ill and paralyzed lie near the fire to enjoy the sweets sent by "good citizens." Charity is a requirement of Judaism and all *shtetls*, no matter how small, supported a poorhouse. The ill and poor trade stories, conversing about the cold, about wolves, and about encounters with "demons, imps, and sprites" (*P*, 75). But the story told by a tall white-bearded stranger is not about the supernatural. It is a tale all too true.

The stranger is Russian and tells the Polish Jews, when they begin to discuss the "harsh decrees" against them, that they live in a paradise compared to Russia. The old man says his life has been "one great riddle." Asked by the others to tell his story, he replies, "If you have the patience to listen." With characteristically pragmatic Jewish humor, the warden of the poorhouse responds, "Here we *must* have patience" (*P*, 76).

". . . I am one of those who are called the captured ones," says the narrator, who introduces himself as Jacob. His nickname, Yankele, is formed in the traditional way by adding the diminutive "ele," pronounced "el-eh," two syllables, both with short "e" sounds. The child is affectionately called Yankele by his parents, but the Russians who capture him rename him Yasha, in the Russian manner:

> The child catchers would barge into a house or a cheder, where the boys studied, catch a boy as if he were some animal, and send him away deep into Russia, sometimes even as far as Siberia. He was not drafted immediately. . . . He had to learn Russian and forget his Jewishness. Often he was forced to convert to the Greek Orthodox faith. The peasant made him work on the Sabbath and eat pork. Many boys died from the bad treatment and from yearning for their parents. (*P*, 77)

When the story begins, young Yankele loves Reizel, his neighbor's girl. In several stories Singer depicts young love as strong and serious, similar to the way he remembers his own young love for his frail girl-next-door in Warsaw, the vulnerable, childish Shosha. With her he could feel protective; she appears in several of his stories and the novel *Shosha*; the extent of his prepubescent passion he makes clear in "A Hanukkah Eve in Warsaw" from *Naftali the Storyteller and His Horse, Sus*. To prevent him from being captured, Yankele is to marry Reizel when the girl is eight. As with other such marriages, the children will not live together until they are much older. But only three days before their wedding, while her mother is still preparing Reizel's trousseau, the Cossacks invade the *shtetl* and Yankele is one of the boys dragged from his home. He has time only to call out to his little fiancée the hope that she will wait for him, and the child responds, "Yankele, I will wait for you" (78).

Yankele is sent deep into Russia, far beyond the Pale of Settlement to which the Jews were restricted. He suffers overwork, loneliness, fear, and prejudice in the home of the peasant Ivan and his six children, all of whom try to convert him. Nonetheless, the boy vows to remain a Jew. To remember his heritage, he holds imaginary conversations in Yiddish with Reizel and his family and determines to celebrate Hanukkah, even if it costs his life. Finally Yasha is old enough to be conscripted. Despite the personal danger, he continues in secret to "light a candle and recite a prayer" during Hanukkah (*P*, 81).

The narrator describes his "great joy" at clandestinely meeting another Jewish soldier who leaves a small Hebrew prayer book with him. Calling it "the greatest treasure of my life," he tells his listeners he still carries it in his sack.

One night 22 years after his capture—years passed in isolation without any communication with his family, for mail written in Yiddish was not delivered—Yasha is caught with his Hanukkah candles by his enemy, "a vicious corporal by the name of Kasputin." Knowing he will be court-martialed and sent to Siberia, he hits the corporal with his gun and runs away.

He walks and rides rails, begging for food, until he reaches western Russia and his hometown of Vibetsk. Fortunately, it is Purim, an early spring holiday during which costumes are worn. To spare his aged parents the shock of reunion, he disguises himself and returns to the home he left as a child. He is welcomed and fed generously, according to Jewish customs of hospitality to strangers. Asking his parents about their children, he is told about their children who are married and have children. But his mother is unable to keep from crying and, by way of explanation, his father tells him the sad story of their boy Yankele, who "got lost like a stone dropped in water" (*P*, 85).

"What happened to his bride-to-be?" asks their disguised son. He learns he is not to be as fortunate as Odysseus; Reizel has died murmuring Yankele's name.

Gradually the son reveals his identity. To protect him from arrest as a deserter, he is introduced to the town as a widowed nephew. This suits Yankele, for he has always thought of Reizel as his wife and knows he could never "remarry." He takes care of his parents for the next six years, "the happiest days" of his adult life, but after their death, he finds nothing to hold him in Vibetsk.

In the tradition of Gimpel the fool, Yankele spends his remaining years as a wanderer, keeping all his possessions in the same sack that he proceeds to show his audience in the poorhouse, including the prayer book he received some 60 years earlier as a young soldier. He goes from town to town, helping the sick and poor. And, sometimes, when he feels especially forlorn, he hides in the woods and lights Hanukkah candles, even when it is not Hanukkah.

Like Gimpel, Yankele spends his remaining nights thinking of his one love. There is no irony in Yankele's sweet reminiscences of Reizel, as there is in Gimpel's memories of his less than perfect Elka. Yankele sees his betrothed dressed in a white silk gown; it is Hanukkah. He lights the *minorah* she has prepared, and then Singer, as he frequently does, elevates the story of this lonely, ruined life into one of miraculous import. Yankele relates that in his vision the sky itself glows like a lighted *minorah*, its flames made of stars. The rabbi to whom Yankele has told his dream observes that love coming from the soul radiates the light of the soul. He is certain, Yankele tells his poorhouse listeners, that when he dies, waiting for him in heaven will be the soul of his betrothed, Reizel.

Human emotion is capable of lighting the sky, and love lasts beyond life. It is the expression of this faith that children respond to in Singer's writing. Even when his stories concern ill-fated lovers, as with "Hanukkah in the Poorhouse" or *The Golem*, there is poetic justice when one believes that this world is, as Gimpel says, "Only once removed from the real world" of eternity, and that in the other, higher world, no child is captured and kidnapped; there, rather, everyone is at home.

A Hanukkah Ghost

In "The Extinguished Lights," from *The Power of Light*, the universal story of the unquiet dead is presented by Singer as a Eastern European Jewish children's story. Singer often wrote ghost stories; for a clear demonstration of the difference between a Singer story for children and one with the same theme written for adults, the reader may wish to see his adult stories "The Power of Darkness" and "A Crown of Feathers."

Singer's setting in "The Extinguished Lights" is Bilgoray, that generic *shtetl* which, like Faulkner's Yoknapatawpha County, is as much a character in the author's universe as any other like Naftali or Zlateh. It is a personal symbol, in contrast to the cultural symbol, Chelm; it is his symbol for the isolated and introverted *shtetl*; it is the locale of his first novel, the seventeenth-century-set *Satan in Goray*, and it is the actual town his grandfather dominated where Singer spent several years as a teenager.

In the children's story version of Bilgoray, Reb Berish roasts potatoes in the studyhouse on the first night of Hanukkah for a few urchin friends who come to hear his stories. After Singer's introductory frame establishes the setting, the story evolves into a monologue by Reb Berish. As he characteristically does, Singer writes into his character's narration the oral teller's tricks; "Now hear something," says the Reb to the boys and proceeds to spin the ghost story not of those tortured by ghouls such as Roderick Usher or Heathcliff, but of a village in the grips of an uncanny omen.

The winter is fierce. Wolves roam the town while horses neigh in fear, and the "snow [is] up to the rooftops" (12). Worse, none of the candles in anyone's *minorahs* will stay lit. Upset, elders forget to give children their Hanukkah *gelt*, or money, and women forget to fry *latkes*. The story-telling Reb builds momentum through mystery: who or what is responsible for extinguishing the Hanukkah candles all over the village? On the seventh night, an old woman comes to the rabbi's door and, within the story Reb Berish is recounting, tells the rabbi an astonishing story.

The ghost is her granddaughter Altele. The name means "little old one" in Yiddish superstitiously meant to trick evil spirits. "Alt" is old, and the Yiddish suffix "eleh" is somewhat equivalent to "y" or "ie" appended to a name in English, for instance, "Stevie." Another of these significant nicknames used by Singer is the moniker of the midget in the circus Naftali goes to see. The midget is called "Pitzele," which affectionately means "little one," "runt," or "baby." The youngest child in a Yiddish-speaking family might be called "the pitzele."

While a critic such as Irving Howe might object that a story such as "The Extinguished Lights" takes place in very familiar territory for Isaac Singer, no other ghost story in children's literature is similar to it. As Dina Abramowicz, reference librarian at YIVO, New York City's

Institute for Jewish Research, observed, "Secular literature for children in Yiddish did not exist until fairly recent times,"[5] and Singer is the foremost source of it. His setting in "The Extinguished Lights" is unique— Hanukkah at the graveyard. Singer's characters are vividly Eastern European: Reb Berish, the rabbi, the old grandmother, Altele herself. Their motivations are very specific—to restore harmony to one and all. In a very few pages, Singer manages to populate a town and bring it to life; he shows the superstition in the village as well as the skepticism. Bilgoray becomes center stage for a miracle.

In terms of its opening exposition of poverty, Singer's story could have been written by Hans Christian Andersen, but the authors' plot paths and tones are profoundly divergent. "Altele" is an unusual name, but so are "Thumbelina," "The Little Mermaid," and "The Little Match Girl." All are names more descriptive than personal. Like the Little Match Girl, Altele is an orphan and doomed. As they waste away in winter, both children realize they are going to die. Thumbelina is abused and exploited. The Little Mermaid suffers in painful silence. The Little Match Girl freezes in solitude and dies, period. But the Little Jewish Girl, part of a cohesive community, asks the entire town to pray for her so that she can live until the first night of Hanukkah.

Still, she dies a day short of this. Her disappointment is the genesis of the mystery, for, a year later, the angry ghost vents her displeasure by blowing out everyone's holiday candles. Her ghostly message to the living, while emphatic, is nonetheless pacifistic. In Singer's story, the ghost's goal is not revenge but rectification. In contrast, a late-twentieth-century American story would probably be called "The Revenge of the Hanukkah Howler" in the style of the R. L. Stine's popular *Goosebumps* series.

Altele does not ask much. She tells her grandmother in dreams that the town must celebrate the last night of Hanukkah at her grave, lighting the *minorah* in the graveyard. Hearing this, the rabbi first expresses regret that he did not pray hard enough for the child to live. This is emotionally satisfying; the girl's grievance is recognized and responded to with real feeling, rather than rejected or ignored. The rabbi checks the holy books to see that what she requests is not forbidden. Finding nothing, he takes upon himself the responsibility for deciding and comes down on the side of active compassion rather than fearful withdrawal. The candles will be lit that night on Altele's grave.

The rabbi enlists everyone in town. There is fasting and prayer for a windless night. But the wind howls and unbelievers snicker. Suddenly, halfway through the evening prayer, the weather breaks; skeptics are silenced. Once all the candles are successfully lit, the party begins. After the blessing, food is served, children play *dreidel*, and a bright light shines over Altele's grave, "a sign that her soul enjoyed the Hanukkah celebration" (*P*, 15). It was the best Hanukkah the graveyard had ever seen.

A different writer might have ended the story there, but Singer's use of the frame allowed him, in this as in many other stories, to conclude by philosophizing in his storyteller's voice. Reb Berish tells the children he remembers the event he has told, although it happened more than 80 years ago. As the studyhouse lamp sputters, the old man gingerly pulls potatoes from the fire and distributes them to the boys, a poor man's fare but clearly shared with good company. Then, a boy asks Reb Berish, "What do all the souls do when they are with God?"

Reb Berish answers most satisfactorily that they sit in Heaven on golden chairs, treated like royalty, while God teaches them about the Torah.

The equating of heaven and learning is a clearly cultural characteristic. What other ethnic group conceives of paradise as endless study and of God as a teacher?

Singer's children's stories present children who cope well. Like Aaron and David in *Zlateh's Goat*, Altele solves her own problem. Presumably her now-healed soul is eternally studying with God, a reassuringly happy resolution to a ghost story. Like the children in *A Tale of Three Wishes*, Singer's young protagonists are capable of understanding trial and adversity; they can plan and wait for change. Good wins, but not deus ex machina. Entire communities participate, sharing the ups and downs of characters such as Shlemiel, Lemel, Atzel, and Altele. Singer's characters support communal action, accept the unusual, and emphasize nonmaterial things. Thus, when these characteristics are rewarded, readers accept the outcome. The often ambiguous universe inhabited by characters in Singer's adult stories is not where his child characters live. As pointed out by Mark A. Bernheim,[6] Singer is subversive as an adult author, but conservative and underlyingly moralistic in writing for children.

For example, he excluded "The Purim Gift," a story from his autobiography *In My Father's Court*, from *A Day of Pleasure*, his subsequent version for children, because it depicts a young betrothed couple nearly estranged after playing nasty practical jokes on each other during the holiday. The first three pages of "The Purim Gift," an instructive story for discerning Singer's standards for age-appropriate literature, chronicle the Singer family celebrating Purim. The holiday is a costume festival,

the Jewish version of Carnival when participants let loose of everyday
restrictions. Rabbis receive the most luxurious gifts their congregations
can afford. But Singer's father only rues the extravagance and shallow-
ness of the manner in which the festival is marked. He gives away most
of what the family receives because he cannot be certain it is truly
kosher. Thus far there is no distinction between the opening of this story
and that of one like "A Hanukkah in My Parents' House." But "The
Purim Gift" is not really about the Singer family and the gifts they are
given; it concerns the gifts exchanged by a fiancé and fiancée. The young
man has tricked his fiancée by sending her a wrapped box containing a
dead mouse. Infuriated, the girl sends her fiancé a cake baked with
refuse, giving rise to an ugly spat. Before calling off the wedding, with
their families they come to Rabbi Singer for a judgment, or *Din Torah*,
over the couple's disgraceful behavior. Although the story ends well—
Singer's father remonstrates with both the young man and young
woman, and they reconcile—Singer deemed what the betrothed did to
each other to be inappropriate for children.

Indeed, as a children's author, Singer plays a role for his readers much
like his own mother played for him, making him leave the room when
grown-up matters were discussed. Nevertheless, in their small apartment Singer overheard a good deal he was not meant to and his memory
of the confused and passionate feelings he had as a child listening to
adult conversation provides much of the tension in his memoirs. But—
as an adult, he is every bit as strict as his mother; the world he presents
by conscious design to his young readers is untroubled in contrast to his
own. The storytellers in his tales also uphold a high moral standard. Reb
Berish, *The Power of Light*'s equivalent to Naftali, is another incarnation
of Singer's own father, instilling a sense of wonder and a fierce ethic in
his listeners. Singer asserts that conservatism is natural to children: ". . .
the child has become the guardian of those moral and religious values
which adults have rejected. . . . Our children refuse to mock or subvert
family life. Daddy and mommy, brother and sister, remain for them serious and stable institutions."[7]

In addition to "The Extinguished Lights," Reb Berish narrates two
more miracle stories in *The Power of Light*, "The Squire" and "Hershele
and Hanukkah." This same frame, the Reb handing potatoes to his
young listeners, is repeated in both of the other stories. The frame also
brings to mind "The Lantuch." In it, like Reb Berish, Aunt Yentl tells a
story to her young audience and then hands out food. Singer recalls and

repeats this fond association of intimacy, food, and storytelling established in his youth.

Elijah, a favorite biblical and folklore figure identified with wonder, appears in "The Squire" and "Hershele and Hanukkah." He is said to visit every Jewish household during Passover, drinking a sip of the wine traditionally left for him and occasionally to return to earth unexpectedly to work miracles. But not too often: Reb Berish begins "The Squire" by telling the boys in the studyhouse that miracles have always been rare, now as before, for if miracles were common, people would cease to exercise free will.

Sometimes, however, the Reb continues, only a miracle will do, as in "The Squire." Life together for the loving Falik and Sarah starts well but soon she dies, leaving behind three young children. Falik also falls ill but refuses the town's charity. Finally one Hanukkah the family has only the *minorah* in to sell for food. Falik asks his children to wait until after Hanukkah to sell the lamp. The children are hungry, but Mannes, the oldest boy, convinces them to pretend the holiday is Yom Kippur, when fasting is required. They do, but they are downcast. A knock sounds at the door. There stands a magnificent Polish squire. He tells Mannes the glow of the Hanukkah candles has caught his attention and he wishes to see the lamp. Visits from Polish squires were very rare, especially from squires who ask to hear the Hanukkah story. The personable nobleman insists on buying the *minorah* for 1,000 gulden, and then advances the children half of the money to play *dreidel* with him. They win even more. Having lost all his money to them, the squire then rises to leave, telling the children that their ailing father will soon recover. When the children look outside to watch the departure of the squire and his retinue, the squire, his coach, and servants have all disappeared.

"I will make it short," says Reb Berish by way of conclusion and sums up the story with facts and philosophy. No sooner does the squire leave than Falik recovers. The Reb tells his audience, "Nothing but a miracle could have saved him, and so the miracle occurred" (*P*, 49).

The boys ask if the squire was Elijah. The Reb says only that he surely was not a Polish squire. The boys ask if the squire ever returned to pick up the *minorah*. Reb Berish replies, "Not as long as I was in Bilgoray" (*P*, 49). But human time and divine time are not the same. Perhaps Falik's grandchildren received another visit from the mysterious squire to claim the lamp he had paid for, the old man continues as he takes roasted potatoes out of the fire to share with the boys.

The effect of the story is one of quiet optimism; God's finesse surpasses human comprehension. Faith and goodness are rewarded, and in determining to celebrate the holiday by spending their last money on candles, the family of Falik had shown itself to be worthy of a miracle.

Animal Friends

Reb Berish's next story in *The Power of Light*, "Hershele and Hanukkah," reads like a fairy tale, but because it is really a miracle story, it diverges in one important way. In a fairy tale, a key characteristic is the lack of surprise or comment at the involvement of the supernatural; any such comment breaks the spell of the story. In a miracle tale, the point is precisely that a miracle has occurred. It occurs because the recipients have faith in God's omnipotence, and in their thankfulness and conscious sense of wonder, characters in these stories express a religious awareness not found in fairy tales.

Other differences are found between a typical fairy tale and Singer's tale. In Grimms' tales, poetic justice is as cruel as it is common; the victors, although they be sweet as Cinderella, are either incapable or undesirous of ameliorating retribution. Poetic justice in Singer's fairy tales is just as common, but it is less graphic than in the Grimms' tales. Evil characters are not rolled down hills in spike-studded barrels, blinded by birds, or forced to dance to death in red-hot shoes—however much they deserve it. Evil ones are diminished by being bested by the good—thus losing their power to do harm—and are banished to lands hard as metal. Exile, however, because of the Jewish history of exile and diaspora, or dispersion, was a harsher punishment, perhaps, than might appear to many readers. To be cast out of the community was to be doomed because only by sticking together did the Jews survive at all.

Furthermore, in the Grimms' tales, the mighty have power, as royalty, based not on character but on blood. No such hierarchies exist in Yiddish children's literature. Singer's characters triumph in the service of the family and the community, not in the seeking of their own fortunes. And, whatever historic validity there is to the common situation in Grimms' tales of children being abandoned by their starving parents, Singer's stories have none of this bleakness.

However, like many familiar Grimms' tales, "Hershele and Hanukkah" begins with the dilemma of a childless couple. Singer develops a history for them: they are hard-working, well-to-do, and generous in sharing the good fortune that has resulted from their honesty and industriousness as the managers of a ne'er-do-well Polish squire's estate. One Hanukkah, Reb Isaac hears a sound at the door and opens it onto a real surprise; a fawn shivers on the threshold, cold and hungry. The family, especially his wife Kreindl, babies the fawn and nurses it until Passover, a period of several months. Although the children wish to name the pet "Hershele," which means "fawn" in Yiddish, Kreindl says, "You are not going to give this name to the animal" (*P*, 66). Instead, the family agrees to call it "Hanukkah," an unusual name for an animal. Later the Reb asks his wife about her refusal but she insists on keeping her secret from him, adding that the reason will soon be obvious.

Here Reb Berish tells his audience of "dear children" that he is going to tell them the secret even before the wife tells it to her husband, giving the audience—and the readers—an exciting piece of privileged information. The secret is that a few weeks before the fawn appeared, a hungry old man had come to the estate. Naturally, the charitable Kreindl feeds him. He takes a Torah out of his sack and begins to read it. Seeing she is dealing with a learned man, Kreindl tells him her troubles. He blesses her, promising she will have a child within the year. When Kreindl asks for a sign, the old man predicts that before her child is conceived, a forest animal will appear at her door. He tells her to name her child after the animal.

To the joy of everyone, Kreindl does become pregnant. As her pregnancy advances, the fawn Hanukkah begins to long for the outdoors. After one last meal of chopped potatoes and carrots, the deer is set free into the wild.

Reb Berish and Kreindl are soon the parents of a healthy boy. They name him Hershele. Soon it is winter again, a colder one than the year before, and the children hope Hanukkah the deer will return. He does, and he happily licks the hand of his newborn namesake. The third Hanukkah the deer again returns, this time with a doe. As the story ends, the family expresses its gratitude at the blessed fertility and continuity of life and friendship.

When Reb Berish's boys ask this time about the mysterious stranger, the Reb states outright that the old man who visited Kreindl was the prophet Elijah. "He always comes disguised as a poor man," says the Reb—thus contradicting Elijah's disguise in "The Squire," where Elijah is a rich Pole but if anyone in the audience notices, he doesn't mention it. Instead, they ask if their old friend will tell them "another story tomorrow. . . ."

And, as Singer might have replied, the old Reb says, "With God's help
. . . I have more stories to tell than you have hair in your sidelocks" (*P*, 72).
The prophet Elijah is also the miracle worker in one of Singer's picture books, *Elijah the Slave*, discussed in chapter 7.
In addition to Hanukkah, another animal in *The Power of Light* is the
key figure in "The Parakeet Named Dreidel." Singer spun this first person story out of an actual event. As his widow Alma told me, one winter
the two of them were sitting at home in New York City when they heard
a sound at the window. Isaac spotted a little bird shivering on the window ledge and brought it inside. It was the first of many parakeets the
Singers kept as pets over a 15-year period. Dorothea Straus details
Singer's devotion to the bird he named "Matzoh," calling it an "old
Soul." Matzoh used to perch on Singer's bald head. When, one summer,
it flew out a window accidentally left open, she says Singer was devastated. The parakeet was replaced by two new little birds, but Singer said
between the two, they did not equal the soul of Matzoh (*P*, 24–25).
The parakeet later named "Dreidel" appears the same way in this
story. This fictional couple has a child, a son of marriageable age, and,
indeed, the homey tale spins out so that the parakeet—lost by the girl
but found, raised, and, eventually returned to her by the boy when he
and the girl marry—is the thread through which the otherwise slight
romance runs.

The Power of Light

"The Power of Light" and "Menashe and Rachel" are both stories in
which a modest bit of light has long-lasting effects, just like the light
from the Maccabees' *minorah*. Singer's stories both concern romantic love
and the survival of the underdogs through acts of great personal courage
inspired by Hanukkah. That a single candle can affect one's world
proves true in "The Devil's Trick," when young David, lost in a blizzard
trying to save his parents from the devil, is able to find his way home in
the dark by virtue of a tiny Hanukkah candle burning in his hut, and in
"A Hanukkah Evening in My Parents' House," when the young saint
Zaddock follows a candle in the forest. The turning point in "The Power
of Light" is also a single slender candle; it inspires two desperate children
to begin a journey that takes them from the ruins of the Warsaw Ghetto
to freedom in Israel.
This story is set, alone among Singer's children's stories, during
World War II in Poland. Although replete with Singer's comments, such

as ". . . the light of the candle brought peace into their souls," (*P*, 57) the tale has a more matter-of-fact tone to it than most of his other stories. The reason for this is explained in the story's final paragraph. Singer reports that the story he has told is a true one; he heard it from the two people involved, David and Rebecca, at their home near Tel Aviv during one of his visits to Israel in the 1950s. The escape of the two nearly starved teenagers seems to validate Singer's father's faith that miracles even now occur.

Schindler's List, among many other virtues, provides a concrete picture for its audience of what the Nazi occupation of Warsaw meant. For 14-year-old David and 13-year-old Rebecca, the destruction of the ghetto has orphaned them and left them without siblings. With only each other, they crouch in a pitch-black cellar, hungry and extremely cold. David occasionally leaves their hiding place to scrounge for food, but both children know that, unless they escape, they will soon either starve or freeze to death. The problem is, escape is impossible. The Nazis patrol the barbed wire perimeter of the ghetto, shooting anyone they see. Although the children have heard of Jewish partisans in the forest near the capital, there is no chance of reaching them; the situation is hopeless. Still, in the face of this, David and Rebecca vow to marry should they somehow live through their ordeal.

One cold night, David, finally returning with some food, tells Rebecca he is saving a surprise for her. The surprise is small but ultimately saves their lives: a single Hanukkah candle David has found, along with a few matches. David says the Hanukkah prayer and lights the candle. The tiny spark among the shadows brightens their future.

They determine to escape the ghetto that night, and before the candle flickers out, they have packed the few things they possess and begun their perilous journey. With the help of the extreme cold that has kept the Gestapo guards to a minimum and frozen the sewage through which they must crawl, David and Rebecca reach the outskirts of the forest. Still, they must survive for a difficult week before they are found by the partisans known as the Haganah, Israeli Jews who have returned to the Old Country to help Jewish refugees. It is the last night of the holiday, and, surrounded now by friends, one of whom gives them a *dreidel*, the children celebrate a Hanukkah in the woods. Trying weeks lie ahead as they walk most of the way to the occupied Yugoslav coast, where they secretly join other Jews on a boat heading for Israel. Pursued by Nazi war planes and submarines, all they can do is pray; they land safely. Greeted joyously by Israeli Jews who take them in, they learn Hebrew;

David goes to engineering school and Rebecca studies literature in Tel Aviv. They marry when she turns 18.

Like the adult story "A Sabbath in Portugal," this story includes Singer as a character, or at least as an audience at the table of Jews whose experience has been very different than his. Singer has joined the young couple in Israel for Hanukkah, and, over the traditional *latkes* and apple-sauce, Rebecca tells him that it was the little candle David lighted that saved their lives, awakening in them "a hope and a strength we didn't know we possessed" (60). Just as Singer preserves their story to pass down to generations of readers, the couple has preserved the actual *drei-del* given them in the Polish forest to pass down to their young son, with whom, as the story ends, Singer is playing *dreidel*.

"Menashe and Rachel" is a more typical Singer story, set in the Lublin poorhouse, which has a special room for orphaned and sick children. The main characters are both orphans; they are also blind. By now, the read-er familiar with Singer's themes will know to expect a tale involving inner sight and a miracle suitable to the setting, a subtle story of inner strength, imagination, and awareness.

Menashe is a prodigy in learning the Torah and skillful with his hands; he carves *dreidels* for himself and Rachel. Moreover, he is a born storyteller around whom even the adults gather. Rachel, a year younger, is also studious; her cornflower blue eyes shine so that people can hardly believe she is blind. The children, eight and nine years old, are deeply in love and refuse to be separated.

In this story, the true miracle is just how deeply these devoted chil-dren do indeed see. On the sixth night of Hanukkah, pressed by Menashe to tell him a story, Rachel begins a tale about them. Everyone thinks them blind, says the child, but she knows they see. Rachel, she says, sees "from the inside," just as seeing people can see in their dreams. This is an interesting thought, one quite compatible with Singer's fasci-nation with the dream state. Rachel says she sees colors, and angels, and, in her head, she sees the Hanukkah lights.

Menashe tells her he too can see; in fact, he can remember sights from before he became blind. Rachel then describes for him the moon, moun-tains, rivers, and dancing children. The boy, too, has seen what no one else can see, and he emphasizes the truth of such visions, as might Wolf Bear from Singer's own childhood, depicted in "A Hanukkah Evening in My Parents' House," or Reb Zebulun explaining to the nascent story-teller Naftali that to create a fiction is not to lie, for all things are possi-ble. Menashe and Rachel feel no need to convince anyone else that they too can see. They are secure in the accuracy of their own sight.

The children plan their married life. They will dream about each other, and they will have seeing children who also have inner vision, divine vision—just as God sees into the heart. Singer introduces the passions of the young again by having Rachel persuade Menashe to give her a brief kiss, an innocent kiss that nonetheless leaves them both breathless. The outer world obtrudes when the poorhouse warden comes to ask them why they are sitting alone. Menashe then makes up a new story to tell the warden, yet it again is a vision of the future life to be shared by the loving children, including their dozen offspring and a sailboat that arrives at their deserted island to take them all to the Land of Israel.

Will these two poor blind orphans one day marry and travel from the Lublin poorhouse by sailboat with their dozen children to the Land of Israel? Probably not, thinks the adult reader—the likelihood is no more realistic than, say, that of the crippled Porgy in the Gershwins' musical *Porgy and Bess* traveling by cart all the way to New York City to find his Bess. But in Singer's stories, anything is indeed possible. And in all the stories in *The Power of Light*, one of his most loved works, the scarcely possible becomes sanctified fact. Either the stories' narrators themselves speak of the miracle, as in "The Power of Light," or an unimpeachable storyteller affirms the unlikely truth, as Reb Berish confirms when asked if he remembers it clearly, "As if it took place yesterday."

In an article that originally appeared in *The Christian Century*, Bernheim concludes his essay on Singer's children's stories with an overview especially pertinent to Singer's book of wonders: "Singer has fully succeeded in portraying the sense for and of the miraculous which we know as the best of children's literature" (36).

Singer, however, writes Jewish children's literature. What makes it Jewish, besides its authorship? In his essay "The Genius of Isaac Bashevis Singer," Ted Hughes philosophizes on the apt association of Judaism and "choice." His observations throw light on the coherent core of *The Power of Light*. Hughes's comments also illuminate Singer's oft-repeated remark that he chose to believe, a choice artistically communicated by his myriad storytellers to both fictional audiences and real-life readers: "The core of the Jewish faith . . . is one long perpetually-renewed back-to-the-wall Choice . . . to affirm a mode of survival against tremendous odds. . . . So it is not surprising if Singer, in his books, gravitates back toward it as a way out of the modern impasse, salvaging at the same time the life of spirit and all the great human virtues."[8]

Chapter Seven

Tales, Histories, and Picture Books

The Fearsome Inn, Mazel and Shlimazel, Alone in the Wild Forest, The Reaches of Heaven: A Story of the Baal Shem Tov, Elijah the Slave, Why Noah Chose the Dove, The Wicked City, The Fools of Chelm and Their History, The Golem

1967

The Fearsome Inn was published by Charles Scribner's Sons in 1967, immediately after *Zlateh the Goat*. Elizabeth Shub had moved as editor from Harper and Row, publisher of *Zlateh the Goat*, to Scribner's, and Singer followed her there with his manuscript. Beginning with *Mazel and Shlimazel: or, The Milk of a Lioness*, however, Singer published almost exclusively with Farrar, Straus and Giroux, in most years producing a children's book or two. Only one other children's book, *The Topsy-Turvy Emperor of China*, was published by another press—Harper and Row—and probably, were it written by anyone but Singer, it would not have been published at all.

Singer's first single-story book, *The Fearsome Inn* was a runner-up for the Newbery Medal in a year of strong competition. The award went to Elizabeth Konigsberg for *From the Mixed-Up Files of Mrs. Basil E. Frankweiler*; other runners-up besides Singer were Scott O'Dell for *Black Pearl*, and Zilpha Keatley Snyder for *The Egypt Game*: all still enjoy steady sales. Contrasted to the others, Singer's book is both more "ethnic" and more "fantastic" in its setting, plot, and characterizations, fully illustrated, and much shorter. In truth, *The Fearsome Inn* was an unusual selection for a Newbery Honor Award; perhaps its bestowal was as much an honor to Singer as to this particular book.

Despite its brevity in contrast to the other Newbery Honor books, *The Fearsome Inn* is many times as long as any single story in *Zlateh the Goat*. In it, Singer spends time here and there, and sometimes it is time not well spent. The tale is literally oneiric, for each of three male protagonists tells a long dream within the story. The denouement fills many pages, rather a let-down akin to several of L. Frank Baum's endings to his Oz stories. Overall in regard to *The Fearsome Inn*, Naomi S. Morse was led to comment, "I find a labored, convoluted quality here" (19). The same general criticism was repeated about several of Singer's longer works for children that varied greatly in terms of plot pacing and subject matter: *Alone in the Wild Forest*, for example, and *Mazel and Shlimazel*, called by one reviewer ". . . rather long."[1]

The Fearsome Inn is difficult to categorize; as with many of Singer's illustrated books, there is a mismatch between the length and complexity of the stories and the putative audience. Although its large format suggests a picture book, *The Fearsome Inn* is generally considered to be for ages 8 through 12. Because of the extraordinary prose and the philosophy embedded therein, it is an excellent choice for older readers too, especially ones who may be looking for respite from recent reality-based, issue-focused literature. The unease about age level some critics express may also be due to the feeling that there is more to his longer single-story books than they know. This intuition is accurate. Eric A. Kimmel writes: "Kabbalistic speculation about reincarnation, demons, and the Messiah are major elements in Singer's writing and are as important in appreciating juvenile works such as *The Fearsome Inn*, *Mazel and Shlimazel*, and *Alone in the Wild Forest* as they are in understanding such adult works as *Satan in Goray*, "The Spinoza of Market Street," and "Gimpel the Fool."[2]

Readers will find themselves enriched in understanding by Kimmel's explanations and by those of Grace Farrell and others who also interpret mystical references in Singer's stories.[3]

Like the Danish Andersen, the Polish Singer uses the cold itself as a character. He begins *The Fearsome Inn* by describing the snow swirling like a "dog chasing its tail." A wind-blown scarecrow laughs "madly."[4] Singer's next sentence is a gem; it starts with a string of prepositional phrases, each compounding the wild, wintery scene. Midsentence Singer introduces the inn; the end of the sentence is reserved for identifying the woman who owns the inn, Doboshova the witch: "On a hill overgrown with thistles, by a windmill with a broken vane and a smithy whose forge had long been cold, stood the inn that belonged to Doboshova, a witch" (n.p.).

Through their witchcraft, Doboshova and her husband Lapitut hold three girls captive. The girls' Yiddish names are a euphonious, playful rhyme: Reitze, Leitze, and Neitze—all pronounced as two syllables. The girls are whipped when they try to escape; rescue by their families is impossible.

Winter storms bring three new victims to the inn: Herschel is an Orthodox scholar; Velvel a merchant; and Leibel a Hasidic mystic who holds a magic piece of chalk. In other cultures' tales, the magic item might be a horse, a wolf, an amulet, or a piece of clothing bestowed by the mother, as in "The Goosegirl." In Singer's version, the magic is bestowed by Leibel's teacher and is transmitted through an item of the *cheder*, or boys' school, and the studyhouse, a commonplace piece of chalk. A circle drawn with this chalk will trap anyone caught within its perimeter.

By this point, Singer's extended fairy tale has a fine balance of absolutes—good and evil, human and devil, male and female—and a distinctive Yiddish-gothic flavor. All the key characters, exposition, and plot complications are in place, so Singer is ready for the next stage. While drawing water to wash, the boys are drugged. Each has a nightmarish dream. In his dream, Leibel, the Hasid, sees an evil creature who looks much like Lapitut. Singer's characters, young and old, pay attention to their dreams and Leibel is no exception. Later, just before the victims are about to eat enchanted food that will leave them completely powerless, Leibel calls out. He claims he has lost a ring in the water barrel; this ring, he says, dates back to King Solomon. Doboshova and Lapitut cannot resist the temptation to steal it and run over to the barrel, bending over it to fish for the treasure. As he had planned, Leibel springs up to draw a circle around them with his magic chalk.

Singer stretches the tale out at this juncture with lively dialog and action as the evil ones realize they are trapped. Leitze, Reitze, Neitze, Herschel, and Velvel are astonished, too, by Leibel's feat. Doboshova and Lapitut rail and rage, but Leibel holds firm. As night falls, the wicked ones call upon their compatriots. The horde includes one of Singer's favorite demons, the mighty river spirit Topiel, who lures humans to their death by drowning. Topiel plays a major role in Singer's story "Topiel and Tekla," discussed in chapter 8. To distract his friends from the onslaught, Leibel asks the girls to relate their stories of capture and slavery . . . he is not the boorish hero who only boasts of his exploits. Finally, hungry and defeated, the inn's proprietors sign an oath, in blood, that they will depart and never return. A long, legalistic-sounding declaration, the oath of Doboshova and Lapitut promises that no evil will approach the inn for 10 generations and that all their treasure now belongs to their "guests" and former "servants." Singer here pokes fun at the slipperiness of language, for the so-called "guests" and "servants" were, of course, the captives.

The climax, when the witch and her guileful half-devil husband are overcome, is vintage Singer—demons and ogres turn into sensuous humans and tempt the girls and boys. In many ways, including symbolically, Singer considers these powers of temptation real. They inhabit this and other plots with the assurance of necessary beings. In fact, when considering these single-story books as a whole, the climactic similarity of several of them becomes clear: *The Fearsome Inn, Joseph and Koza*, and *Alone in the Wild Forest* all describe ferocious combat between incarnate spirits of evil and spiritually well-endowed humans. In the children's stories, evil is ultimately impotent—although it puts up one hell of a fight.

With the break of day, the thwarted witch and her consort depart to the desert wastelands where "dusk is eternal." The incantation of exile, reminiscent of that in "The Devil's Trick" and several other stories, has the sound of the formulaic to it; perhaps this ending was characteristic of Singer's mother's stories.

But one reviewer found this vivid passage and the earlier description of the young men's nightmares to be a problem: "We're not sure this is a children's book, although it looks like one. It is pure Singer and . . . might give some children nightmares."[5] June H. Schlessinger and June D. Vanderryst disagree, however, finding that the value placed in Judaism on compassion ameliorates the punishment from a violent death to simple removal: banishment. Actually, for the Jewish psyche there is hardly a fate worse than exile; it has happened in Jewish history so many times that, as a punishment, it bears more weight than non-Jewish readers might imagine.

Schlessinger and Vanderryst also comment that the very everydayness of the legal document the wicked ones sign is a reassuring reminder that evil can be contained and controlled. Further, they note that in many of Singer's stories where there is a battle between good and evil, the evil characters are encouraged to change their behavior, and only failing any cooperation are they punished.[6] Eric A. Kimmel points to a religious reason for these endings, a belief that the young Singer would have been inculcated with by his Hasidic father: that the entire world cannot be saved until *all* evil has been collected, transformed, and consolidated into good.

The Fearsome Inn continues for several pages as "three nice Jewish girls" meet "three nice Jewish young men"[7] and fall in love. Accordingly,

Singer's description of winter changes; now rainbows sparkle in the icicles. The romantic circumstances are initially confused, for the hero—and clearly the best catch—is Leibel the Hasid—a bit of wishful plotting, perhaps, on Singer's part. Leibel's mystic power is the power of the righteous—it is *efficacious* power, useful to the community. This force is exemplified also by Rabbi Leib in Singer's *The Golem*, discussed below, whom God selects to perform mystical magic because of the rabbi's Jewish virtues: he is studious, humble, and faithful to the Torah, as is the Leib in this story. Eventually, *The Fearsome Inn*'s couples are matched and marry under a canopy, according to the Talmud.

But there is more resolution. Mirroring the healed home, the countryside around it is reborn, and all the newlyweds' families come for the spring celebration. After seven days it is departure time, but one couple has chosen to remain to keep the inn open as a free wayside hostel: Leibel and Neitze. The other couples gain renown in the wide world, but return to the inn annually with their children for a celebration.

Singer's final paragraph is reserved for his traditional benediction: the light from the inn, he writes, calls to it angels and cherubs, but the light is not generated artificially. It illuminates all who see it, for it comes from within.

The theme of the home gained after a battle is frequently found in children's literature, for example, in Russell Hoban's *The Mouse and His Child* and Kenneth Grahame's *The Wind in the Willows*. Hugh Nissenson, writing in *The Horn Book*, observes another theme, "'No matter how strong the Devil,' Leibel said, 'God is stronger.' This is the theme of all of Singer's work." Nissenson is critical, however, of the book, describing it as "too sketchy. . . ." He finds Nonny Hogrogian's illustrations "pale" and "thin."[8] Morse, on the other hand, finds Hogrogian's "moody, grainy watercolor illustrations" to be the "redeeming features of the book" (19).

Singer's second picturebook for 1967 was a much livelier tale described as "exceptionally winning" by *The New York Times Book Review*.[9] Praised by Zena Sutherland and Ruth Hill Vigeurs for its art as well as its content, *Mazel and Shlimazel: or, The Milk of a Lioness* was illustrated by Margot Zemach. For the full-color book, Zemach used watercolor earth tones, muted reds, and turquoises. A "remarkably fine set of pictures" wrote *The Detroit Jewish News*, and "a most magnificent children's story."[10] *Mazel and Shlimazel* was published the same year not only as *The Fearsome Inn*, but as *The Manor* and the reissue of *The Family Moskat*, both colossal family saga novels set in Eastern Europe. Singer continued to publish also in Yiddish in *The Jewish Daily Forward*. He was now at his creative and productive peak.

Mazel means "good luck"; *shlimazel* "bad luck." Personified, the opponents battle over a young man's destiny. The main plot complication is a twist itself on a familiar theme: a wager made over the fate of a human. Good-natured Mazel bets the dour Shlimazel that, if given a year, he can completely change the lackluster life of the peasant Tam. *Tam* is a generic Yiddish noun for "fool," a rather mild term among the many words used to describe the incompetent; the Yiddish title of "Gimpel the Fool" is "Gimpel tam." Shimazel bets he can undo in just one second all the good Mazel can do for Tam in a year.

Mazel arranges for the king's carriage to break down in front of Tam's hut. With Mazel's help, Tam repairs the carriage and ingratiates himself with the king. "Luck sometimes changes very quickly," the king says to Tam, opening the door of the carriage. When he invites Tam to accompany him to the palace, ". . . the villagers [can]not believe their eyes."[11] Being taken to the palace is just the beginning of Tam's changed luck, however, for soon he is the "best-loved" man in the kingdom. Only he is not loved by the envious prime minister; Shlimazel, also, is scheming to trap Tam when his one second comes.

It comes in this way: the king falls ill and the great doctors declare that only milk from a lioness can save him. With Mazel behind him, Tam bravely offers to bring lioness's milk to the king. For this, the monarch promises Tam his daughter's hand.

Again, all the elements are in place: the conflicts, the attachments, the pivotal problem. Shlimazel bides his time while the luck-inspired Tam milks a lioness and returns to the castle. At the king's bedside, Tam loudly proclaims that he has indeed brought the milk of a . . . "dog" (*M*, 28). His slip of the tongue is pure Shlimazel, and he is dragged off to await execution.

Mazel magnanimously congratulates the victor Shlimazel—but he does not give up. That hope—or call it luck—is never finished off completely is another of Singer's main themes, one he felt to his bones. "In the history of my people," he said in a lecture, "the difference between being *sick* and being *dead* is a big one."[12] Mazel invites Shlimazel to taste his prize, for their wager was that, if bad luck won, good luck would give him a barrel of the wine of forgetfulness. Good luck gets bad luck drunk. Boozily, Shlimazel begins to blubber about his unhappy childhood, "in the way drunkards sometimes do" (*M*, 32). Zemach's circular

In a faraway land, on a sunny spring day, when the sky was as blue
as the sea, and the sea is as blue as the sky, and the earth is green,
and in love with them both, two spirits were passing through a village.
One was called Mazel, and his name meant good luck. The other's name
was Shlimazel, bad luck.

Spirits are not seen by man, but one spirit can see another.
Mazel was young, tall, slim with pink cheeks and curly hair. He wore
a green jacket, red riding breeches and a hat with a feather on it. He wore
silver spurs on his high boots. Mazel seldom walked. He usually rode
his horse which was also a spirit. On this particular day, he felt like
strolling through the village on foot.

Shlimazel limped along beside him, an old man with a wan face and
angry eyes under his bushy eyebrows. He wore a long black
coat, and on his head a pointed hat, and supported himself on a knotty-wood cane. His
nose was crooked. His beard was
as grey as spider webs. Mazel spoke and Shlimazel listened.

Mazel was in a boasting mood. "Everybody wants me, everybody
loves me. Wherever I go I bring joy. Naturally the people can't see me
because I am a spirit, but they all long for me just the same: merchants
and sailors, doctors and shoemakers, lovers and card players. All over the
world they call, 'Mazel come to me.' Nobody calls for you, Shlimazel.
You'll have to admit that what I say is true."

Shlimazel winced and clutched his beard. "Yes, I must agree that
you're a charmer." he said. "But the world is ruled by the strong and not
by the charming. What you can build in a year I can destroy in one second."

Shlimazel had made a point and now Mazel bit his lip with annoyance.

Figure 5. Page one of the draft manuscript of "Mazel and Shlimazel" showing the collaborative
editing process (Fales Library, New York University)

painting of the imp's memories is a playful swirl of wings, hooves, huts, and peasants.

Grandly, Shlimazel also invites Mazel to join him in conquering the world. Like many of Singer's impish characters, this antagonist is gregarious, as is the imp sent by Cunegunde to Rabbi Leib in "Rabbi Leib and the Witch Cunegunde." He would rather be joined than beaten. Mazel has other plans, however. Just before the noose is to tighten around Tam's neck the next morning, Mazel emboldens the boy to call out for his last wish—to see the king. Tam tells the king what can only be called a glib lie to win back both his favor and his daughter, Nesika. Convinced of Tam's innocence, the king drinks the lioness's milk (which Nesika has saved), immediately regaining his health. All is well—Tam and Nesika marry and have seven children. The nasty prime minister becomes the plaything of Shlimazel, who, having drunk the wine of forgetfulness, has fortunately forgotten all about Tam.

A true moralist, Singer ends: "Tam had learned that good luck follows those who are diligent, honest, sincere, and helpful to others. The man who has these qualities is indeed lucky forever" (*M*, 42). The reader has, somewhat glibly, to ignore the contradiction over diligence provided by the opening exposition, in which the hero is sitting apathetically picking at the toadstools on his hut's walls until Mazel shows up. Such matters are minor, however; the *Chicago Sun Times* calls *Mazel and Shlimazel* "timeless."[13] In 1982, Mark A. Bernheim declared the book a "classic," and "Singer's most popular single children's story."[14]

A Number of Josephs

Singer himself was, at this stage in his career, being called timeless, too. On the book jacket for *Mazel and Shlimazel* are reprinted excerpts from Singer's reviews: "Singer is more than a writer; he is a literature"[15] and ". . . thousands of years of Jewish history are embodied in him. . . ."[16] Once in a while, however, Singer did not span the culture gap sufficiently.

Alone in the Wild Forest was illustrated by Margot Zemach and translated by Singer and Shub. Because it is puzzling, it is not one of Singer's more popular works. In fact, *The New York Times Book Review*'s D. Keith Mano calls it "spare, severe, oddly humorless. . . . For the sort of child who arranges elaborate funeral services for dead birds and mice."[17] Zena Sutherland writes the story is too long and digressive.[18] But, as Kimmel points out, there is more to the story. In fact, *Alone in the Wild Forest* is one of Singer's most closely felt works, a cabalistic tale of redemption.

Wolkstein observed to Singer in an interview that he had used this as the title of the book his character Menaseh is reading when he runs away from home and into the forest in "Menaseh's Dream" (Wolkstein, 145). He expresses surprise, but *Alone in the Wild Forest* seems to have been a story ordained to be told by Singer.

This story more than any other resembles the sort of fantastic tale Singer pictures himself telling as a boy in Poland. It is Singer's version of Aladdin and the Magic Lamp and it has the feel of the extemporaneous to it, Scherazade-like. Of all the settings of all the fairy tales, arguably the most archetypally significant is the Wild Forest—and to be Alone in it is extremely evocative. The story has trap doors, past lives, a beautiful princess, a magical amulet, a selfish first minister, incredible coincidences, and bizarre transformations: the hero disguises himself by growing two horns out of his head. The fluid narrative demonstrates the creative process described by the blind Menashe in "Menashe and Rachel" from *The Power of Light* in which the teller follows wherever the impulse leads.

Young Joseph is a strange child; even his conception is touched by the divine. Orphaned like Menaseh, he is mistreated and runs alone into the wild forest. There, like Roland, Sir Lancelot and many other heroes, he eats berries and mushrooms, undergoing a symbolic purification. In return for his help, an angel gives Joseph an amulet that will bring him whatever he desires. Wealth? Power? Women? No, indeed. Joseph's first request is for a prayer book. Only with it in hand does he then ask for food—all vegetarian, mind you. His next request is for company, but the amulet tells him that is his responsibility.

Joseph heads for the royal capital, arriving auspiciously when the king has just announced he will give his daughter Chassidah's hand to the man who can replenish his treasure. For this good king has just spent all his money making his subjects happy. Unlike the greedy king in "Rumplestiltskin," Singer's monarch wants his wealth to serve the public good, and Singer's hero, unlike the reluctant daughter in "Rumplestiltskin," goes willingly to serve the king. When the king introduces Chassidah to Joseph, destined to be her husband, she seems to recognize him, as if "in a former life."[19] This *heiros gamos*, or marriage of the gods, is one of the mystical elements in Singer's story. In Judaism, the earth, the world, is called the *Shekinah*, God's bride, the incarnate evidence of divine love; and each human couple ideally embodies this relationship, a relationship both spiritual and erotic as expressed in the Bible's "Song of Solomon."

In Singer's story, however, the descent from divinity comes quickly—and in a gender-stereotypical manner. The evil minister Bal Makane persuades the gullible Chassidah to test her fiancé's love by making him show her the source of his power. Like so many stories, *Amor and Psyche* or "Samson and Delilah," we are on disappointingly familiar ground here. Like the manly Adam, like Rabbi Leib in *The Golem*, discussed below, for the sake of a woman Joseph consents to do what he knows he should not do. He shows Chassidah his amulet. The ingenue goes directly to tell Bal Makane what she has found out, enabling him immediately to trap Joseph and steal the amulet. The minister's first wish is to exile Joseph.

Joseph finds himself on a paradisiacal island where he learns that he is an old soul brought back to earth to correct a former mistake. The idea that one keeps coming back to the incarnate world until one lives a just life is a key occult element of the story. Like a Jewish Odysseus, Joseph sails from one magical environment to the other until he returns home just as the king begins the celebration announcing the engagement of Chassidah and Bal Makane. Chassidah, like Penelope, is, of course, reluctant. And like Odysseus, Joseph sneaks into the ball disguised. His masquerade is unique; he does not, ultimately, like Odysseus, win by force of arms but by appealing for justice. While on another mysterious island, Joseph has collected two pieces of those symbolically potent fruits—apples—one for growing horns on the head, the other for removing them. Joseph grows horns on his head to cloak his true identity.

Once inside the ballroom, he tricks Bal Makane into eating the horn-growing apple. At the same time, Joseph removes his own horns by eating from the other apple. His identity now publicly confirmed, Joseph accuses Bal Makane of attempted murder and is believed. He refuses to remove Bal Makane's horns; only a change of heart brought about by Bal Makane's own free will can accomplish his return to normalcy. Bal Makane is exiled to the land of the sexually hungry witch Zlichah.

All thus ends well, but the 80-page book is only half over. In the long digression objected to by *The New York Times*'s reviewer, the action shifts to Bal Makane. Zlichah loves his horns and tries to seduce him with one of the best lines in the files of femme fatales: "I've been surrounded by demons, devils, goblins, hobgoblins, imps, and sprites, but what I've always longed for was a man" (*A*, 59). Bal Makane, however, is having trouble warming up to a creature comprising a pig, ape, and frog parts. Meanwhile, the hideous witch gives her groom-to-be something to play with—a feral female named Zeivah. Then, conveniently, the witch

drinks too much of her own brew and passes out for seven days and
seven nights.

Bal Makane cares for the wolf-raised woman the witch has given him.
Zeivah, it turns out, like Bal Makane also requires redemption to atone
for sins in a former life. Together they escape from the witch. Hiding
deep in the forest, repentant, both pray. Moreover, prayer works:
reformed, Bal Makane and Zeivah fall in love. The first city they
approach happens to be Joseph and Chassidah's capital, formerly Bal
Makane's as well. Because they look like beggars and charity is part of
the nuptials, he and Zeivah are invited in to celebrate the impending
royal wedding. There, sitting at table as a supplicant, Bal Makane is
confronted by his former enemy, Joseph.

Joseph realizes there is only one explanation for Bal Makane's presence and for his escape from the horrible witch: genuine repentance. In
recognition of this transformation, Joseph changes Bal Makane's name
to Bal Tshuvah . . . from "man of envy" to "man of repentance." Bal
Tshuvah and Zeivah are married, but they decline high positions in government in order to travel the country bearing religious witness. Singer
tidies up by accounting for the fate of the ghastly witch the unreformed
minister was sent to live with—she misses him so much she drinks herself to death and is escorted to hell.

Most authors would have ended the story there, if not sooner. But
Singer has one paragraph left, and that one is very important. It expresses both the mystic quest for universal redemption and also the certainty
that redemption will come: "But even [Zlichah] will not remain [in hell]
forever. All souls must be cleansed and at the End of Days appear before
God, their Father. He has prepared for them a heavenly feast and the
eternal joys of Paradise" (A, 80).

Here again Singer is stating the mystic belief that before the world
can be purified and returned to God, *all* souls must be redeemed. Bal
Makane, Zeivah, even Zlichah must be reformed as well as Joseph.
Zeivah's name, in fact, indicates this—it means "brightness," or "intense
light," spiritual light, that is, the dispersed holy light from creation that
must be regathered, in Jewish mystic lore, before the world's redemption. Chassidah, from the same root as Hasid, means "pious one," a suitable name for Joseph's wife. Providing the opportunity for sinners to
choose the good and to be transformed by it are fundamental tenets of
Singer's upbringing, and in *Alone in the Wild Forest*, these are expressed in
fictional form. The story is actually a weighty book of religious philosophy as much as—or even more—than a story for children. Readers inter-

ested in an excellent discussion of the four symbolic, religious stages in the story will be enlightened by Eric A. Kimmel's "I. B. Singer's *Alone in the Wild Forest*: A Kabbalistic Parable."

Another Joseph story, *Joseph and Koza: or The Sacrifice to the Vistula*, was published at about the same time as one of Singer's major adult novels, *The Slave*. More than one critic has observed that *Joseph and Koza* is a children's version of the adult novel, notably Clive Sinclair writing in the *Times Literary Supplement*. In fact, the protagonists of *Alone in the Wild Forest* and *Joseph and Koza* share the same name as the protagonists of both *The Slave* and Singer's National Book Award winner, *The Penitent*.[20] And all share similarities with the biblical Joseph: they are reformers in foreign lands who rise in government and they listen to their dreams. Singer was aware of these similarities and commented, "Tolstoy said that the [biblical] Joseph story is the greatest story ever written. All writers can learn from it" (Wolkstein, 142).

It is likely that *Joseph and Koza* spun out effortlessly from the more complex and graphic *The Slave*. This kind of cross-fertilization of efforts for children and for adults is attested to by other cross-over authors, such as Russell Hoban. For example, a key character of Hoban's adult novel *Pilgermann*, one Bembel Rudzuk, becomes the hero of a children's book published at the same time, *The Flight of Bembel Rudzuk*.

Singer's *The Slave* and *Joseph and Koza* both concern the pagan rituals of preenlightened Poland: namely, human sacrifice. The heathen king Wilk, or "Wolf," rules that part of ancient Poland called Mazovia, but only as advised by the witch Zla. Zla worships the great witch Baba Yaga, a dominant figure in Slavic-Russian mythology. Annually Zla selects the most beautiful Mazovian maiden to sacrifice to the Vistula. As the story opens, the stars tell Zla that Wilk's lovely only daughter, the kind-hearted Koza, must be the next sacrifice. Koza accepts this and comforts her grieving parents.

The 90-day period granted the sacrificial maiden during which time she lives with her girl friends in an apple orchard is reminiscent of the biblical story of Jephthah's daughter. But unlike that girl, Koza is saved from death by a dark-eyed stranger named Joseph, a Jewish goldsmith from Jerusalem. His arrival in Wilk's kingdom alters everything. Joseph persuades Wilk to see whether not sacrificing Koza will truly bring down upon the Mazovians the wrath of Baba Yaga. Zla fiercely fights the king's decree, predicting disasters such as the rising of Topiel, but Joseph says, "I do not fear. . . . The word of God is stronger than all witches and devils."[21]

Joseph and his God prevail. Zla is humiliated and Koza is promised to her rescuer. Many Mazovians, especially younger ones, flock to Joseph and study his ways. All is not well, therefore, for Wilk realizes that "if Joseph remained among them, there would be a rebellion in Mazovia" (*Stories*, 150). Wilk resolves his dilemma by saying good-bye to his newly married daughter, thereby ridding his land of too much of a good thing. Joseph and Koza begin a new and prosperous life in Jerusalem.

Clive Sinclair writes that the opposition of good and evil "works beautifully" (1199), but May Sarton, writing for *The New York Times Book Review* has to "confess to some disappointment. . . . With everything apparently going for it, this large pretentious book appears to be a dud."[22]

Surprisingly, *Joseph and Koza* was transformed into a comedy by A Renegade Theatre Ensemble (ARTE) of Los Angeles, performing at the West End Playhouse in 1993. The story, and three others, "The Day I Got Lost," "Menashe and Rachel," and "Tashlik" were adapted for the stage by Joe Megel and produced by Philip Sokoloff. In the audience myself, I was amazed. Through gestures and expressions and imaginative costuming, the heavy-handed story acquired a different tone, delighting the spectators, mostly children. Even Singer's "Tashlik" and "Menashe and Rachel," not dramatic stories in terms of action, were successfully modified for live performance. The audience's clear favorite was the *shlemiel* story, "The Day I Got Lost." ARTE's production will, one hopes, be restaged frequently.

Bible-Based and Traditional Stories

Elijah the Slave was published in 1970, the same year as *Joseph and Koza*. *Why Noah Chose the Dove* followed in 1973, the same year as *The Fools of Chelm and Their History* and the magnificent adult collection *A Crown of Feathers and Other Stories*. *A Tale of Three Wishes* came out in 1975, the same year as *Passions and Other Stories*. During the same time, Singer was also publishing elsewhere and also lecturing. This was a peak period in his career.

Elijah the Slave, Why Noah Chose the Dove, and *A Tale of Three Wishes* are truly picture books, that is, accessible to preschool listeners and lookers. *The Wicked City,* based on the story of Sodom, although dramatically illustrated by Leonard Everett Fisher, is for older children. The three books for preschoolers also contain engaging and imaginative illustrations: *Elijah the Slave* by Antonio Frasconi, *Why Noah Chose the Dove* by Eric Carle, and *A Tale of Three Wishes* by Irene Leiblich, who also illustrated Singer's subsequent collection for children, *The Power of Light.*

In *Elijah the Slave* the poor but pious scribe Tobias is visited by the prophet long associated in Jewish tradition with the miraculous. Tobias is tested and found fit for a divine intervention. Elijah appears, instructing Tobias to sell him in the market as a slave where he states—not boasts—that he can do anything. He is bought by a rich man for whom he promises to build a palace more magnificent than the emperor's. The huge sum the prophet brings at auction is given to his putative owner, Tobias—whose lot does immediately improve. Despite this, Tobias continues a life of righteousness and piety.

Meanwhile, back at the building site, Elijah implores God to fulfill what he, God's servant Elijah, has promised. The next day, angels descend to build what is indeed the most splendid domicile in the land. This culmination is important, for Elijah's, and by extension, God's, credibility is at stake.

Elijah the Slave is satisfying, if not particularly memorable. Booklist's reviewer says that, although it may "lack general appeal, [the] illustrations . . . are a feast for the eyes."[23]

Why Noah Chose the Dove is a colorful parade of animals vying for the honor of scouting for land after God's flood. But none of the animals contending for supremacy is selected by Noah. It is the shy dove that catches the patriarch's eye, precisely because of its modesty. Once the device of competition is established—pick me, I'm bigger/stronger/smarter/prettier/and so on—the narrative quickly becomes repetitive.

The Tale of Three Wishes, 1975, is a longer illustrated story, although straightforward enough for younger children. Its illustrations, too, are very straightforward, simple oils by Irene Leiblich. Singer translated it with Elizabeth Shub.

Three companions, Solomon, Moses, and sister Esther, miss a chance at three genuine wishes, but they mature and accomplish by their own efforts what they had wanted done for them by magic. *The Tale of Three Wishes* is pleasant. The desires of the three children, however, stereotype the boys as wanting either power or wisdom, and the girl as wanting to be pretty. Moreover, it is the girl's frivolous wish that sets the disaster in motion.

The Reaches of Heaven: A Story of the Baal Shem Tov is a sensitive and respectful biography of the founder of Hasidism, a great evangelical teacher called the Baal Shem Tov, the BeSHT, or Master of the Good

Name. Set in the 1700s just after the time of Sabbatai Zevi, the false messiah, and the Chiemlincki Massacre, which changed Eastern European Jewish history, *The Reaches of Heaven* provides a picture of the ferment among Jews. The Baal Shem Tov's ecstatic, experience-based worship included dancing and singing. This was the way to overcome the horror of history, but the Hasidic worship scandalized the Orthodox, leading later to deep divides. Singer brings forward the sweetness of the founder, the BeSHT, and what a comfort his democratic, hope-filled teaching was to the devastated Jewish community. The book is interesting too because, through the Baal Shem Tov, Singer criticizes Judaism as a religion for women. *The Reaches of Heaven* has value as a text in history and in religious and cultural studies courses. Singer also collaborated on an adult book about Hasidism with Ira Moskovitz.

It is difficult to find anything good to say about *The Topsy-Turvy Emperor of China*, published by Harper and Row in 1971. Even the illustrations by William Pene du Bois are unappealing. It was Elizabeth Shub's least favorite book, and it received very poor reviews. Singer wrote that he had heard the story from his mother, Bathsheba. Like *Joseph and Koza*, which was also a departure from Singer's exclusive use of a Yiddish setting, *The Topsy-Turvy Emperor of China* seems forced and overlong.

As amiable as is *The Tale of Three Wishes*, *The Wicked City* is fierce and stark. Illustrated powerfully by Leonard Everett Fisher, translated by Singer and Shub, and published in 1972, it is not one of Singer's best. He retells the tale of Sodom, of Abraham and his reprehensible nephew Lot. The book's main interest is less as a successful children's book—for it is hard to imagine most children really enjoying this story—than as one of Singer's most intriguing short stories.

While discussing *The Wicked City*, Singer joked, "I feel that we are living partially in Sodom and partially in Chelm."[24] It's even probable that he was being serious. At any rate, there are hardly two more noticeable antipodes in Singer's range than the fulmination of *The Wicked City* as opposed to the broad comedy of *The Fools of Chelm and Their History*.

Singer and Shulevitz

The fools of Chelm, the ruling council of the *shtetl*, reappear in a book devoted exclusively to their ridiculous solutions to the town's very real poverty. Gronam Ox, Dopey Lekisch, Zeinvel Ninny, Treitel Fool, Sender Donkey, Shmendrick Numskull . . . and the secretary, Shlemiel, the best minds of their generation, concoct one absurd scheme after the other until they are on the verge, as usual, of giving up—and, a bit of trenchant humor here—postponing the discussion "until a future meeting."[25] This satirizes the powerlessness of the verbally formidable but otherwise helpless Jews. But suddenly Gronam, wearing his preposterous horned hat, is struck by inspiration: ". . . only a war can save Chelm" (12). Naturally, Gronam's army loses ignominiously at night to the minuscule town of Mazelborsht, a laughable name meaning "Lucky Beet Soup." There is inevitably a rebellion against the leadership of Gronam and his sages. His wife, Yenta Pesha, is disgusted, too. "Emperor, shmemperor. . . . To me you're nothing but a fool of Chelm," (21) she says, thereby joining the succession of Singer wives harnessed to husbands for whom they have no respect.

The first of the successive rulers to follow the sages, who hastily depart, is Bunem Pokraka. He posts nine rules, one of which is to abolish money so everyone will be "equally poor" and "the city will not have to pay salaries to Chaikel the policeman and Lemel the jailer." Singer personalizes the story by providing names for the functionaries; this also emphasizes what a small village Chelm is: everyone knows everyone else by first names. Singer's satire comes complete with a sniveling revolutionary poet whose ode begins: "It shall be known for now and ever / Bunem Pokraka is mighty and clever" (33).

Bunem, however, is every bit as idiotic as his predecessor. Bunem has two Sages of Sages, Berel Pinhead and Shmerel Thickwit. In a last ditch effort to prevent the return of money, Bunem and his sages open markets where all Chelmites can come to barter their skills for what they need. Only . . . many find out they own or can do nothing of value, including the poet Zeckel. The people rebel against the rebel Bunem.

The new leader is Feivel Thief. First he distributes paper money plentifully. Then he decrees his own rules, characteristic of which is that every Thursday, Chelm's housewives shall make him two pieces of gefilte fish (45). Feivel and his bullies conquer the outlying towns: Mazelborsht and Gorshov. The poet predicts the conquest of "India . . . Frampol, and Madagascar" (47). But the conquered towns fight back and overthrow Feivel, forcing the poet to change the title of his oft-revised epic once more: "The Shame and Downfall of the Tyrant Feivel" (51).

In newly "liberated" Chelm, Gronam is reinstated as ruler. It is not long before his botching of absolutely everything leads his wife to inaugurate a protest party, the Women's Party. Despite his dislike of the role reversal that sees him and his fellow sages doing dishes and changing diapers, when the book ends Gronam is optimistic. Someday, he declares, "all the world will be one great Chelm" (57).

In her essay "Fools and Sages: Humor in Isaac Bashevis Singer's *The Fools of Chelm and Their History*," R. Barbara Gitenstein writes, ". . . full understanding of some aspects of the humor, especially the satire on scholarly tradition, presupposes knowledge of both politics and Jewish tradition not usually found in a child."[26] As Gitenstein makes clear, however, Singer employs so many kinds of humor that this is a book for most age levels.

By the time artist Uri Shulevitz, himself an Eastern European Jew but much younger than Singer, began working on *The Fools of Chelm and Their History*, he and Singer had mutual publishers and friends, such as Elizabeth Shub. Shulevitz already casually knew Singer—he had once given him and his wife Alma a ride to New Jersey. Shulevitz was an admirer of Singer's writing and had been instrumental in bringing Sendak in as illustrator of *Zlateh the Goat*. As Shulevitz remembers it, it was Elizabeth Shub who suggested to him that he contact Singer's editor at Farrar, Straus and Giroux about illustrating *The Fools of Chelm*, which she, Elizabeth, had just helped Singer translate.

Shulevitz was so tickled by the book's opening paragraphs that he chose to "make his contribution" by expanding upon them in his frontispiece.[27] The lively drawing sets the book's comic tone. Shulevitz recalls: "I was familiar with some stories of Chelm; there are so many. But Singer's *The Fools of Chelm* is really his own and has little to do with traditional stories. It is more like a satire of the development of various movements . . . poking fun at the foibles of people and recent history: communism, women's lib . . ." (Interview, 1992).

Shulevitz was to create a picture per chapter. But he found that all the characters were doing in the first chapter was sitting in a room having a discussion. When he moved on to the next chapter, they were still sitting, still discussing, and still in the same room. From an author's point of view there was no problem, but Singer wasn't thinking visually; he was thinking in terms of content. Shulevitz, however, had an artistic problem to solve; he couldn't repeat the same scene. "I wasn't in touch with [Singer] about how to illustrate the book or anything of that sort because that was not his way of thinking. He was very much a writer when it came to illustration; [art] wasn't his field. What I did was, in the first picture they are sitting down and in the second they are standing up" (Interview, 1992).

If Shulevitz's illustrated characters are contrasted to Sendak's and Zemach's, one observes that Sendak's are stolid, static, and staring. Zemach's look as if they could be blown over with a feather. Shulevitz's Chelmite stooges are bulbous dimwits whose gestures mirror the narrative; to indicate their deep thought, they stick out their tongues, pull their beards, and scratch their chins. They partake of the same spirit as Rabelais's and Breugel's pot-bellied art or William Carlos Williams's poem "The Round" about Breugel's painting. Shulevitz's illustrations remind me also of *klezmer* music, the raucous, emotional music once played by traveling bands of Jewish musicians throughout Eastern Europe. Each of Shulevitz's expressive noodleheads is distinctive, as is each of the instruments in a *klezmer* band: trumpet, clarinet, violin. This music can be heard on the Rabbit Ears' audio cassette and also video cassette production of an old Russian tale, "The Fool and the Flying Ship." The music is by The Klezmer Conservatory Band and the narration is by Robin Williams, whose Yiddish accent and vocal antics coincide with the impassioned music.

The way Shulevitz uses the space around his characters received high praise, too. For example, the illustration of the dark night in which the pitchfork, scissors, and kitchen knife-wielding Chelmites attack their neighbors is a riot of perspective: the confused Chelmite army trips over its own feet and disappears into the nothingness of the page.

Only once did Shulevitz contact Singer about illustration: It was about "the description of the main character, Gronam Ox. There was something there about a headdress with horns and I didn't know exactly what Singer meant by that. I asked him whether it would be okay with him if I gave Gronam a hat with horns, as you can see in the picture. He gave me the go ahead" (Interview, 1992).

Many years passed. Shulevitz had already gotten word through his editor from Singer's editor that Singer was pleased with the way the illustrations for the *The Fool of Chelm* came out and that Singer had suggested Shulevitz illustrate *The Golem*. In the interim between *The Fools of Chelm* and *The Golem*, Shulevitz turned down two other Singer stories: *Why Noah Chose the Dove* and *Joseph and Koza*, saying, "I have the greatest admiration for Singer as a writer; that doesn't mean everything he wrote I would feel I want to illustrate and those two stories I turned down. One of them was *Why Noah Chose the Dove*, which later I made a couple of pictures of for *Cricket*, but as a book I didn't feel I could illustrate it" (Interview, 1992).

Shulevitz says *The Golem* was in a drawer for a long time at Farrar, Straus and Giroux. "They were busy on other matters," he laughs. The story was originally published a good decade earlier in the *Jewish Daily Forward*.[28] Once it resurfaced, Shulevitz said he would be happy to illustrate it: "In connection with *The Golem*, everything seemed to be quite clear to me. I didn't need to talk to Singer" (Interview, 1992).

The Golem is one of the best-known of legendary characters, a gigantic creature constructed out of clay and brought to life for the sole purpose of helping the Jews overcome their much stronger enemies. *Golem* means "dummy," "ignoramus." Yet despite the specificity of the Golem's raison d'être and his profound limitations, he nonetheless strikes at the deepest chords of archetypal resonance. Like Frankenstein's monster, this inferior intelligence is nonetheless a feeling creature. He has appeared in every art form. Versions and commentaries continue to be produced, even picture books. Readers can consult several bibliographies, anthologies, and contemporary children's renditions of the story, for example, the version by Elie Wiesel.[29]

Singer's version conflates several of the episodic Prague legends into one story with two climaxes: the first when the Golem fulfills his mission in a courtroom scene, and the second when he is destroyed after having, through no fault of his own, overstayed his welcome in the land of the living.

No one is more surprised than the humble rabbi Leib of Prague himself when he is visited at midnight by one of the 36 hidden Jewish saints. The holy man instructs the rabbi as to how and why the *golem* should be brought to life. The rabbi is enjoined to use the *golem* only to "save the Jews," and to "take care that he should not fall into the follies of flesh and blood."[30]

The Jewish community must rely on the *golem* to save them from the "Blood Libel," an accusation more horrifying and lethal than any monster: that they have killed a Christian child to bake her blood into the Passover *matzoh*. The calumny was actually fairly common and greatly feared by Jews. When the accusations were investigated with sincerity, they would be found, of course, to be set-ups staged by some fanatical priest or disgruntled borrower of money, as it is in Singer's story.

The first part of Singer's version climaxes when the *golem* dramatically appears in court, carrying the supposedly dead child in his arms. The Jews are freed and the Golem is a hero. But questions about human nature and *golem* nature become more complex as the story continues.

Because there is no longer an immediate danger to the Jews, the rabbi decides to erase from the *golem*'s forehead the Holy Name that brought the clay to life. But the rabbi's wife, a charitable woman named Genedel, remembers the tale of a huge treasure in the rabbi's backyard, covered by an immovable rock. She persuades her husband to use the *golem* to lift the rock, "pointing out how many people could be helped with the gold. She so appealed to the rabbi's compassionate nature that he gave in and reluctantly promised to do what she was pleading for" (57).

This clouds the *golem*'s purpose and begins a tragic chain of events. For the first time, the *golem* refuses to do as the rabbi bids; he won't uncover the treasure, nor will he bend down so the rabbi can rub out his existence. The rabbi realizes he has "made a mistake he is unable to correct" (58). The reader realizes Singer has chosen to make it the wife, who, like Eve, leads her husband astray for the sake of the apparent, but short-term, good.

Singer's *golem* becomes more and more human, an overgrown child with a huge appetite and no sense of limit. He goes to *cheder* and remains a part of the rabbi's family, even after he sprouts a beard and consistently gobbles everyone's dinner.

Along with the rabbi's family, the *golem* is served by a young orphan girl. "Miriam nice girl," the monster observes, and when she playfully asks him if he would like her for a bride, he lifts her up and kisses her. Like Frankenstein's monster, the *golem* wants only to be human. To the rabbi he cries the saddest of cries, "Golem alone," and "golem no want be golem" (67).

But the *golem* is beyond control, either the rabbi's or his own. Emperor Rudolph complains. The *golem* must be returned to lifelessness before his destructiveness brings repercussions onto the Jewish community. The rabbi implores Miriam to aid him; "Rabbi," Miriam responds, "I feel as if you had asked me to kill a man" (78). This is poignant; human values here conflict—the rabbi valuing the overall needs of the community; the orphan valuing the needs of the *golem*, and her own needs as well. ". . . clay must return to clay," the rabbi tells her, "You must make him helpless, but I myself will erase the name." Weeping, Miriam gets the *golem* drunk. But this is what the saint earlier in the tale had warned against. Just at the point when it appears the Golem is ready to enter into the follies of humanity, with Miriam in one hand and wine in the other, he passes out. His last words are, "Golem love wine" (82). The rabbi erases the holy name, kisses the now lifeless forehead, and leaves to meditate, but it is Miriam who is tragically affected. One morning Miriam's bed is empty. The ending, typically Singer, mixes love and sadness, the perverse and the marvelous: "There were rumors that Miriam was seen walking at dawn toward the river, most probably to drown herself. Others believed the golem was waiting for her in the darkness and took her to a place where loving spirits meet. Who knows? Perhaps love has even more power than a Holy Name. Love once engraved on the heart can never be erased. It lives forever" (83).

The lines "Love once engraved on the heart can never be erased. It lives forever" is about as fine an ending for any story as one can find. Love is more mysterious and holy than even the Name of God, even if— or perhaps especially if—it is between a monster and an orphan.

In somewhat the same "outcast" vein, Singer dedicates his book to "the persecuted and oppressed everywhere, young and old, Jew and Gentile, in the hope against hope that the time of false accusations and malicious decrees will cease one day." Barbara Novak writing for the *New York Times* agrees, "Mr. Singer ends quite properly on this note of love—perhaps the last thing left to draw upon."[31]

Margaret Meek in the *Times Literary Supplement* compares *The Golem* to *Pilgrim's Progress*.[32] Neil Philip, reviewing for the same publication, notes that Singer translated this story himself and adds "Children . . . will have no difficulty at all responding to the moral and emotional complexities . . . rich in implications."[33] Shulevitz's illustrations were praised; "velvety . . . sensitively complement the tone of the text," wrote Novak (48); Meek stated they were, "dignified, fine-grained illustrations" (776).

One reviewer, however, was critical of Singer. In his essay "Isaac Bashevis Singer and the Legend of the Golem of Prague," Arnold Goldsmith comments, ". . . the two halves of Singer's novella do not fuse, and the sugary closure is an unsatisfactory ending to one of the greatest legends in Jewish culture."[34] I understand Goldsmith's awe for the folklore story and agree, but Singer's is a children's story, which by most definitions includes a large element of hope at the end. An example of telling children the starker adult ending—the Golem is, in essence, killed, period—is Beverly Broderick McDermott's child's picture book. Its uncompromising portrayal of "things fall apart" provides no reason for the chaos and downslide that ensue.

In discussing this potent legend, Goldsmith's essay is very informative, as is Gershom Scholem's classic "The Idea of the Golem," from his 1965 *On Kabbalah and Its Symbolism*.[35] Scholem, it should be noted, is a major source of information about Jewish mysticism.

The Golem is one of Singer's best books—for all ages. It has a much greater affective pull than the more abstract *The Fearsome Inn*. Its characters are more developed and vivid. *The Golem* is a much more dramatic story than *Alone in the Wild Forest*, and although both stories are bipartite, the former is more coherent and tighter. I think it is the *golem*'s fight to be someone, his fight to survive even though he feels like—and in fact is—a lonely outcast, that resonates with adolescents . . . that resonates with us all.

The story, too, is intrinsically interesting, and part of the enjoyment of Singer's version is the knowledge of how it fits in, and yet alters, the basic folktale. Singer here contributes directly to a corpus of literature where his version is one of many.

Singer, then, for 15 years wrote for children: from 1967 when *The Fearsome Inn* came out, to 1982 when *The Golem* was published. He ranged in his material from private storehouse—such as a tale told to him by his mother, *The Topsy-Turvy Emperor of China*—to cultural archetype, the legend of the Golem. Some of his illustrated stories cross age lines, some appeal to young readers largely through their art, and some are mystical speculation put in fictional form.

Zena Sutherland uses Singer's picture book's *Why Noah Chose the Dove* to establish an overall assessment: "Singer is not at his best when writing within the limitations of the picture book for young children."[36] Naomi S. Morse concurs; some of the stories "appear misdirected at this (children's) audience" (22). Whereas a weak story in among a brilliant collection could be overlooked, a weak story by itself could not.

Agreement is general that Singer's finest work for children is found in his collections, as opposed to his single books. *Stories for Children*, the definitive collection of 36 stories discussed in chapter 8, contains selections from the four previous collections and also reprints many of the individual stories discussed in this chapter. Together in a single volume, they are unsurpassed as a literary and cultural contribution.

Chapter Eight

Last and Foremost

Stories for Children

A One-Man Grimm Brothers

The 1984 *Stories for Children* is the definitive collection; Singer and Stephen Roxburgh, Farrar, Straus and Giroux's children's book editor, selected its 36 stories. Following his definitive collection for adults, *Collected Stories*, by two years, it furnished critics and reviewers with the opportunity to place the author's children's works in a complete context; they found that Singer's children's and young adults' stories complement his adult ones. The *Wall Street Journal* writes that *Stories for Children* "belongs on the shelf beside 'The Collected Stories'" [*sic*]. Singer, the review continues, "knows the ludicrous and the pleasurable, but also the awesome and the holy."[1] In fact, as with "Topiel and Tekla," discussed below, the many gradations and overlappings of adult and children's stories require that all of Singer's stories be considered as a continuum, and then his prodigious command of the form is all the more stunning.

The Horn Book writes of *Stories for Children* that ". . . one is reminded of Dryden's comment on Chaucer, 'Here is God's plenty.'"[2] *Time* magazine reviewer Stefan Kanfer points to T. S. Eliot and Rudyard Kipling as other Nobel Prize laureates who wrote for children, but observes that "both men sought relief from their vocation in child's play; Singer has declared juveniles to be his ideal audience." Kanfer places Singer "in the long line of moral fabulous from Aesop and La Fontaine to Kafka and Italo Calvino."[3] Probably the latter two would be less to Singer's liking than the former ones, for, as his editor Cecil Hemley expressed, "He . . . considers most of the modern literary innovations debasements."[4]

Commenting in the *New York Times Book Review* on Singer's "sheer storytelling power" in the same vein as this book's first paragraph, reviewer Leonard Michaels writes, "in this respect, he has no peers among contemporaries." Michaels discusses "Growing Up," calling it the "most psychologically realistic story in the collection and the most revealing of the artist himself." Michaels agrees with Joshua Singer that the fabulating Reb Bear is a liar, not a true storyteller. Yet Wolf Bear's tale-spinning facility overwhelms the young Isaac, who is already planning with his friend Feivel to publish and sell his own stories. Comparing his own neophyte skills to the older man's, the child seems to feel what Harold Bloom calls the "anxiety of influence" and weeps in frustration. Michaels also praises "Hanukkah in the Poorhouse," adding that "at the most basic level, Mr. Singer treats the theme of innocence and experience."[5]

In *The Listener*, Nicholas Tucker writes, "At his best Singer bridges both the inner and the outer worlds he describes so well, setting his readers' imagination alight in a way few other modern writers can begin to rival." While stating that the collection is "good news for everyone," Tucker finds not everything in the book to be of equal quality. According to his review, Singer relies on "once credible supporting characters which may seem fairly corny to today's better informed young readers . . ."[6] Tucker agrees with another British reviewer in the *Times Literary Supplement* who writes that "occasionally one feels that non-Jewish readers need a little more help than they are given. . . ."[7] He refers to terms such as *dreidel* (spinning top) and *shammes* (sexton). Preponderantly, the reviews were very favorable, and the collection was designated "Notable" by the ALA.

Upon publication of *Stories for Children*, critics were also able to reassess their favorite stories. As one of his favorites, for example, Kanfer selects the traditional "Shrewd Todie and Lyzer the Miser," with its punch line, "If spoons can give birth, candlesticks can die."

Other critics noted four stories previously unpublished in book form: "The Day I Got Lost," "Ole and Trufa," "Topiel and Tekla," and "Tashlik," stories that confirm Singer's range: the former a slapstick Shlemiel story, the latter a memoir of passionate—if unfulfilled—adolescent love. The collection was the last work produced by Singer for children. New editions and combinations of Singer's children's stories are frequently reissued, but in the late 1980s Singer's health declined and he gradually withdrew from the public attention he had so enjoyed.

"The Day I Got Lost," subtitled "A Chapter from the Autobiography of Professor Shlemiel," is an easily understood first-person tale. Originally published by *Puffin* magazine and translated by Elizabeth Shub, it is not one of Singer's Chelm stories. This *shlemiel* is a professor who resides in New York City. His problem? He is indeed a *shlemiel*— which means he is dressed in ill-fitting clothes, has lost one of the lenses of his spectacles, carries with him reams of meaningless papers and a broken umbrella, and constantly misplaces things he needs. Such lapses are only to be expected of a *shlemiel*, but this *shlemiel* has a particular dilemma. His wife is throwing a big birthday party for him, but he has forgotten where he lives. He cannot call friends for directions because they are all waiting to greet him at his home. Characteristic, too, of Singer's *shlemiels* is that, despite his absent-mindedness, Professor Shlemiel has friends and family who care about him.

In his attempt to find his house, the professor phones a friend, only to be told by the babysitter that the friend is at Professor Shlemiel's house for a birthday party. The babysitter asks for his name, thinking she will take a message. The professor identifies himself. "They went to your house," says the babysitter. "Can you tell me where they went?" asks the professor. "I've just told you," says the babysitter, "They went to your house." "But where do I live?" "You must be kidding," says the babysitter, and hangs up (*Stories*, 118).

Unable to resolve his impasse, the professor begins to muse over one of his favorite problems: which came first, the chicken or the egg? Standing in the rain (he has lost his umbrella), he sights a kindred spirit, a lost-looking, soaking wet black dog. Immediately, the kind professor makes a new lifelong friend to whom he says, "I'm a man shlemiel and you're a dog shlemiel." The man promises to take care of the dog and the dog, raising his paw, obviously understands. He thus becomes another of Singer's faithful and profound animal characters.

Just then, a taxi passes and suddenly stops. In it is one of the professor's friends, on his way to the party; he asks the *shlemiel* what he is doing out in the storm. When the professor explains, the friend immediately gives both the birthday celebrant and his canine friend a ride home. The Mrs. Shlemiel opening the door upon her missing husband in this story sounds much like the Mrs. Shlemiel in "When Shlemiel Went to Warsaw," in which another husband gets lost and comes home under confused circumstances. The professor's wife "shrieks" and "scolds," but these are cultural expressions of caring. Both husband and dog find a welcoming home, and the wife thenceforth focuses on reminding them not to forget again where they live. By way of epilogue, the professor adds that he has given up trying to solve the-chicken-or-the-egg riddle and is now writing his autobiography, which children will soon be able to read—that is, if he doesn't forget the manuscript someplace or other.

Characters like these in Singer's stories are a lot like children in that they are uninhibited in their emotional lives. Not being competent adults, they do not dissemble, they are not confused by moral ambiguities, and, as Leonard Michaels observes, they don't recognize evil—being themselves free of it.[8] They say what they mean and mean what they say. Jerome Griswold observes in "The Fool and the Child" that fools used to be considered so valuable that some cultures paid them to be present because ". . . it is important that there be someone who can say whatever he wants to anyone." The fool, Griswold states, "sees things with his heart."[9] Singer sees it this way: "God was very frugal . . . in bestowing gifts on us. He didn't give us enough intellect, enough physical strength, but when it came to emotions, passions, He was very lavish . . . every human being . . . is a millionaire in emotion . . . emotions are the very topic of literature."[10]

Singer's culturally resonant characters are demonstrative, excitable, compassionate, and contentious. They scream and shriek—the Yiddish word for this is the onomatopoeic verb *kvitcher*—they groan, they pull their beards; but they also hug, dance, toast each other, stick together, and "commit random acts of kindness." Does Singer's story say that Professor Shlemiel's ride home providentially shows up just at the moment the protagonist commits a random act of kindness toward the dog? Not in so many words: but as Singer said in one of his public appearances, "You find the message. I don't have to do everything for you."[11]

A very different story originally appeared in the *Atlantic*. Praised by both the *Wall Street Journal* and the *New York Times Book Review*, "Ole and Trufa" is summarized by the latter: "the characters are leaves who fall from their home, in autumn, to die and be reborn into the greater life of the universe."[12] The *Wall Street Journal*'s reviewer states, "As an image of enduring love it is worthy to stand beside Ovid's 'Baucis and Philemon,' although it has no human characters."[13]

Ole means "leaf" in Hebrew, and *trufa* means "healing,"[14] so here again, as in Sus's name, which means "horse," and *shlemiel* used as a proper name, Singer is emphasizing the typical or generic. The two personified leaves have been in love since being born into this world in spring. As we have seen in Singer's children's stories, true love usually means that whatever the lovers' fates—even falling helplessly from the highest branches and dying on the ground with their kinsfolk—they will in consciousness remain together. As with humans, the leaves are aware of their transitoriness, their insignificance with regard to the main body of the tree, the trunk that will survive without them and, somewhat mechanically, will produce new leaves in due time. The metaphor to human life beneath the divine dome is made explicit when Singer writes that the leaves looked upon the trunk as a god. In fact, Singer's two leaves have the same metaphysical, questioning bent as any number of his main characters. They wonder why they have been spared thus far, and think it may be because of their fidelity. But, like most of us, they really do not know.

The leaves are Singer's rendition of the ideal old couple, solicitous and supportive; it is all too rare in contemporary literature to read a portrayal of beatification through lifelong conjugality. In fact, this may be the most sentimental of all Singer's stories. He wrote elsewhere, "literature has neglected the old and their emotions . . . in love, as in other matter, the young are just beginners. . . ."[15] Nevertheless, beatified or not, Ole and Trufa's loving bond is soon to be dissolved forever. Ole falls first. The story shifts to Trufa. She spends one night alone, the last leaf on the tree. Then, like the old joke, Trufa wakes up literally to find herself dead, although Singer is not being funny. Quite the opposite; here his prose takes flight, for it turns out that dissolution is not forever. His two protagonists meet on the ground to begin life on a higher plane: "A breeze came and lifted Ole and Trufa in the air, and they soared with the bliss known only by those who have freed themselves and have joined with eternity" (*Stories*, 253).

This metaphysical conclusion is reminiscent of the final paragraph of "Menaseh's Dream," which also concerns the afterlife. In that story, unseen woodland beings dance and sing, but only for those who "know that everything lives and nothing in time is ever lost" (*Stories*, 321). Leaves, elves, crickets, orphans, goats, *lantuchs*—the characters in Singer's animated, democratic universe are all spiritually aware, fully contributing members to the music of the spheres. So unassuming is their harmony that it mostly goes unnoticed: the powerful, the prejudiced, the rich, the manipulative, the self-involved live and die confined merely to the plane of history. Singer knew well that, because of history's incomprehensible cruelties, seeking personal meaning in that impersonal realm could often be profoundly puzzling, both to children and adults. For if history teaches anything, it is that things are not as they should be. Israel Knox succinctly writes, "Judaism . . . has never yielded to the enticement of cutting off the ideal from the actual, the spiritual from the natural, elevating the religious above, and in effect, separating it from—the ethical."[16] Singer's final sentence in *Stories for Children* is from "Are Children the Ultimate Literary Critics?" It addresses the fundamental bafflement of serious seekers for meaning, and provides an outlet: "Many adults read and enjoy children's literature. We write not only for children but also for their parents. They, too, are serious children" (*Stories*, 338).

Rivers of Love

First appearing in *Nimrod*, "Topiel and Tekla" exemplifies that crossover between children's and adults' literature of which few writers are capable. The stark theme of human sacrifice is ameliorated by the spirituality of poor Tekla's fate in a tale to be considered for older, that is, young adult, readers.

Topiel is an indigenous river god from times predating the arrival in Poland of either Christianity or Judaism. Like a heathen deity from the Bible, Topiel is bloodthirsty, or, more precisely, his worshipers fearfully perceive him to be so. To assuage his tempers, expressed in devastating floods, Topiel is offered human sacrifices. This story, with its Polish characters, is thus much like "Joseph and Koza," discussed in chapter 7. But in the other story, the sacrificial Polish princess Koza is saved by the religious reforming Jewish hero Joseph. Tekla is not so fortunate. Her father, as penniless as he is callous, sells his daughter's unborn child to the townsfolk to be sacrificed to Topiel. For this, Tekla's family is to receive a pig. Singer's distaste is revealed in the association of the ancient Poles with pigs, which are disgusting to kosher Jews and especially, therefore, disgusting to the vegetarian Singer.[17] Tekla has gotten herself pregnant; she has neither husband nor sympathy. She does, however, have feelings. She is disgusted not only by her fate and the insult of the price—a pig—but horrified by the parallel fattening of the two respective sacrifices. As her pregnancy grows, so does the pig insincerely coddled by the family that so hungrily anticipates butchering it.

Tekla is described like so many Singer women—Shosha, for example, as frail, neurotic, and silent, with "watery blue eyes" and pale skin. An outsider within her own family, she is easily seduced by a "vagabond" who leaves before she even knows she is pregnant. Tekla has always been strange, fatalistic, and drawn to the supernatural. More than any other female character in Singer's children's stories, she resembles the lost and horrified women of his adult stories, such as Akhsa from "A Crown of Feathers," Hodle from "The Gentleman from Cracow," Risha from "Blood," Lise from "The Destruction of Kreshev," or Miriam Leiba from *The Manor*. Lawrence S. Freidman provides a discussion of these characters in "The Short Stories" from *Understanding Isaac Bashevis Singer*.[18] Unlike the soon-to-be sacrificed daughter of the biblical Jephtath, the time remaining for Tekla is spent without friends or dignity or comfort.

As in the stories featuring Akhsa, Hodle, Risha, and Lise, Singer's atmospherics in "Topiel and Tekla" are superb. Tekla leaves the hut where the family is oblivious to her and moves, with the animals, into the hay. There, as the child jerks and pushes within her, "the wind barked and wailed like a pack of wolves" (*Stories*, 264). In what Tekla interprets as rage at having to wait for the sacrifice, Topiel overflows its banks. Tekla is also sure that, whatever the terrors of the river, Topiel is a mighty god who cares for the many wives he is said to sing with when it storms. This is a Singer story, so when the climax comes it is less a surprise than it is an ineluctability, ". . . maybe she should become one of his wives and bring up her child together with him" (*Stories*, 265).

Weiprz, the pig promised to the family, is slaughtered; Tekla is tortured by its screams and by her family, which is preprandially savoring its flesh. This section of the story, the slaughter and Tekla's rage, would not be good bedtime reading for a child. The pregnant woman is described as "yellow and bloated"; in fact, the prose here is as hair-raising as anything in "The Slaughterer" or *Satan in Goray*, works by Singer known for their poetic prose and gruesome events. Tekla sacrifices herself on Christmas Eve, while her family is at church and chunks of Wieprz simmer on the stove. Here Singer fills in the kind of details he only suggested in *The Golem* when Miriam commits suicide the same way. "The sky swayed on the waves," Singer writes, "Tekla's hair tried to tear loose from her skull." She sees Wieprz on the river gesturing toward her, remembers suddenly he is dead, and interprets the vision as a sign that the animal's spirit has come to say good-bye: the pig is more spiritually evolved than the family who murdered him. Tekla throws herself headfirst into the water. The climax occurs with Topiel rising from the icy deeps and taking her in his arms to his "glittering castle" (*Stories*, 268).

The last of the story's four sections is the denouement, providing ironic justice. The villagers, believing that Tekla's father has hidden her away, descend upon his shack in a fury and take all the pork, even the pot on the stove. Topiel goes wild—we readers know it is because of his fury on behalf of his new consort Tekla, but the villagers see in the vicious storm that topples the church only confirmation that the river has been denied its due by Tekla's father's swindle. Things fall apart. Eventually the ruling Russian authorities hear of the intended human sacrifice and arrest Tekla's family, sending them to Siberia. Locusts descend upon the deserted village, and "the last inhabitants swore that . . . their huts crawled toward the river like snakes" (*Stories*, 270). The ending is consummated with an unforgettable image: ". . . Topiel came out at night onto the dunes and danced in a whirl with Tekla—she in a shawl of pearls over her naked body, with a child in her arms, and he with a beard of foam-sparkling curls, and a crown of ice" (270). The vision is chillingly beautiful; at last Tekla is protected.

The prose in this story, translated by Joseph Singer, is so extraordinary that the non-Yiddish reader must wonder at the power, novelty, and nuance of Singer's word choice in his native language. His editor Cecil Hemley wrote, "I am told by those who know the language well that the English equivalent of any Singer is inevitably a watering down" (225). In "Topiel and Tekla," Singer's use of language—any language—is dazzling.

"Tashlik," the final story in Singer's *Stories for Children*, is a small masterpiece. It was translated by Singer and Cecil Hemley and first appeared in the *London Jewish Chronicle*. Instructors of young adult literature who assign Goethe's *Young Werther*, Twain's *Huckleberry Finn*, or Salinger's *Catcher in the Rye* will find in Singer's 10-page story a complete rendition of love and longing, conflict with tradition, family, and conscience, and local color of rare intensity.

The autobiographic story begins with some exposition: the main character, a teenaged Isaac, is a city boy whose exciting life in Warsaw is changed when the depression brought on by World War I forces his family to move back to the country, and back in time, to the tiny *shtetl* of Bilgoray. This village where an entire extended family of his lived is described by Singer as far from a railway line and "stuck" in the middle of "a pine forest"; he writes, "I never stopped longing for Warsaw" (*Stories*, 323).

Whereas in other memoirs Singer typically depicted his fierce boy's devotion to his backward, dependent neighbor Shosha, the Isaac in this story is older by many years, and the object of his attention, Feigele ("Little Bird") is a fully functioning, intelligent young woman. And what is more, she actualizes in her life and in her independent thinking much that Singer both admired and envied. The only household in the "hamlet" with a telephone, her "emancipated" family is everything his pious one is not. Aaron the watchmaker, her father, has a substantial library, plays chess, reads Polish newspapers and German translations of the Bible. Therefore, he is viewed with suspicion of heresy by the majority of Jews in Bilgoray, including Singer's family.

Across from his room at night, Isaac can see Feigele in her attic window. Isaac feels a kinship to her, recognizing she, too, is "living in exile" (324). She has gone to school in the big city, Lublin, and returned to Bilgoray with a diploma. In her isolation and the uncertainty of her own future as an educated Jewish girl, does she presage the numerous female

characters in Singer's adults' stories who are in no-win situations? Their
native intelligence leads them inexorably to seek knowledge, which
alienates them from their culture. However, to stifle their intelligence is
also an untenable choice. This story is about Isaac's attraction to Feigele,
so we see her only from his eyes. Yet so evocative is Singer's description
of Feigele's outcast position in the *shtetl* that it does not take much imagination to feel the bleakness of her future—if she had one. The adult
reader frequently remembers that Singer's characters, often based on
reality, in reality had no future, for these are precisely the people
destroyed by the Nazis.

Isaac rejects the majority view of Feigele's family, but despairs that
Feigele would ever see him beyond the identification with his father and
grandfather, both rabbis. Like his feeling of being an outsider because of
his old-fashioned dress in "A Hanukkah Evening in Warsaw" when he
was a boy, in "Tashlik" the adolescent Isaac too is acutely aware of his
garb. His appearance does not represent who he, Isaac, truly is, the Isaac
who is secretly reading Knut Hamsun, Strindberg, and Spinoza. Equally
unacceptable to his father, Isaac is studying the *Cabala*, the book of mysticism Jews are not considered mature enough to study until they reach
middle age. The scandal would be of monumental proportions were any
of these heretical activities of the rabbi's son to become public, threaten-
ing the family's standing in the community and Isaac's father's liveli-
hood (325).

Nonetheless, Isaac yearns for Feigele, and in the fervor and naivete of
his mystical leanings, sends out psychic messages to bring her magically
to his side; he writes, "I wrapped a phantom net around her like some
sorcerer from the *Arabian Nights*." He focuses on the "totally illogical"
belief that their relationship will begin on Tashlik, the holy day when the
pious march to the riverbanks to recite the prayer by which they throw
their sins into the water (325–26).

Singer describes the colorful parade of Bilgoray's residents to the river
as if he were still there watching it, the townsfolk in their New Year's
best, the "traditional tashlik jokes." Filled with disappointment that he
has not succeeded in pulling Feigele to him, and full of the ineffable
power of the star-filled night, young Singer, standing outside the group,
prays to the vibrant universe with visionary ardor, "'Gather me to you. I
am weary of being myself'" (329).

Suddenly, Feigele is standing next to him. Her eyes twinkle and the
flustered boy sees that her request for his help in finding the Tashlik
prayer in her book is really only an excuse to talk to him. In his confu-

sion, Isaac's elbow brushes Feigele's; this only increases his disorienta-
tion. Finally, he finds the prayer for Feigele; she suggests they say it
together. Isaac is acutely aware of many things; he is exultant that his
amorous sorcery has worked, but at the same time, he feels the town is
watching him and Feigele, and he knows he will be in "a great deal of
trouble at home." The memoir ends, significantly, with the two disparate
outsiders standing together on the river bank as Feigele murmurs the
prayer. Readers are not told what happens next: the teenagers stand on
the brink, fixed in Singer's memory representing both the unknown
future and the rejected past. The quoted section of the Tashlik prayer
itself is meaningful here too, an obvious contrast to the *shtetl* mentality.
It states that the Lord looks upon all "the sons of men. . . . He fashioneth
all their hearts alike. He considereth all their works. . . ." (330–31). The
words of the prayer restate the boy's maturing conviction that there is no
orthodoxy by which one can distinguish human values. Decades later,
Cecil Hemley said of his friend, "Singer, although a religious man, is not
an Orthodox Jew . . . he, himself, resists any dogma."[19] In "Tashlik," the
adolescence of Singer's consistent, insistent individuality is portrayed.

An Alien Plant

Singer's universal appeal grows out of the insider/outsider dichotomy
expressed in "Tashlik." The audience Singer has attracted are for the
most part, non-Jewish. This is a necessity, a matter of statistics as well as
appeal; not many authors who write only in Yiddish wind up with read-
erships like Singer's. There simply aren't that many Jews in the world.

In the essay "What It Takes to Be a Jewish Writer," Singer writes,

> The creative man . . . is always an alien plant . . . a mutant . . . an exper-
> iment: The creative writer must have deep roots in his milieu, but he
> himself must not be entirely of it. He cannot be typical of it. On the con-
> trary, he must have something that divided him from it. . . . The true
> artist is simultaneously a child of his people, and a stepchild.[20]

Singer is describing the creative margins of an author who bordered
several fronts. Singer's dualities offer a rich field for a multicultural
analysis: Hasidic/traditional; Jewish/Christian; believer/skeptic; Yiddish-
speaking/English-speaking; Polish/Jewish/American. And, most perti-
nently for our study, as a writer Singer negotiated the border between
childhood and adulthood.

Wherever he went, Singer never lost sight of where he was from or what he had experienced during the first 31 years of his life in Poland. He drew strength from the continuity of his culture while ultimately rejecting its demands as represented by the extremism of his father:

> [The author] must be the product of a home which had tradition and stability. He must trace his lineage to his grandmothers and grandfathers. . . . The great masters were all deeply bound to the culture of their people. They knew the people's language, their habits, their idiosyncracies. . . . Moreover . . . no great artist has been produced by a people . . . still in the process of formation. ("Jewish Writer," 55)

In Singer's literary theory, this is true of creativity not only on an individual level but on a cultural one as well. Writing in the 1960s, Singer appears prescient in regard to border studies and multiculturalism. Singer expresses the late twentieth century's salad bowl—or parfait—image of multiculturalism, as opposed to the predominantly melting pot assimilationalist paradigm of the earlier twentieth century. ". . . Jewish art is strongest where the Jews lead their own distinct life, speak their own language, cultivate their own customs and maintain their own traditions from generation to generation. The richer the soil, the stronger the plant" ("Jewish Writer," 54–56).

One of the key traits of Singer's greatness and his complexity, this insider/outsider opposition accounts for the ambivalence with which he was typically viewed by the rest of the Yiddish community. He was perceived as an outsider, and he felt like one: "Yes, as a matter of fact, I still am outside. I'm far from being an insider even today."[21] Isaac Singer, as Irving Howe and others pointed out, was neither sentimental nor socially active, the two most traditional features of Yiddish literature. Or, more precisely, Singer saved his sentimental writing for the Yiddish language *Jewish Daily Forward*, and he seldom, if ever, undertook political causes. Writing as "Isaac Warshovsky" (Isaac from Warsaw) in untranslated works, Singer often reminisced about the Old Country with considerable nostalgia, painting a one-sided, almost idyllic world. But with regard to social justice, Singer was a disappointment to intellectuals such as the influential Irving Howe. See, for example, Howe's "I. B. Singer."

But Singer was actually full of protest. His was not, however, protest against social institutions; he had very little faith in humanity and expected very little from it. His conservatism was political, best

explained by Chaim Potok's comment on the basic conservatism of the
Polish Jews. It was not good when the boat rocked in Eastern Europe,
for no matter who wrestled for the helm, the Jews were inevitably
pushed overboard first. War and revolution were bad for them.[22] This is
the attitude ingrained in Singer.

But God, on the other hand, was inexplicable in perpetuating iniqui-
ty. Singer's "deep resentment" was against "the Almighty," in whom he
maintained faith and doubt at the same time. He called humanity blind
and God permanently silent.[23] Singer told Richard Burgin:

> I often say to myself that God *wants* us to protest. He has had
> enough of those who praise him and bless him for all His cruelties to man
> and animal.
>   . . . If I could, I would picket the Almighty with a sign: "Unfair to
> Life." ("Conversations," 115–16)

The impact of reading Singer's Yiddish prose in the 1950s led Howe
to champion Singer's work for the English-speaking audience, although
with waning enthusiasm over the decades. His comments here criticize
Singer's subject matter and style. "I . . . fail to see any principle of
growth within his work. Singer seems almost perfect within his stringent
limits, but he . . . plays the same tune over and over again, and with
a self-confidence that is awesome he keeps modelling his work largely
on . . . his work" (52).

Also noting the repetition of remarks made by Singer's storyteller
characters from Gimpel to Naftali, Thomas P. Riggio recalls the fat boy's
complaint from "Gimpel the Fool": that he had heard "Grandpa"
Gimpel tell the same story to the children during his last visit.

There is validity in this charge of repetitiveness; Howe felt it strongly. When I asked him in New York City in 1991 whether his opinion of
Singer's work had changed from his essays of decades ago, he said he
would stick to what he had written earlier. But the irony, which Howe
acknowledged, was that the best work Singer did was that which stayed
within the narrowest confines. Thus, essentially, Howe was criticizing
Singer for doing what Singer did best—revealing the complexity of the
shtetl world and of his own passionate mix of memory and imagination.
Singer was well aware of this: "I keep going back to 10 Krochmalna
Street in my writing. I remember every little corner and every person
there. I say to myself just as other people are digging gold God put

there millions of years ago, my literary gold mine is this street"
("Conversations," 9).

It is true that Singer sometimes repeated his best lines, for example,
"We have to believe in free will. We have no choice." This is repeatedly
quoted in interviews. And for 17 years, from its first recording in 1961
to his use of the line in his Nobel Prize acceptance speech, he saved the
joke about liking to write ghost stories and therefore continuing to write
in Yiddish—which is a dying language.

In a well-known tongue-in-cheek essay, "Envy: Or, Yiddish in
America," Cynthia Ozick defends Singer: "They hated him for the amazing things that had happened to him—his fame. . . ." At the same time,
in a tone similar to Woody Allen's, she spoofs Singer's ironic sense of
humor as seen on his lecture tours to places such as Massachusetts
Institute for Technology and Harvard University:

Q.   . . . Can you tell me please if you believe in hell?
A.   Not since I got rich.[24]

Ozick is not the only contemporary Jewish woman to use Singer as a
vehicle for humor; Sandra Bernhard wrote an often anthologized essay,
"My Date with Isaac Bashevis Singer" that pokes fun at Singer's Old
World persona by pairing him amorously with a liberated woman—
Bernhard herself.[25]

Alfred Kazin responds to another criticism, that Singer frequently
portrayed the Eastern European Jews unattractively. Singer, Kazin
writes, is not like "certain American Jewish writers who cannot get over
mama and can displace her only by reproducing her legendary force of
invective": "Singer swims happily in the whole . . . tradition—Jews are
his life. But he would certainly agree with Mark Twain's reply to anti-
Semites: 'Jews are members of the human race; worse than that I cannot
say of them.'"[26]

A more telling critique of Singer is that he did not distinguish in what
he wrote between what was good and what was mediocre or worse. He
suffered less from narrowness than from unchecked fertility. This is the
negative side of an author who repeatedly professed to have no favorites
among his writings and who seldom, if ever, went back to reconsider a
piece after it was in print. He published some real clunkers, for children
as well as for adults. An example is *The Topsy-Turvy Emperor of China*, an
unlikable book by most standards. It actually serves to prove Singer's
rather than Howe's point: that an author must write what he knows. In

this picture book, Singer tells a convoluted charmless tale set coyly on the other side of the earth. Like "The Dog Who Thought He Was a Cat and the Cat Who Thought She Was a Dog" and *Joseph and Koza*, which are stories with Polish characters rather than Yiddish ones, Singer does not meet his usual high standard in this single Asian-set story. It is heavy-handed, and although Singer attributes *The Topsy-Turvy Emperor of China* to his mother, it is certainly not one of her best.

Singer left behind a massive amount of unorganized material, the bulk of which is housed at the University of Texas in Austin. The curator expects it will take a few years to sort through the miscellany. One hopes the author's reputation will not be damaged by publications he might not have wanted. Speaking to Richard Burgin in 1980, Singer said he had written a number of pieces in Yiddish that he did not have translated because they were unsuccessful: "I hope that no one is going to translate them after my death" ("Conversations," 55). Now, with new novels being published by Farrar, Straus and Giroux—none to terrifically good reviews—the question of quality obtrudes all the more.

We have no way of currently knowing whether additional Singer children's stories exist. After all, in Singer's world, anything is possible.

Isaac in Wonderland

Anyone who has seen the end of the PBS's *American Masters* biography on Isaac Bashevis Singer, when he solemnly accepts the Nobel Prize from the King of Sweden, must have been impressed by the sight of the frail old man tottering purposefully in his tuxedo to the stage. Seconds after receiving the prize, Singer the performer is in total command of his glittering audience—and posterity—addressing them in a heavily accented English, or "Enklish," as he would have said it. Amazingly, the impoverished rabbi's boy, now 74 years old, is cracking them up in Stockholm. On the world's center stage, he is making ironic jokes about Yiddish, his *mama loshen*, or mother-tongue. He likes to write ghost stories, he states, and Yiddish, as a dying, or "dyink," language is the favorite language of ghosts: "They all speak it," he says. As a believer in resurrection, the bespectacled laureate adds, he continues to write in Yiddish because, when the day comes that all dead souls arise, their first question will be, "What new thing is there to read in Yiddish?"

Spanning the better part of the century, Singer's literary legacy ranges from 2- to 3-page picture books to trilogies of well more than a thousand pages. Like Plato, Augustine, Voltaire, Wordsworth, Balzac, and

Twain, Singer represented, on the one hand, an entire culture and a philosophical outlook, and on the other, a distinct style and aesthetic. Eric A. Kimmel writes in *Children's Literature*, "The greatest children's writers are great writers by any standard: Defoe, Carroll, Stevenson, Twain. The twentieth century will add no more than a handful of names to that number. One of them, however, will surely be that of Isaac Bashevis Singer" (889). In order to appreciate this, *Collected Stories*, *Stories for Children*, a novella such as *The Penitent*, a novel or two such as *The Slave*, a major saga such as *The Family Moskat*, and any number of his articulate interviews are basic reading. All in all, critics agree on the pre-eminence of his shorter works. And, thus, no evaluation of Singer can fail to note in particular his legacy to that literature which includes children in its readership.

The day Singer died in 1991, July 25, the news made front pages around the world. The *New York Times*'s lengthy obituary included biography, photographs, sidebars, excerpts from major works, and several interviews. Stefan Kanfer wrote in *Time*, "It was easy for Isaac Singer to believe in miracles. He was proof they existed." That Singer's work was impossible to categorize was just the way the author wanted it; Kanfer quotes Singer, "'The various 'isms' and schools of literature were invented by professors. . . . Only small fish swim in schools.'"[27] *Newsweek*'s Malcolm Jones, Jr. wrote ". . . his universe had the outlines of a fairy tale and the smell of a police blotter, and to countless readers, it felt like home."[28] His uniqueness was noted in the *Los Angeles Times* in Burt A. Folkart's obituary: "He wrote, until his final illness, in splendid isolation—tending a mythical universe inhabited by his own creations."[29] And the magnitude of his accomplishment in winning the globe's foremost creative award was noted in the *San Diego Times* by an admirer, Rabbi Wayne Dosnick: ". . . an amazing feat for a writer who . . . pound[ed] out his words on an old Yiddish typewriter. . . . His picture hangs on my wall."[30]

Singer's death elicited diverse memories. Hugh Nissensen, writing in *USA Today*, reminisces about a trip to the circus with Singer. Just before the end of the show, the ringmaster had the spotlight directed at the surprised author, and, with a drum roll, introduced him to the audience as "the great writer and Nobel laureate."[31] Writing for the *Denver Post*, newspaper intern Reed Martin recalls the many times he and his mother met Singer at soda fountains; later he and Singer corresponded. The details are fascinating: "He always wore a lot of blue," and strolled Collins Avenue in "royal blue nylon sneakers," a bright blue shirt, and a straw hat with a blue band. Evidently he felt more whimsical sartorially in Miami than he did in Manhattan.[32]

Pictures on walls, anecdotes, books on shelves, reviews, panels, admirers, imitators: these are the signs of survival. Singer's wholehearted entry into children's literature; his uniqueness and his refusal to assimilate any aspect of his native culture; the humor, depth, and passion of the characters he created—these ensure for him a place in the highest ranks of literary masters who shared their gifts with the young. Although social education was far from his primary motivation, he nonetheless set an example for other writers, and just perhaps the work of Buchi Emecheta, Rudolfo Anaya, and many others has found a more receptive audience because of his extraordinary and uncompromised success. Singer knew well the vagaries of fortune and fate, literary and otherwise. He was characteristically philosophical about his literary legacy: "Time is a broom which sweeps away everything which is of no value and leaves sometimes the things of value. And every writer has the hope that his works will not be swept away by this broom. So do I."[33]

The work of a genius is, of course, ineffably more than the sum of any and all analyses and interpretations: Singer's work will last because it is, simply put, so good.

Notes and References

Chapter One

1. Roger Sale, "Good Servants and Bad Masters," *Hudson Review* 20 (Winter 1967–68): 674.
2. Stanley Edgar Hyman, "The Yiddish Hawthorne," in *On Contemporary Literature*, ed. Richard Kostenlanetz (New York: Avon Books, 1964), 586–90, 586.
3. Isaac Bashevis Singer, *Stories for Children* (New York: Farrar, Straus and Giroux, 1984); hereafter cited in text as *Stories*.
4. See also Singer's autobiography *Love and Exile* (New York: Doubleday, 1984), which combines the earlier memoirs *A Little Boy in Search of God: or, Mysticism in a Personal Light* (New York: Doubleday, 1975), *A Young Man in Search of Love* (New York: Doubleday, 1978), and *Lost in America* (1981) with a new introduction, "The Beginning." In *A Young Boy in Search of God*, Singer again details his fears of the tenement's stairway (13).
5. Isaac Bashevis Singer, *A Day of Pleasure* (New York: Farrar, Straus and Giroux, 1963), 17, 21; hereafter cited in text as *Day*.
6. Diane Wolkstein, "The Stories behind the Stories: An Interview with Issac Bashevis Singer," *Children's Literature in Education* 18 (Fall 1975): 142; hereafter cited in text.
7. Isaac Bashevis Singer, in "On Translating My Books," *The World of Translation* (New York: P. E. N. Center, 1984), 111–12; hereafter cited in text as "Translating."
8. Roderick McGillis, "Reactivating the Ear: Orality and Children's Poetry," *The Voice of the Narrator in Children's Literature*, ed. Charlotte F. Otten and Gary D. Schmidt (New York and London: Greenwood, 1989), 252.
9. Laurie Colwin, "I. B. Singer, Storyteller," *New York Times Book Review*, 23 July 1978, 23; hereafter cited in text.
10. Irving Howe, "I. B. Singer," *Encounter* 26 (March 1966): 62; hereafter cited in text.
11. Isaac Bashevis Singer, *In My Father's Court* (New York: Farrar, Straus and Giroux, 1962), 195; hereafter cited in text as *Court*.
12. Alfred Kazin, "His Son, the Storyteller," *Book Week*, 24 April 1966, 10.
13. Isaac Bashevis Singer, *The Power of Light* (New York: Farrar, Straus and Giroux, 1980), 5.
14. I. L. Peretz, "If Not Higher," *Short Shorts*, ed. Irving and Alana Howe (New York: Bantam, 1983), 63–66.
15. Isaac Bashevis Singer, *Love and Exile* (New York: Doubleday, 1984), xvii.

16.   Isaac Bashevis Singer, *The Penitent* (New York: Farrar, Straus and Giroux, 1983).

17.   Hinde Esther (Singer) Kreitman, *Deborah* (London: Virago, 1983); hereafter cited in text. I. J. Singer, *Of a World That Is No More* (New York: Vanguard, 1970); hereafter cited in text as *World*.

18.   Dorthea Straus, *Under the Canopy* (New York: Braziller, 1982), 23.

19.   Isaac Bashevis Singer and Richard Burgin, *Conversations with Isaac Bashevis Singer* (New York: Doubleday, 1985), 107; hereafter cited in text.

20.   Isaac Bashevis Singer, *A Little Boy in Search of God: or, Mysticism in a Personal Light* (New York: Doubleday, 1975), xviii.

21.   Isaac Bashevis Singer, *The Fools of Chelm and Their History* (New York: Farrar, Straus and Giroux, 1973), and "The Elders of Chelm and Genedel's Key," *When Shlemiel Went to Warsaw* (New York: Farrar, Straus and Giroux, 1968).

22.   Clive Sinclair, "A Conversation with Isaac Bashevis Singer," *Encounter* 2 (February 1979): 23; hereafter cited in text.

23.   Elizabeth Shub, interview by Alida Allison, June 1992, New York, unpublished tape recording, transcribed July 1992; hereafter cited in text as Interview, 1992.

Chapter Two

1.   My thanks to Melissa Meade, assistant editor at Farrar, Straus and Giroux, for information on Singer's children's books sales and on the artistic techniques used by his illustrators.

2.   Isaac Bashevis Singer, "I See the Child as a Last Refuge," *New York Times Book Review*, 9 November 1969, 1, 66.

3.   Ibid., 66.

4.   Isaac Bashevis Singer, *Nobel Lecture* (New York: Farrar, Straus and Giroux, 1978), 13–14.

5.   Paul Kresh, *The Story of a Storyteller* (New York: Dutton, 1984), 124.

6.   Saul Bellow, introduction to *Great Jewish Short Stories*, ed. Saul Bellow (New York: Dell, 1963), 13.

7.   Isaac Bashevis Singer, foreword to *Zlateh the Goat and Other Stories* (New York: Harper and Row, 1966); hereafter cited in text.

8.   Naomi S. Morse, "Values for Children in the Stories of Isaac Bashevis Singer," in *Children's Literature: Selected Essays and Bibliographies*, vol. 9, ed. Anne MacLeod (Baltimore: College of Library Information Services, University of Maryland, 1977), 17.

9.   Francelia Butler, "An Interview with Isaac Bashevis Singer," in *Sharing Literature with Children* (Prospect Heights, Ill.: Waveland Press, 1977), 158.

10.   Isaac Bashevis Singer, "On Writing for Children," in *Children's Literature*, vol. 6 (Philadelphia: Temple University Press, 1977), 252.

11.   McGillis, 252.

NOTES AND REFERENCES

12. Grace Farrell, ed., *Isaac Bashevis Singer, Conversations* (Jackson: University Press of Mississippi, 1992), 255; hereafter cited in text as *Conversations*.
13. Thanks again to Melissa Meade for this information.

Chapter Three

1. Ben Siegel, "Sacred and Profane: Isaac Bashevis Singer's Embattled Spirits," *Critique* 6 (Spring 1963), 30.
2. See Thomas Yoseloff, *The Further Adventures of Till Eulenspiegel* (New York: n.p., 1957). I am grateful to my colleague Peter Neumeyer for this reference.
3. Nathan Ausubel tells a version of this in his comprehensive *A Treasury of Jewish Folklore* (New York: Crown Publishers, 1948).
4. Isaac Bashevis Singer, review of *Russian Fairy Tales*, collected by Aleksandr Afanas'ev, *New York Times Book Review*, 16 November 1975, 27.
5. Here, as often throughout this book, I am grateful to my colleague Yitz Gefter for his assistance with the Yiddish and Hebrew languages and with Jewish customs.
6. Morse, 16–31, 25.
7. Michael John O'Donnell, class assignment, San Diego State University, spring 1994.
8. Most of the verses in Singer's books were written by Elizabeth Shub. As his first attempt at writing for children revealed (see ch. 2, 23), Singer had no facility for poetry and did not write it well (Interview, 1992).
9. Henry Spaulding, *Encyclopedia of Jewish Humor* (Middle Village, N.Y.: Jonathan David, 1969), 115.
10. Straus, 21.
11. One of my students gave me a copy of a short Japanese Buddhist play about young acolytes who discover their guardians have similarly tricked them by telling them the jam is poison. The neophytes eat the jam nonetheless, and then manuever the elders into collusion, lest they have to admit they lied to their charges. I do not have a citation for this.
12. Morse, 18–19.
13. Alison Lurie, review of *Zlateh the Goat,* by I. B. Singer, *New York Review of Books*, 15 December 1966, 29.
14. Irving Feldman, "Fool's Paradise," review of *Zlateh the Goat*, by I. B. Singer, *Book Week*, 30 October 1966, 4.
15. Thomas P. Riggio, "The Symbols of Faith: Isaac Bashevis Singer's Children's Books," in *Recovering the Canon: Essays on Isaac Bashevis Singer*, ed. Jacob Neusner (Leiden: E. J. Brill, 1986), 133–44, 134; hereafter cited in text as "Symbols."
16. Mark A. Bernheim, "The Five Hundred Reasons of Isaac Singer," *Bookbird* 1–2 (1982): 31–36, 32.

Chapter Four

1.   Isaac Bashevis Singer, foreword to *When Shlemiel Went to Warsaw*, trans. Singer and Elizabeth Shub (New York: Farrar, Straus and Giroux, 1968); hereafter cited in text as *S*.

2.   Hanan J. Ayalti, *Yiddish Proverbs* (New York: Schocken Books, 1963), 85.

3.   See, for example, Isaac Bashevis Singer, "What It Takes to Be a Jewish Writer," *National Jewish Monthly*, November 1963, 54–56.

4.   Ruth Wisse, *The Schlemiel as Modern Hero* (Chicago: University of Chicago Press, 1971), 59.

5.   Israel Knox, "The Traditional Roots of Jewish Humor," *Judaism* 12 (Summer 1963): 327–47, 332.

6.   Leo Rosten, *The Joys of Yiddish* (New York: McGraw Hill, 1968), 287.

7.   Bernheim, 31.

8.   Cunegunde is also the name of an evil woman in Singer's story of that name from *Short Friday*.

9.   Eugene Goodheart, "The Demonic Charm of Bashevis Singer," *Midstream: A Quarterly Jewish Review* 6, no. 3 (Summer 1960): 88–93, 88.

10.   Alfred Kazin, "His Son, the Storyteller," *Book Week*, 24 April 1966, 1, 10.

11.   Isaac Bashevis Singer, "Indecent Language and Sex in Literture," trans. Mirra Ginsburg, *Jewish Heritage*, Summer 1965, 51–54.

12.   Joseph della Reina is also mentioned in "Growing Up" and "Tashlik." He was a mystic of the Safed school associated with Lurianic mysticism.

13.   *Conversations,* 152.

14.   *Conversations*, 75.

15.   Milton F. Hindus, "Isaac Bashevis Singer," *Jewish Quarterly*, Fall 1992, 44–52, 48.

Chapter Five

1.   Norma Rosen, review of *Naftali the Storyteller and His Horse, Sus*, by I. B. Singer, *New York Times Book Review*, 14 November 1976.

2.   Isaac Bashevis Singer, *Naftali the Storyteller and His Horse, Sus* (New York: Farrar, Straus and Giroux, 1973), 20; hereafter cited in text as *N*.

3.   Grace Farrell, *From Exile to Redemption: The Fiction of I. B. Singer* (Carbondale: Southern Illinois University Press, 1987), 22–23.

4.   *Conversations*, 255.

5.   Isaac Bashevis Singer, review of *Russian Fairy Tales*, collected by Aleksandr Afanas'ev, *New York Times Book Review*, 16 November 1975, 27.

6.   *Conversations*, 253.

7.   Edward Blishen, review of *When Shlemiel Went to Warsaw*, by I. B. Singer, *Times Educational Supplement*, 9 December 1988, 23.

8.   Again I wish to thank Yitz Gefter for his help with linguistic and religious questions.
9.   Allison interview with Alma Singer, unpublished, June 1994, Miami Beach.

Chapter Six

1.   Isaac Bashevis Singer, *The Power of Light* (Farrar, Straus and Giroux, 1980), 3; hereafter cited in text as *P*.
2.   Saul Maloff, review of *The Power of Light*, by I. B. Singer, *New York Times Book Review*, 18 January 1981, 30.
3.   Theodor H. Gaster, *Festivals of the Jewish Year: A Modern Interpretation and Guide* (New York: William Morrow, 1952), 237–46.
4.   *Conversations*, 119.
5.   Dina Abramowicz, "Yiddish Books for Children," *Booklist*, 15 December 1989, 841. Another excellent overview of Jewish children's literature—or the lack thereof—is Leonard R. Mendelsohn, "The Travail of Jewish Children's Literature," in *Children's Literature*, vol. 3 (Philadelphia: Temple University Press, 1974), 48–55.
6.   Bernheim, 31.
7.   Isaac Bashevis Singer, "I See the Child as a Last Refuge," *New York Times Book Review*, 9 November 1969, 66.
8.   Ted Hughes, "The Genius of Isaac Bashevis Singer," *New York Review of Books*, 22 April 1965, 8–10, 10.

Chapter Seven

1.   Review of *Mazel and Shlimazel*, by I. B. Singer, *The Booklist and Subscription Books Bulletin*, 15 January 1968, 595.
2.   Eric A. Kimmel, "Isaac Bashevis Singer," in *Twentieth Century Children's Writers*, ed. Tracy Chevalier (Chicago: St. James Press, 1989), 889; hereafter cited in text.
3.   Grace Farrell, "Belief and Disbelief: The Kabbalic Basis of Singer's Secular Vision," *From Exile to Redemption: The Fiction of I. B. Singer* (Carbondale: Southern Illinois University Press, 1987), 12–24; Edith Mucke, "Isaac B. Singer and Hassidic Philosophy," *Minnesota Review* 7, no. 3 (1967): 214–21.
4.   Isaac Bashevis Singer, *The Fearsome Inn* (New York: Charles Scribner's Sons, 1967), 1.
5.   *National Jewish Monthly*, 8 April 1968, 52.
6.   June H. Schlessinger and June D. Vanderryst, "Supernatural Themes in Selected Children's Stories of Isaac Bashevis Singer," *Journal of Youth Services in Libraries*, Summer 1989, 333.
7.   "Books in Brief Review," *National Jewish Monthly*, 8 April 1968, 52.

8. Hugh Nissensen, review of *The Fearsome Inn*, by I. B. Singer, *The Horn Book* 72 (8 October 1967): 38.

9. Review of *Mazel and Shlimazel*, by I. B. Singer, *New York Times Book Review*, 3 December 1967, 30.

10. Review of *Mazel and Shlimazel*, by I. B. Singer, *Detroit Jewish News*, 22 December 1967, 43.

11. Isaac Bashevis Singer, *Mazel and Shlimazel: or, The Milk of a Lioness* (New York: Farrar, Straus and Giroux, 1967), 15; hereafter cited in text as *M*.

12. Isaac Bashevis Singer, "My Personal Conception of Religion," *Flora Levy Lectures in the Humanities*, 1980 (Lafayette: Southwestern Louisiana Press, 1982), ix–x.

13. *Book Week, Chicago Sun Times*, 3 March 1968, 11.

14. Bernheim, 35.

15. Stanley Edgar Hyman, review of *Mazel and Shlimazel*, by I. B. Singer, jacket of *Mazel and Shlimazel*.

16. Alfred Kazin, review of *Mazel and Shlimazel*, by I. B. Singer, jacket of *Mazel and Shlimazel*.

17. D. Keith Mano, review of *Alone in the Wild Forest*, by I. B. Singer, *New York Times Book Review*, 17 October 1977, 10.

18. Zena Sutherland, review of *Alone in the Wild Forest*, by I. B. Singer in *Bulletin of the Center for Children's Books*, 9 February 1972, 7.

19. Isaac Bashevis Singer, *Alone in the Wild Forest* (New York: Farrar, Straus and Giroux, 1971), 23; hereafter cited in text as *A*.

20. Clive Sinclair, review of *Joseph and Koza*, by I. B. Singer, *Times Literary Supplement*, 19 October 1984, 1199; hereafter cited in text.

21. Isaac Bashevis Singer, *Joseph and Koza: or, The Sacrifice to the Vistula* (New York: Farrar, Straus and Giroux, 1970), no page numbers in the book; hereafter cited in text as *J*.

22. May Sarton, review of *Joseph and Koza*, by I. B. Singer, *New York Times Book Review*, 18 October 1970, 34.

23. Review of *Elijah the Slave*, by I. B. Singer, *The Booklist*, 1 February 1971, 453.

24. Diane Wolkstein, "The Stories Behind the Stories: An Interview with Isaac Bashevis Singer," *Children's Literature Education* 18 (Fall 1975): 143.

25. Isaac Bashevis Singer, *The Fools of Chelm and Their History* (New York: Farrar, Straus and Giroux, 1973), 10; hereafter cited in text.

26. R. Barbara Gitenstein, "Fools and Sages: Humor in Isaac Bashevis Singer's *The Fools of Chelm and Their History*," in *Studies in American Jewish Literature*, ed. Daniel Walden, no. 1 (Albany: State University of New York Press, 1981), 107.

27. Alida Allison interview with Uri Shulevitz, unpublished, 1992; hereafter cited in text.

28. Arnold Goldsmith, "Isaac Bashevis Singer and the Legend of the Golem of Prague," *Yiddish* 6, no. 2–3 (1985): 39–50, 39.

29. For children's versions of the legend, see books by Elie Wiesel, Beverly McDermott, Sulamith Ish-Kishor, and others.

Maureen T. Krause is compiling two anthologies on the *golem*, one for *Journal of the Fantastic in the Arts* and the other for a scholarly press. See Arnold Goldsmith, *The Golem Remembered, 1909–1980: Variations of a Jewish Legend.* Detroit: Wayne State University Press, 1981.

See also Alida Allison, "Guess Who's Coming to Dinner: The Golem in Jewish Children's Literature," *The Lion and the Unicorn* 14, no. 2 (December 1990): 92–97.

30. Isaac Bashevis Singer, *The Golem* (New York: Farrar, Straus and Giroux, 1983), 23; hereafter cited in text.

31. Barbara Novak, "Lonely Monster," *New York Times Book Review*, 14 November 1982, 48.

32. Margaret Meek, review of *The Golem*, by I. B. Singer, *Times Literary Supplement*, 22 July 1983, 776.

33. Neil Philip, review of *The Golem*, by I. B. Singer, *Times Educational Supplement*, 25 February 1983, 34.

34. Goldsmith, "Isaac Bashevis Singer and the Legend of the Golem of Prague," 44–48.

35. Gershom Scholem, "The Idea of the Golem," *On Kabbalah and Its Symbolism* (New York: Schocken Books, 1965).

36. Zena Sutherland, *Why Noah Chose the Dove, University of Chicago Bulletin of the Center for Children's Books*, September 1974, 17.

Chapter Eight

1. Review of *Stories for Children*, by I. B. Singer, *Wall Street Journal* 104, no. 85 (30 October 1984): 28.

2. Review of *Stories for Children*, by I. B. Singer, *The Horn Book*, 183.

3. Stefan Kanfer, review of *Stories for Children*, by I. B. Singer, *Time*, 29 October 1984, 94.

4. Cecil Hemley, "Isaac Bashevis Singer," in *Poetry and Prose*, ed. Elaine Gottlieb (Athens: Ohio University Press, 1968), 222.

5. Leonard Michaels, review of *Stories for Children*, by I. B. Singer, *New York Times Book Review*, 11 November 1984, 51.

6. Nicholas Tucker, review of *Stories for Children*, by I. B. Singer, *The Listener*, 5 March 1987, 25.

7. Review of *Stories for Children*, by I. B. Singer, *Times Literary Supplement*, 1 May 1987, 472.

8. *New York Times Book Review*, 51.

9. Jerome Griswold, "The Fool and the Child," in *Sharing Literature with Children*, ed. Francelia Butler (Prospect Heights, Ill.: Waveland Press, 1977), 153.

10. *Conversations*, 85–86.

11. "Isaac Bashevis Singer," *American Masters*, Public Broadcasting System television program, 1985.

12. *New York Times Book Review*, 51.

13. Review of *Stories for Children*, *Wall Street Journal*, 30 October 1984, 28.

14. Once again, my thanks to Yitz Gefter for his help with terminology.

15. Eric Pace, "I. B. Singer, Narrator of Jewish Folkways, Dies," *New York Times*, 25 July 1991, sec. B, p. 9.

16. Israel Knox, "The Traditional Roots of Jewish Humor," *Judaism* 12 (Summer 1963): 332.

17. It is no coincidence that Art Spiegelman represents Poles as pigs in his Holocaust books *Maus I* (New York: Pantheon, 1986) and *Maus II* (New York: Pantheon, 1992).

18. Lawrence S. Friedman, *Understanding Isaac Bashevis Singer* (Columbia: University of South Carolina Press, 1988), 222–25.

19. Cecil Hemley, "Isaac Bashevis Singer," in *Poetry and Prose*, ed. Elaine Gottleib (Athens, Ohio: Ohio University Press, 1968), 217–33, 219.

20. Isaac Bashevis Singer, "What It Takes to Be a Jewish Writer," *National Jewish Monthly* (November 1963), 54; hereafter cited in text as "Jewish Writer."

21. "Isaac Bashevis Singer," in *The Contemporary Writer: Interviews with Sixteen Novelists and Poets*, ed. L. S. Dembo and Cyrena N. Pondrom (Madison: University of Wisconsin Press, 1972), 112.

22. Chaim Potok, *Wanderings* (New York: Alfred A. Knopf, 1978), 336

23. Richard Burgin, "A Conversation with Isaac Bashevis Singer, *Chicago Review* 31, no. 4 (Spring 1980): 55.

24. Cynthia Ozick, "Envy: or Yiddish in America," in *Isaac Bashevis Singer: A Study of the Short Stories*, ed. Edward Alexander (Boston: G. K. Hall, 1990), 123–25.

25. Sandra Bernhard, "My Date with Isaac Bashevis Singer," *The Big Book of Jewish Humor,* eds. William Novak and Moshe Waldoks (New York: HarperCollins, 1990), 17.

26. Alfred Kazin, "Isaac Bashevis Singer and the Mind of God," in *Recovering the Canon*, ed. Jacob Neuser (Leiden: E. J. Brill, 1986), 151.

27. Stefan Kanfer, "The Last Teller of Tales," *Time*, 5 August 1991, 61.

28. Malcolm Jones, Jr., "The Century's Storyteller," *Newsweek*, 5 August 1991, 59.

29. Burt A. Folkart, "Isaac Bashevis Singer: Yiddish Cultural Archivist," *Los Angeles Times*, 26 July 1991, sec. A, p. 1.

30. Wayne D. Dosnik,"Rabbinic Insights: Of a World That Is No More," *San Diego Jewish Times*, 19 August 1991, 14.

31. Hugh Nissenson, "An Insightful Day at the Circus with Isaac Bashevis Singer," *USA Today*, 8 August 1991, sec. D, p. 4.

32. Reed Martin, "Famed Fiction Writer Singer Was Lad's Soda Fountain Confidant," *The Denver Post*, 28 July 1991, sec. D, p. 5.

33. Paul Rosenblatt and Gene Koppel, "Isaac Bashevis Singer on Literature and Life," *On Literature and Life* (Tucson: University of Arizona Press, 1971), 40.

Selected Annotated Bibliography

PRIMARY SOURCES

Children's Stories, Fiction

Singer, Isaac Bashevis. *Alone in the Wild Forest*. Illustrated ⸱ ; Margot Zemach; translated by Singer and Elizabeth Shub. New York: Farrar, Straus and Giroux, 1971.

———. *Elijah the Slave*. Illustrated by Antonio Frasconi; translated by Singer and Elizabeth Shub. New York: Farrar, Straus and Giroux, 1970. Singer's books had been for the upper-elementary- or middle-school reading level. This is a picture book, brightly illustrated and suitable for 4- to 8-year-olds. Elijah is sent from heaven to be sold as a slave in order to help the worthy family man and pauper Tobias.

———. *The Fearsome Inn*. Illustrated by Nonny Hogrogian; translated by Singer and Elizabeth Shub. New York: Charles Scribner's Sons, 1967. This book was awarded the Newbery Honor Award. No question of the existence of demons in this story; good triumphs as evil is banished by a young Hasidic scholar.

———. *The Fools of Chelm and Their History*. Illustrated by Uri Shulevitz; translated by Singer and Elizabeth Shub. New York: Farrar, Straus and Giroux, 1973. The fools of Chelm, the ruling council of the *shtetl*, reappear in a book devoted exclusively to their ridiculous solutions to the town's very real problems. The book has some of the feeling of *Animal Farm*. Here, somehow, everything works out, but only because the entire town is comprised of fools.

———. *The Golem*. Illustrated by Uri Shulevitz; translated by Singer and Elizabeth Shub. New York: Farrar, Straus and Giroux, 1982. This book was designated an ALA Notable book for Children. A magnificently told rendition of a very old motif in Jewish folklore, one of Singer's best books for children.

———. *Joseph and Koza or, The Sacrifice to the Vistula*. Illustrated by Symeon Shimin; translated by Singer and Elizabeth Shub. New York: Farrar, Straus and Giroux, 1970. Definitely only for older children, this takes place during bloody times of human sacrifice in the Polish province of Mazovia. The ruler Wilk annually allows the witch Zla to select for sacrifice to the river Vistula the land's most beautiful maiden. Eventually his own daughter Koza is chosen. Despite Zla's fearsome summoning of

Baba Yaga herself, Koza is saved and the people are civilized by a young traveler from Jerusalem, Joseph, who teaches them about a loving God.

———. *Mazel and Shlimazel: or, the Milk of a Lioness.* Illustrated by Margot Zemach; translated by Singer and Elizabeth Shub. New York: Farrar, Straus and Giroux, 1967. The first of several books illustrated by Zemach, the first published by Farrar, Straus and Giroux, Singer's publisher ever since. *Mazel* means "good luck"; *schlimazel*, "bad luck." Personified, they battle in this fairy tale and again good triumphs.

———. *Naftali the Storyteller and His Horse, Sus.* Illustrated by Margot Zemach; translated by Singer and Elizabeth Shub. New York: Farrar, Straus and Giroux, 1976. The third of Singer's fine collections of varied tales. The title story is about a storyteller like Singer.

———. *The Power of Light.* Illustrated by Irene Leiblich. New York: Farrar, Straus and Giroux, 1980. A lovely collection, including stories of Hanukkah in Singer's childhood home, and a powerful tale of two adolescent escapees from the Nazis.

———. *The Reaches of Heaven: A Story of the Baal Shem Tov.* Illustrated by Ira Moskowitz; translated by Singer and Elizabeth Shub. New York: Farrar, Straus and Giroux,1980. A sensitive and respectful account of the life of the founder of Hasidism that provides a picture of the ferment and difficulties among Jews in the 1700s just after the time of Sabbatai Zevi. Interesting as well because, through the Baal Shem Tov, Singer expresses his criticism of Judaism as a religion for women.

———. *Stories for Children.* New York: Farrar, Straus and Giroux, 1984. This book was designated an ALA Notable book. Singer's own selections from the best of his many children's works.

———. *A Tale of Three Wishes.* Illustrated by Irene Leiblich. New York: Farrar, Straus and Giroux, 1975.

———. *The Topsy-Turvy Emperor of China.* Illustrated by William Pene du Bois; translated by Singer and Elizabeth Shub. New York: Harper and Row, 1971. This is very diffucult to get; perhaps providentially, for it received very poor reviews.

———. *When Shlemiel Went to Warsaw and Other Stories.* Illustrated by Margot Zemach; translated by Singer and Elizabeth Shub. New York: Farrar, Straus and Giroux, 1968. A Newbery Honor book. A delightful collection, similar to *Zlateh the Goat* in its variety and with many of the same characters, the same profound silliness, the same naturalness and supernaturalness.

———. *Why Noah Chose the Dove.* Illustrated by Eric Carle; translated by Singer and Elizabeth Shub. New York: Farrar, Straus and Giroux, 1972. The third of Singer's biblical tales, this picture book imagines the animals' competition for the honor of being Noah's messenger. The dove is selected because it doesn't compete.

———. *The Wicked City*. Illustrated by Leonard Everett Fisher; translated by Singer and Elizabeth Shub. New York: Farrar, Straus and Giroux, 1972. Singer retells the tale of Sodom, Abraham, and his reprehensible nephew Lot. Not one of Singer's best.

———. *Zlateh the Goat and Other Stories*. Illustrated by Maurice Sendak; translated by Singer and Elizabeth Shub. New York: Harper and Row, 1966. A Newbery Honor book. This collection remains the standard by which all of Singer's works are judged—a high standard. In this book several of his recurrent kinds of characters make their first appearance: *shlemiels*, fools, devils and spirits, affectionate animals, storytellers, working people—Singer's rich, unforgettable, and doomed world is defined. Humor, acceptance, warmth, charity, patience, and wisdom characterize the interplay.

Nonfiction

Singer, Isaac Bashevis. *A Day of Pleasure, Stories of a Boy Growing Up in Warsaw*. Photographs by Roman Vishniac; translated by Channah Kleinerman-Goldstein et al., New York: Farrar, Straus and Giroux, 1969. A National Book Award winner. One of the best books about childhood ever written, this is a moving recreation of several episodes in Singer's early life. The characters—family members, friends, petitioners at his Rabbi father's court—are vividly present, the scene setting is sure and skillful, the child's dilemmas are universal. This book is essential to understanding Singer's work, world, and the wisdom he represents.

———. *In My Father's Court*. Translated by Channah Kleinerman-Goldstein, Elaine Gottlieb, and Joseph Singer. New York: Farrar, Straus and Giroux, 1966. Singer's award-winning autobiography told in numerous short stories set in Poland before World War I. It contains most of the stories in *A Day of Pleasure*, and many others.

———. *A Little Boy in Search of God; or, Mysticism in a Personal Light*. Translated by Joseph Singer. Garden City, N.Y.: Doubleday, 1976.

———. *Nobel Lecture*. New York: Farrar, Straus and Giroux, 1978.

———. *On Literature and Life*. Tucson: University of Arizona Press, 1971.

———. "Are Children the Ultimate Literary Critics?" In *Stories for Children*. New York: Farrar, Straus and Giroux, 1984.

———. "I See the Child as a Last Refuge." *New York Times Book Review*, 9 November 1969, 1, 66.

———. "Indecent Language and Sex in Literature." Translated by Mirra Ginsburg. *Jewish Heritage*, Summer 1965, 51–54.

———. "Introduction." In *Yoshe Kalb*, Israel Joseph Singer. New York: Harper and Row, 1965, v–x.

Here, as elsewhere, Singer extols his older brother, author Israel Joshua Singer. The introduction includes a good deal of interesting family information. There are similarities between *Yoshe Kalb* and I. B. Singer's *The Penitent*.

———. "My Personal Conception of Religion." In *The Flora Levy Lectures in the Humanities, 1980*. Lafayette: University of Southwestern Louisiana Press, 1982.

———. "On Translating My Books." *The World of Translation*. New York: P. E. N. American Center, 1987, 109–13.

———. "On Writing for Children." In *Children's Literature*, vol. 6, Annual of the MLA Group on Children's Literature and the Children's Literature Association. Philadelphia: Temple Univeristy Press, 1977, 9–16.

———. Review of *Russian Fairy Tales*. Collected by Aleksandr Afanas'ev. *New York Times Book Review*, 16 November 1975, 27.

———. "What It Takes to Be a Jewish Writer." *National Jewish Monthly*, November 1963, 54–56.

SECONDARY SOURCES

Books

Alexander, Edward. *Isaac Bashevis Singer: A Study of the Short Fiction*. Boston: G. K. Hall (Twayne Publishers), 1990. The book includes analyses of many of Singer's major short stories and also major essays about Singer's work.

———. *Isaac Bashevis Singer*. New York: G. K. Hall, 1980. Biography and general themes in Singer's work are discussed in the first chapter. The rest of this perceptive book's nine chapters discuss Singer's adult works only; the author does not mention his books for children.

Achievement of Isaac Bashevis Singer, The. Ed. Marcia Allentuck. Carbondale: Southern Illinois University Press, 1969. The first four of these eleven essays discuss Singer's work overall; the last seven treat individual works. Especially interesting in the former group is William Gass's "The Shut-In": Singer's world, although insulated, is shown to be one in which "everything is possible." In the latter essays, "Singer's Children's Stories and *In My Father's Court*" is the only one to deal with his work for children. Given the book's 1969 publication, the essay naturally covers very few of these works. Also, as the article's subtitle "Universalism and the Rankian Hero" indicates, the perspective of the essay is narrow but fascinating. Because fools, *shlemiels*, and *shlimazels* figure so prominently in Singer's children's stories, the last of the book's essays, "Gimpel and the Archetype of the Wise Fool," is helpful in understanding these folk characters.

Baron, Salo. *The Russian Jew under the Tsars and Soviets.* New York: Macmillan, 1964.

Bellow, Saul. Introduction. In *Great Jewish Short Stories.* New York: Dell, 1963, 13–16.

Buchen, Irving H. *Isaac Bashevis Singer and the Eternal Present.* New York: New York University Press and London: University of London Press, 1968. This often-quoted study begins with a detailed biography of Singer's life and literary career, then reviews his novels and short stories. Buchen sees the short stories' prose style as a combination of "the realistic, the philosophical, the demonic, and the apocalyptic" (140). These are useful categories because they appear in Singer's children's books, too. However, Buchen treats none of these. His bibliography is excellent, although dated, of course.

Critical Views of Isaac Bashevis Singer. Ed. Irving Malin. New York: New York University Press, 1969. Malin's anthology presents several perspectives on Singer's work that are useful in acquiring a general understanding, although none of the essays treats the works for children. For example, essays by Wolkenfield and Fixler shed light on recurrent themes and images of sexuality, perversion, and corruption in Singer; these do not figure in his children's books. The essay by Gittleman focused on *In My Father's Court* and provides insight into Singer's own childhood in Warsaw.

Davis, Enid. *A Comprehensive Guide to Children's Literature with a Jewish Theme.* New York: Schocken Books, 1981. Davis's thorough, annotated bibliography arranges Jewish children's literature into distinct genres. The chapter "Literature: Folk Tales and Anthologies" provides a useful discussion of folklore in Jewish children's stories. I. B. Singer's contributions in this field are given special recognition and a number of his books are cited.

Farrell, Grace, ed. *Conversations with Isaac Bashevis Singer.* Jackson: University of Mississippi Press, 1992.

———. *Critical Essays on Issac Bashevis Singer.* New York: Twayne Publishers, 1996.

———. *From Exile to Redemption: The Fiction of Isaac Bashevis Singer.* Carbondale: Southern Illinois University Press, 1987. Farrell focuses on Singer's work for adults; she does not deal with his children's books. Yet substantial sections of her book are useful in understanding Singer's beliefs that underlie his work for children as well: chapter 2, "The Kabbalic Basis of Singer's Secular Vision" explains aspects of Jewish symbolism; chapter 3, "Reading the Short Stories," emphasizes the tension between storytelling and reality; the final two chapters discuss the importance in Judaism of community.

Friedman, Lawrence S. *Understanding Isaac Bashevis Singer.* Columbia: University of South Carolina Press, 1988. Although much more recent than

Buchen's book, Friedman's is identical in format: a thorough biography is followed by several chapters devoted to Singer's major novels and short stories. Friedman's book benefits from having more material to discuss, but deals with none of the 16 books for children available by 1988. Friedman's bibliography is excellent, and he indexes major characters as well.

Gibbons, Frances-Vargas, *Isaac Bashevis Singer in Search of Love and God in His Writings for Adults and Children.* Ann Arbor, Mich.: Dissertation Abstracts International, 1993.

Kreitman, Hinde Esther (Singer). *Deborah.* London: Virago, 1983. Singer's older sister's autobiography demonstrates the family's talent for writing and reveals the difficulties of being a Jewish girl in a patriarchal society.

Kresh, Paul. *The Story of a Storyteller.* New York: Dutton Books, 1984. This chatty biography for young adults is an insider's view on Singer's personal and literary life. One chapter concentrates on Singer's children's books, providing useful anecdotes about how he came to write them and their publication and translation histories. There is little interpretation, although the facts are useful. Among these is the story of how Singer's longtime friend Elizabeth Shub persuaded him to write his first children's book, *Zlateh the Goat,* when he was 62 years old.

Pinsker, Sanford. "The Isolated Schlemiels of Isaac Bashevis Singer." *The Schlemiel as Metaphor.* Carbondale: Southern Illinois University Press and London: Feffer and Simons, 1971, 55–86. Pinsker's discussion of Singer focuses on the author's unusual popularity with American audiences. Pinsker evokes the *shtetl* and the Holocaust as undeniably parts of Singer, combining a world that changed little in four centuries with the event that ended it forever. Singer's use of the grotesque as well as the humorous is exemplified in "Gimpel the Fool," his best-known work. Pinsker's information is very useful, considering the recurrence of *shlemiels* in Singer's children's stories. Singer's children's books are not discussed.

Siegel, Ben. "Isaac Bashevis Singer." Pamphlet 86. Minneapolis: University of Minnesota Press, 1969. Siegel's general introduction to Singer's work is comprehensive, authoritative, and well-written, if short. Only a few pages of overall commentary precede his specific discussion of Singer's work available at the time. In this slim pamphlet, Siegel evokes the "integrated and coherent" (8) life of the vanished *shtetl.* Unfortunately, he only mentions that Singer writes for children.

Sinclair, Clive. *The Brothers Singer.* London: Allison and Busby; New York: Schocken Books, 1983. This is the most provocative and substantive of the literary biographies available. Sinclair interweaves the Singer family's personal history with the writing of the siblings, Esther, who died early, Israel Joshua, the elder brother and first to become famous, and Isaac Bashevis. The two very different men are very different authors. Sinclair is notably thorough in his biography of the entire family, beginning with the parents, who embodied the most diverse temperaments as well as elements of Judaism, crucial tensions in Singer's early years. The book, although published in the early 1980s, limits itself to Singer's earlier works. It does not mention his writing for children. It includes a useful bibliography.

Singer, Israel Joseph. *Of a World That Is No More*. Translated by Joseph Singer. New York: Vanguard Press, 1970.

Straus, Dorthea. *Under the Canopy*. New York: Braziller, 1982. The wife of Singer's publisher Roger Straus, the author writes as much about her own reactions to Singer as about Singer. The anecdotes she provides are fascinating, such as the story of Singer's parakeet Matzoh.

Wisse, Ruth R. *The Schlemiel as Modern Hero*. Chicago: University of Chicago Press, 1971. Because Mr. and Mrs. Shlemiel are recurrent characters in Singer's children's stories, Wisse's discussion of the fool's relationship to God, to history, and to Jewish culture is pertinent.

Articles

Bernheim, Mark A. "The Five Hundred Reasons of Isaac Singer." *Bookworld* (1–2), 31.

Blishen, Edward. Review of "Glow Like Fire," by I. B. Singer. *Times Educational Supplement*, no. 3685 (13 February 1987): 42.

Collar, Mary. "In His Father's House: Singer, Folklore, and the Meaning of Time." *Studies in American Jewish Literature*. Albany: State University of New York Press, 1981.

Colwin, Laurie. "I. B. Singer, Storyteller." *New York Times Book Review*, 23 July 1978, 1, 23–24.

Commire, Anne. "Singer, Isaac Bashevis." *Something about the Author*, 3. Detroit: Gale Research, 1972.

"Conversation with Isaac Bashevis Singer, A." *Sharing Literature with Children*. Ed. Francelia Butler. Prospect Heights, Ill.: Waveland Press, 1977.

Daltry, Patience M. "Newbery and Caldecott Medal Winners." *Christian Science Monitor*, 29 February 1968, 5.

De Montreville, Doris, and Donna Hill, eds. "Isaac Bashevis Singer." *Third Book of Junior Authors*. New York: H. H. Wilson, 1972.

Elman, Richard M. "Singer of Warsaw." *New York Times Book Review*, 8 May 1966, 1, 34–36.

———. *A Day of Pleasure*. I. B. Singer. *New York Times Book Review*, 1 February 1970, 30.

Feldman, Irving. "Fools' Paradise," review of *Zlateh the Goat and Other Stories*, by I. B. Singer. *Book Week*, 30 October 1966, 4.

Fiedler, Leslie. "I. B. Singer, or the Americanness of the American Jewish Writer," *Studies in American Jewish Literature*. Albany: State University of New York Press, 1981.

Frongia, Terri, "Tales of Old Prague: Of Ghettos, Passover, and the Blood Libel." In *Journal of the Fantastic in the Arts*, Fall/Winter 1995, 135–51.

Fuller, Edmund. "A Magic Barrel Full of Tales." *Wall Street Journal* 104, no. 85 (30 October 1984): 28.

Goldsmith, Arnold. "Isaac Bashevis Singer and the Legend of the Golem of Prague." *Yiddish* 6, no. 2–3 (1985).

Goodheart, Eugene. "The Demonic Charm of Bashevis Singer." *Midstream: A Quarterly Jewish Review* 6, no. 3 (Summer 1960): 88–93.

Griswold, Jerome. "The Fool and the Child." In *Sharing Literature with Children*. Ed. Francelia Butler. Prospect Heights, Ill.: Waveland Press, 1977, 153.

Hadda, Janet. "The Double Life of Isaac Bashevis Singer." *Prooftexts: A Journal of Jewish Literary History*, 5, no. 2 (May 1985): 165–81.

Hemley, Cecil, "Isaac Bashevis Singer." In *Poetry and Prose*. Ed. Elaine Gottleib. Athens: Ohio University Press, 1968, 217–33.

Howe, Irving. "I. B. Singer." In *Critical Views of Isaac Bashevis Singer*. Ed. Irving Malin. New York: New York University Press, 1969.

———. "I. B. Singer." *Encounter* 26 (March 1966): 60.

Hughes, Ted. "The Genius of (I. B. S.)" *New York Review of Books*, 22 April 1965, 8–10, 70.

Hyman, Stanley Edgar. "The Yiddish Hawthorne." In *On Contemporary Literature*. Ed. Richard Kostenlanetz. New York: Avon Books, 1964, 586–90.

Kanfer, Stefan. Review of "Preacher," by I. B. Singer. *Time* (29 October 1984): 94.

Kazin, Alfred. "His Son the Storyteller: Reversing an Ancestral Pattern, I. B. Singer Has Converted Piety into Fable." *Book Week*, 24 April 1966, 1, 10.

Kimmel, Eric A. "I. B. Singer's 'Alone in the Wild Forest': A Kabbalistic Parable." *Children's Literature in Education*, no. 18 (Fall 1975): 147–58.

Knox, Israel. "The Traditional Roots of Jewish Humor." *Judaism* 12, no. 3 (Summer 1963): 327–37.

Lurie, Alison. Review of *Zlateh the Goat and Other Stories* by I. B. Singer. *New York Review of Books*, 15 December 1966, 29.

Maloff, Saul. Review of *The Power of Light*, by I. B. Singer. *New York Times Book Review*, 18 January 1981, 30.

Mano, D. Keith. Review of *Alone in the Wild Forest*, by I. B. Singer. *New York Times Book Review*, 18 January 1981, 30.

McGillis, Roderick. "Reactivating the Ear: Orality and Children's Poetry." In *The Voice of the Narrator in Children's Literature*. Ed. Charlotte F. Otten and Gary Schmidt. New York: Greenwood Press, 1989.

Mendelsohn, Leonard. "The Travail of Jewish Children's Literature." In *Children's Literature*, vol. 3. Philadelphia: Temple University Press, 1974, 48–55. Mendelsohn speaks of the tension between the lost world of Europe and the new but uncomfortable world of America.

Michaels, Leonard. Review of "Little Creatures Who Leave Home," by I. B. Singer. *New York Times Book Review*, 11 November 1984, 51.

Miller, David Neal. "Isaac Bashevis Singer: The Interview as Fictional Genre." *Contemporary Literature* 25, no. 2 (1984): 187–204.

Miller, Henry. "Magic World of Imps and Villagers." *Life* 57 (11 December 1964).

Morse, Naomi S. "Values for Children in the Stories of Isaac Bashevis Singer." In *Children's Literature: Selected Essays and Bibliographies*, vol. 9. Ed. Anne MacLeod. Baltimore: College of Library Information Services, University of Maryland, 1977; 16–31. Morse's is an excellent discussion of Singer's work for children, focusing on the messages contained within the stories, messages of acceptance and hope clarified through contrast of Singer's work with Andersen's. While another reader might disagree with elements of her evaluations of individual works, her contribution is admirable.

Nissenson, Hugh. Review of *The Fearsome Inn*, by I. B. Singer. *New York Times Book Review*, 8 October 1967, 38.

Patterson, Sylvia W. "Isaac Singer: Writer for Children." In *Proceedings of the Eighth Annual Conference of the Children's Literature Association*. Ed. Priscilla Ord. Boston: Northeastern University Press, 1982. A basic introduction to Singer's work, Patterson's work stresses three factors operative in Singer's children's books: his emphasis on storytelling, his respect for his audience, and his superb abilities. She quotes Singer's uncompromising criteria for children's literature.

Philip, Neil. Review of *The Golem*, by I. B. Singer. *Times Educational Supplement*, 25 February 1983, 34.

Prawer, S. S. Review of *Stories for Children*, by I. B. Singer. *Times Literary Supplement*, 1 May 1987, 472–73.

Ree, Harry. Review of *A Day of Pleasure* by I. B. Singer. *Times Educational Supplement*, 13 June 1980, 23.

Riggio, Thomas P. "Isaac Singer's Books for Young People." *Children's Literature* 5 (1976), 304–10.

———. "The Symbols of Faith: Isaac Bashevis Singer's Children's Books." *Recovering the Canon: Essays on Isaac Bashevis Singer*, vol. 8. Ed. David Neal Miller. From the series: *Studies in Judaism in Modern Times*. Ed. Jacob Neusner. Leiden: E. J. Brill, 1986; 133–44. Riggio's essay is superb, situating Singer within the Jewish folklore tradition and the global tradition, emphasizing Singer's "I choose to Believe" as most clearly operating in his children's books. *Shlemiels* are discussed, and differentiated from fools. Singer's covert politics are discussed too. The volume also contains an essay by Alfred Kazin, "Isaac Bashevis Singer and the Mind of God."

Rosen, Norma. Review of *Naftali the Storyteller and His Horse, Sus*, by I. B. Singer. *New York Times Book Review*, 14 November 1976, 56.

Sale, Roger. "Good Servants and Bad Masters." *Hudson Review* 20 (Winter 1967–68): 666–74.

Sarton, May. Review of *Joseph and Koza*, by I. B. Singer. *New York Times Book Review*, 18 October 1970, 34.

Schlessinger, June H., and June D. Vanderryst. "Supernatural Themes in Selected Children's Stories of Isaac Bashevis Singer." *Journal of Youth Services in Libraries* (Summer 1989): 331–38.

Sheridan, Judith Rinde. "Isaac Bashevis Singer: Sex as Cosmic Metaphor." *The Midwest Quarterly* 23, no. 4 (1982): 365–79.

Shmeruk, Chone. "Polish-Jewish Relations in the Historical Fiction of Isaac Bashevis Singer." *The Polish Review* (The Polish Institute of Arts and Sciences) 23, no. 4 (1987): 401–13.

———. "Bashevis Singer—In Search of His Autobiography," *The Jewish Quarterly* 29, no. 4 (Winter 1981/1982).

Siegel, Ben. "Sacred and Profane: Isaac Bashevis Singer's Embattled Spirits." *Critique* 6 (Spring 1963).

Sinclair, Clive. "A Conversation with Isaac Bashevis Singer." *Encounter* 52, no.2 (February 1979): 20–28.

———. Review of *Joseph and Koza*, by I. B. Singer. *Times Literary Supplement*, 19 October 1984, 1199.

Tucker, Nicholas. Review of "Where Young Love Flourishes," by I. B. Singer. *Listener* 117, no. 3001 (5 March 1987): 255.

Wigan, Angela. "Singer, Isaac Bashevis." *Twentieth Century Children's Writers*. Ed. D. L. Kirkpatrick. New York: St. Martin's Press, 1978.

Wolkstein, Diane. "The Stories behind the Stories: An Interview with Isaac Bashevis Singer." *Children's Literature in Education*, no. 18 (Fall 1975): 136–45.

SECONDARY SOURCES

General Background

Ausubel, Nathan Alexander, ed. *A Treasury of Jewish Folklore, Stories, Traditions, Legends, Humor, Wisdom, and Folk Songs of the Jewish People*. New York: Crown, 1948. The most comprehensive reference work on Jewish folklore, a work of profound scholarship which is delightful to read. In his introduction, Ausubel provides a history of the various books of Jewish religious literature, clarifying differences between, for example, the Talmud and the Agada, the latter a major source in the folk tradition. Many of the characters and themes found in Singer's work are discussed, including the fools of Chelm and the *golem*. The bulk of the book is a valuable collection of traditional stories, serving, for purposes of a book

on Singer, to help locate him in terms of his roots and to emphasize his
    originality.
Browne, Lewis. *The Wisdom of Israel: An Anthology.* New York: Random House,
    1945. This extraordinary selection of Jewish wisdom literature spans sev-
    eral thousand years and includes a glossary.
Buber, Martin. *The Origin and Meaning of Hasidism.* Edited and translated by
    Maurice Friedman. New York: Harper and Row, 1966 (paperback).
————. *Tales of the Hasidim: Early Masters*, Translated by Olga Marx. New
    York: Schocken Books, 1947.
————. *Tales of the Hasidim: Late Masters.* Translated by Olga Marx. New
    York: Schocken Books, 1948.
Gaster, Theodor H. *Festivals of the Jewish Year.* New York: William Morrow,
    1952.
Howe, Irving, and Eliezer Greenberg. *Yiddish Stories: Old and New.* New York:
    Avon, 1974. This anthology of Yiddish stories again locates Singer in
    terms of his tradition and illuminates his originality. The brief introduc-
    tion is useful in summarizing central aspects of Jewish literature and
    experience in Eastern Europe.
The Living Talmud. Selected and translated by Judah Goldin. New York: New
    American Library, 1957 (paperback).
Neusner, Jacob. *The Mishnah: An Introduction.* Northvale, N.J.: Jason Aronson,
    1989. This book presents the Mishnah from several points of view: as lit-
    erature, social vision, religion, and philosophy.
Potok, Chaim. *Wanderings: Chaim Potok's History of the Jews.* New York: Alfred A.
    Knopf, 1978. This is a very readable history, by a well-known novelist, of
    the Jews from the earliest time to the modern day.
Scholem, Gershom. *Major Trends in Jewish Mysticism.* New York: Schocken
    Books, 1961 (paperback).
————. *On the Kabbalah and Its Symbolism.* Translated by Ralph Mannheim.
    New York: Schocken Books, 1969 (paperback).
Shtetl: A Creative Anthology of Jewish Life in Eastern Europe, The. Translated and
    edited by Joachim Neugroschel. Woodstock, N.Y.: Overlook Press,
    1989.
Spalding, Henry D. *Encyclopedia of Jewish Humor.* Middle Village, N.Y.:
    Jonathan David, 1969.
Wiesel, Elie. *Souls on Fire: Portraits and Legends of Hasidic Masters.* Translated by
    Marion Wiesel. New York: Random House, 1972.
Yiddish Folktales. Edited by Beatrice Weinreich. Translated by Leonard Wolf.
    New York: Pantheon, 1988.
Zohar: The Book of Splendor. Selected and edited by Gershom Scholem. New
    York: Schocken Books, 1963 (paperback).

Index

The Author

Alida Allison is associate professor of English and comparative literature at San Diego State University, where she specializes in children's literature and is the director of SDSU's Children's Literature Circle. She received her doctorate in comparative literature from the University of California, Riverside. Her forthcoming volume is on the writing of Russell Hoban. In addition to academic work, Allison is also the author of several children's books and directs the Western Slope Institute, an educational center in Ridgway, Colorado.